Arthur P. Richmond

MASSACHUSETTS LIGHTHOUSES & LIGHTSHIPS

Schiffer Publishing Ltd
4880 Lower Valley Road • Atglen, PA 19310

Other Schiffer Books by the Author:

**Cape Cod
Lighthouses & Lightships**
ISBN 978-0-7643-3545-7

**Lighthouses of
Cape Cod & the Islands**
ISBN 978-0-7643-2460-4

Cape Cod Wide
ISBN 978-0-7643-2776-6

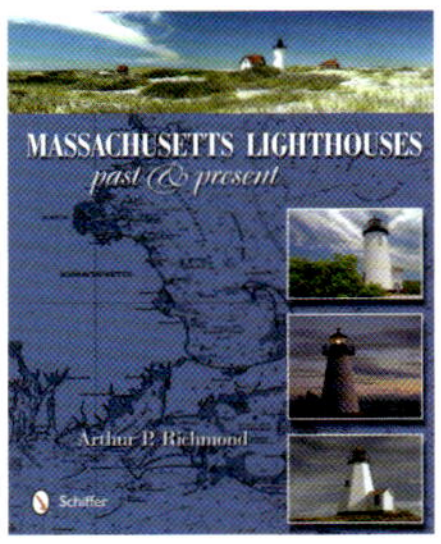

**Massachusetts Lighthouses:
Past & Present**
ISBN 978-0-7643-4305-6

Martha's Vineyard Perspectives
ISBN 978-0-7643-3834-2

Boston Wide
ISBN 978-0-7643-3273-9

Library of Congress Control Number: 2015939908

Cover design by Brenda McCallum
Type set in Adobe Caslon Pro and Arial

ISBN: 978-0-7643-4853-2
Printed in China

Published by Schiffer Publishing, Ltd.
4880 Lower Valley Road
Atglen, PA 19310
Phone: (610) 593-1777; Fax: (610) 593-2002
E-mail: Info@schifferbooks.com

For our complete selection of fine books on this and related subjects, please visit our website at www.schifferbooks.com.
You may also write for a free catalog.

This book may be purchased from the publisher.
Please try your bookstore first.

We are always looking for people to write books on new and related subjects. If you have an idea for a book, please contact us at proposals@schifferbooks.com.

Schiffer Publishing's titles are available at special discounts for bulk purchases for sales promotions or premiums. Special editions, including personalized covers, corporate imprints, and excerpts can be created in large quantities for special needs. For more information, contact the publisher.

To Alexandra Paige

CONTENTS

PREFACE.....6
INTRODUCTION.....7

MASSACHUSETTS LIGHTHOUSES.....20

FALL RIVER.....20
- Borden Flats.....22

BUZZARDS BAY.....27
- Cuttyhunk.....28
- Dumpling Rocks.....30
- New Bedford.....33
- Clark's Point.....34
- Butler Flats.....39
- Palmers Island.....45
- Cleveland Ledge.....49
- Ned's Point.....52
- Wing's Neck.....58
- Bird Island.....61

MASSACHUSETTS BAY SOUTH.....63
- Duxbury Pier (Bug Light).....65
- Plymouth / The Gurnet.....69
- Scituate.....77
- Minot's Ledge.....88

BOSTON HARBOR.....96

Aids to Navigation, Still Active
- The Graves.....99
- Boston.....104
- Deer Island.....114
- Nix's Mate Daybeacon.....117
- Long Island Head.....119

Aids to Navigation, No Longer Active
- Lovell's Island Range.....125
- The Narrows (Bug Light).....128
- Hooper Strait.....131
- Spectacle Island Range & Broad Sound Range.....134

MASSACHUSETTS BAY NORTH.....138
- Egg Rock.....138
- Marblehead.....141

SALEM REGION.....151
- Baker's Island.....152
- Fort Pickering (Winter Island).....157
- Derby Wharf.....162
- Hospital Point.....167

CAPE ANN REGION.....175
- Eastern Point.....177
- Gloucester Breakwater / Dog Bar.....182
- Ten Pound Island.....185
- Thacher's Island.....188
- Straitsmouth Island.....196
- Annisquam.....201
- Ipswich Range.....206

NEWBURYPORT REGION.....210
- Plum Island.....210
- Newburyport Rear Range.....217
- Salisbury Range.....221

MASSACHUSETTS LIGHTSHIPS.....222

- Introduction.....222
- A Brief Survey of Early Lightships.....227
- Massachusetts Lightship Stations.....234

BUZZARDS BAY **238**
Vineyard Sound 238
Hens and Chickens 240
Buzzards Bay 241

MASSACHUSETTS BAY **243**
Minot's Ledge 243
Boston 244
Lightships Today 248
Nantucket *WLV 612* 248
Chesapeake *LV 116 / WAL 538* 251

CONCLUSION **253**
AUTHOR'S NOTE **253**
ACKNOWLEDGMENTS **254**
BIBLIOGRAPHY **255**
INDEX **256**

PREFACE

This is the fourth book on Massachusetts lighthouses and lightships that I have done. *Cape Cod Lighthouses and Lightships* was the first volume. This book, which includes all the lighthouses and lightships along the coast of Massachusetts except for Cape Cod, includes images and a detailed discussion of those aids to navigation.

Several aspects of this volume have been expanded. There are more charts in this book, particularly ones from the eighteenth and nineteenth centuries that were available to mariners at that time. Centuries-old charts that are available online from NOAA have superimposed images that show the lighthouse that would have been there at that time.

There are more interior images of the beacons that are open to the public, as well as those that are restricted. The text explains and describes each aid, but more critical and significant are the archival images. If "a picture is worth a thousand words," then some of these photographs are important manuscripts. Study the images, look for details, and appreciate their explanation.

For the lighthouse enthusiast and all those interested in coastal maritime Massachusetts history, this book is a treasury of these beacons and lights along the shore.

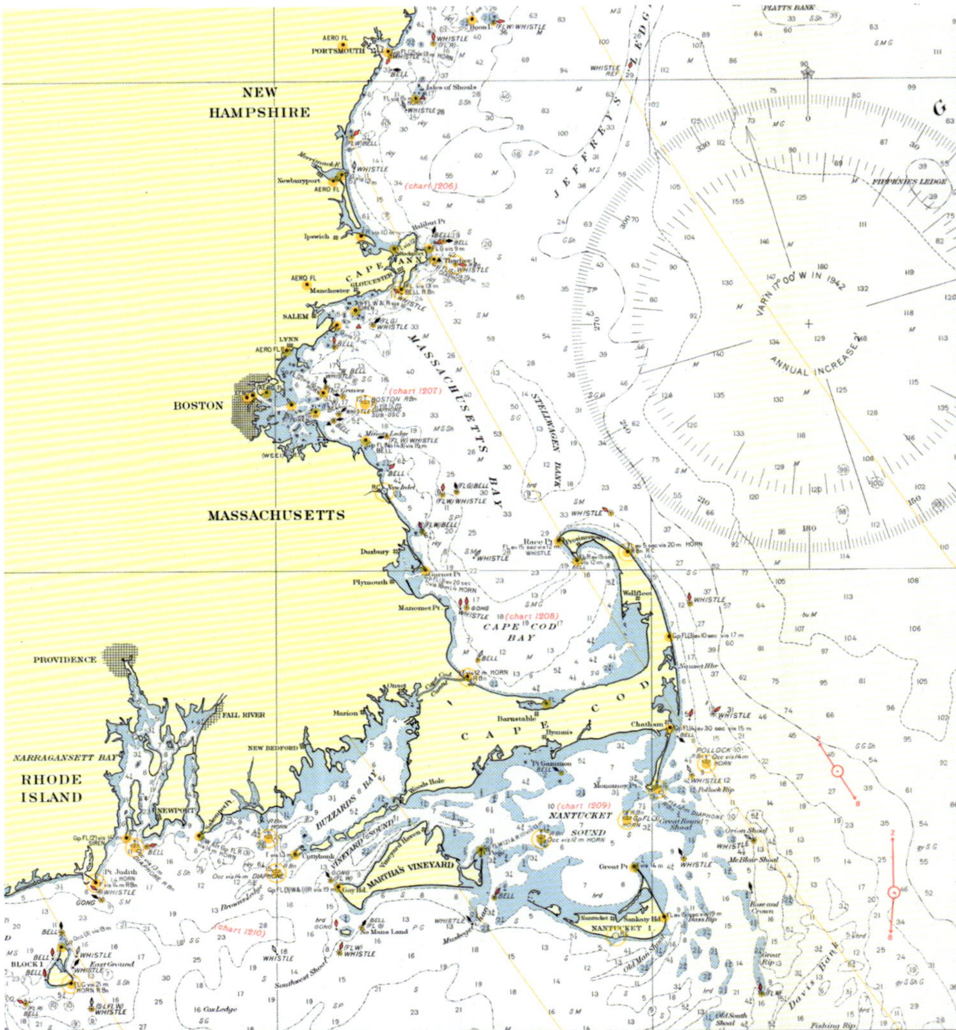

This portion of a 1941 chart is just a small part of the area between West Quoddy, Maine, and Block Island, Rhode Island. Of note are the three identifiable aids to navigation on the chart: lighthouses, lightships, and large, offshore, navigational buoys. The yellow rings represent stations or sites with radiobeacons; the distinctive characteristic signal of each beacon is indicated on the chart. Navigators would also have access to the light and sound characteristics of each aid that didn't have a radiobeacon. This chart has a scale of 1:625,000 (1 inch = 9.86 miles). This chart was to be used only for offshore navigation. Many of the charts used for illustrative purposes in this book have a scale of 1:40,000 (1 inch = .63 miles). Smaller-scale charts, with more detail, would be used when ships were closer to the harbors along the coast. Note that as improvements are made to navigation and technologies become outdated, these changes are either included or deleted as future charts are printed. *(Courtesy of NOAA)*

INTRODUCTION

This book about the lighthouses of Massachusetts is unique. There is no other publication that is quite like it. You will gain knowledge not only about one popular aid to navigation, lighthouses, but also about the once-common floating aids to navigation, lightships. There are numerous and very well written books about lighthouses, a favorite subject of both amateur and professional photographers, history buffs, and authors. There are no recent books about lightships, as they last sailed in these waters in 1983. This book attempts to provide the reader with an illustrated introduction to these two major aids to navigation, lighthouses and lightships.

Images have been collected from a variety of sources to provide the reader with a sequence showing the lighthouse or lightship as it existed years ago. Many of these photographs and plans have not been previously published.

The story begins centuries ago, with little documented history, when men began to venture out to sea. More recently, our narration begins in earnest in the late 1700s, coinciding with the birth of our nation. In fact, the first lighthouse built in Massachusetts, Boston Light, was also the first lighthouse established in North America and was first lit on September 14, 1716. This book is divided into two sections, lighthouses, and then lightships, allowing the reader to examine each independently. Comparing charts from each section will help the reader to visualize the coordination that occurred between these different lighthouse locations and lightship stations. Enjoy the archived images that provide us with such a fascinating history of these aids to navigation.

Adopted in 1869, this is the distinctive flag of the U.S. Lighthouse Service. Lighthouse tenders would fly this flag as well as the national ensign.

In the beginning, before the American Revolution, each colonial government was aware of the need for the safety of vessels visiting their ports, and some of these colonies provided aid in the form of primitive lighthouses. In the mid- to late 1600s in the Massachusetts Bay Colony, a fire burned on Little Brewster Island to warn mariners and guide them into Boston Harbor. Across the channel, in Hull, on Point Allerton, a simple beacon—an open iron basket that burned tar-soaked fiber—was present as early as 1673. On September 14, 1716, the first Boston Light was built and lit, making it the first light station established in North America. (Some sources indicate there may have been an earlier light in Havana, Cuba.) In 1719, the earliest established fog signal was a cannon on the same island as Boston Light, which responded to ships in the fog by firing every half hour. About sixty years later, during the Revolution, colonial troops burned the structure, and on June 13, 1776, British troops using explosive charges completely destroyed the tower when they left Boston. The present tower was rebuilt in 1783 and was the last lighthouse automated in the United States, in 1998. It still has its 2nd order Fresnel lens (1859). The first use of buoys to mark channels was in Boston Harbor in 1797.

Following is a brief history of aids to navigation in America, including lighthouses and lightships from the birth of the country in 1776 to the present time in the second decade of the twenty-first century. For a more detailed discourse, several books in the bibliography offer a closer examination of the various U. S. Government lighthouse administrations, with both their successes and failures, and of individuals, locations, and the application, or lack of it, in the implementation of technological advances.

Prior to 1776, each of the thirteen colonies was responsible for the location, construction, maintenance, and manning of its lighthouses. In August 1789, the federal government, aware of the need for consistency and uniformity, assumed control of all lighthouses (twelve that were built and four that were under construction) and designated the responsibility to the Treasury Department. During the early years, Presidents Washington, Adams, and Jefferson made decisions and signed off on construction details and keeper assignments to the various lighthouses.

As the number of lighthouses increased and remained under the control of the Department of the Treasury, the Fifth Auditor position was established, responsible for all aspects of these aids to navigation. Stephen Pleasanton was appointed to this position in 1820. Hard-working and conservative, Pleasanton was principally a bookkeeper and more interested in the "economics," the bottom line, than in the efficiency or ability of lighthouses and lightships to complete their mission in a successful manner. During his tenure, America was a third-rate nation in respect to its aids to navigation. European countries, particularly Great Britain, were much more advanced, and welcomed the use of the latest technologies in their lighthouses and lightships in order to assist mariners.

Case in point: Augustin Fresnel, a French inventor, developed a series of glass prisms in 1822 that could be combined to form a lens that would produce a light beam significantly superior to other optics of the day. Although they were quickly accepted and widely used throughout Europe, it took nearly twenty years before the first Fresnel lenses were used in America, at the twin tower lighthouse in Navesink, New Jersey. By the Civil War, all the lighthouses in this country had Fresnel lenses. Even today, some lighthouses still retain lenses that were installed more than 150 years ago. Restored and maintained, many of these beautiful pieces of glass are the centerpiece of maritime museums.

Another problem with the administration of the maritime aids was the scope and growth of the facilities as the country expanded and maritime trade increased. At the turn of the nineteenth century, there were sixteen lighthouses. By 1812 there were forty-nine, and by 1822 there were seventy. In

1838, there were 204 lighthouses and twenty-eight lightships, and only four years later the numbers had risen to 256 lighthouses, thirty lightships, thirty-five beacons, and about a thousand buoys. Problems continued to haunt the Pleasanton administration, and after several congressional inquiries and investigations, Congress, in 1852, reorganized the department of aids to navigation. A nine-member Lighthouse Board was created that included military officers, government engineers, and civilian scientists.

With this new and enlightened organization, the aids to navigation improved dramatically and increased the safety of maritime trade. Now ships could be assured of consistent and expanded signals in the lighthouses and lightships that they passed on their way from port to port. One of the significant contributions made by the Lighthouse Board was the annual publishing of the Light List. Described in the list, which included the east and west coasts, the Great Lakes, and the nation's rivers, were all the aids to navigation and their important characteristics, including color of the light, flashing periodicity, and height, to name just a few. Through the years as photography developed, images were added to assist the mariners. Some of the images in this book came from Light Lists that were published over a hundred years ago. In the next fifty years, America's aids to navigation became first-rate and equal to, or better than, any other nation's lighthouses and lightships.

By the beginning of the twentieth century, the Lighthouse Board and its nine members were failing to produce the required tasks to operate and maintain the aids to navigation. By 1910 Congress abolished the Lighthouse Board and created the Bureau of Lighthouses under the control of one individual who was not military, an engineer, or a politician. George R. Putnam was appointed Bureau commissioner by President William Howard Taft, and during his tenure of twenty-five years significant improvements were made to lighthouses, lightships, and other aids to navigation. Radio beacons, automated aids (with the development of electricity), and a retirement system for employees were just some of the contributions that came about in the early part of the twentieth century.

The last governmental reorganization in respect to lighthouses and lightships, in 1939, abolished the United States Lighthouse Service and transferred all the assets to the U.S. Coast Guard. The origin of the modern Coast Guard can be traced to 1915, when Congress formalized the merger of the Revenue Cutter Service and the Life Saving Service. After the addition of the Lighthouse Service, the Bureau of Marine Inspection and Navigation was added in 1942, and in 1967 the Coast Guard was moved to the Department of Transportation and subsequently to the Department of Homeland Security in 2002 after the terrorist attacks of September 11. With the demise of lightships and with the nation's lighthouses becoming automated, the role of the Coast Guard focused on other matters. The mission of today's Coast Guard focuses on the maritime environment regarding homeland security, maritime law enforcement (MLE), search and rescue (SAR), marine environmental protection (MEP), and the maintenance of aids to navigation (ATON). With more than 50,000 men and women and an additional 30,000 Auxiliarists, the United States Coast Guard, like their motto, *Semper Paratus*, is "always ready."

In addition to the Light Lists, books and charts were published that could be used by the captain and navigator to plot their course. One such publication was the *New American Coast Pilot,* which provided navigators at the end of the nineteenth century with critical data for plotting a course. Charts and sketches of the shoreline (see page 18 for an example) also provided important information. In the following partial description, the vessel is sailing into Boston Harbor:

> *Directions for sailing into Boston Harbor, From Cape Ann to Boston light-house, the course is S. W. ½ S distance of 3⅛ leagues. After making the light, with the wind fair, you will bring it to bear W. by N. or W. N. W. and then run for it, till you come within two cable's length of it. If the weather is bad, and you can not get a pilot from the light-house, after running abreast of it so as to bring it to bear N. by E. you may run W. by S. about 1½ miles to Nantasket Road, where you may anchor in 7 to 5 fathoms, in safety. The main entrance into Boston Harbor lies between Light-House Island on the north side, and Point Allerton on the south.*
>
> —*American Coast Pilot, Eleventh Edition, Sept. 1827*

An appendix in the book supplied the sailor with light and sound characteristics that included not only the lighthouses but also the lightships the commercial vessel would encounter on its journey. Signals would change, lighthouses would be discontinued, and lightships or their stations would be withdrawn, so having the latest *Coast Pilot* was necessary for vessels plying these waters.

Although this book is about the primary aid to navigation—the lighthouse—a brief discussion of buoys is essential, since many are found associated with the nearby lighted towers. (The small unlit harbor aids are the buoys discussed here, not large lit offshore buoys usually with sound.) Many older charts, as seen in this book, would have included as part of their legends sailing instructions that indicated time, distance, and significant features on the land to assist the navigator.

The first mention in the literature involving buoys was in 1767, when the state of Pennsylvania placed two sets of barrels in the Delaware River. Through the years, many colonies and later states would install these minor aids to navigation in harbors, bays, and channels. By 1797, with the country still in its infancy, the Congress authorized and provided sixteen buoys for the waters in and around Boston Harbor. By 1820, spar buoys, tree-trunk-like and preferably made of cedar, replaced the less efficient and not-so-reliable barrels. By the early 1840s more than a thousand were found in America's coastal waters. From twelve to sixty feet in length, the buoys marked the channels and indicated hazards to navigation. Fifty years later there were nearly five thousand. By the 1930s, there were more than fourteen thousand buoys in a variety of shapes, color, size, and location. They were susceptible to problems such as becoming waterlogged and losing buoyancy, or being damaged by maritime traffic. These are some of the reasons wood buoys were replaced in the mid-1800s by iron aids made of boilerplate. The first metal can buoy was placed at Egg Harbor, New Jersey. Compartmentalized, with several airtight sections within, these buoys were more buoyant and easier to maintain.

Anyone who has sailed or boated is aware of the saying "red right returning." Color, as also in the early history of lightships, is important to identify these aids that usually mark channels and underwater hazards. In 1850, Congress systematized buoy characteristics. Upon entering a harbor, the red even-numbered buoys were on the right and the black odd-numbered buoys on the left. The numbers increased as you entered the harbor. In the late 1970s and early 1980s, Coast Guard tests determined that green was more visible than black and the buoy color was changed. Other colors, yellow, white, and stripes, were utilized to indicate specific hazards.

The first bell buoy was placed on station in 1854. Familiar to any boater, the present-day can (shaped like a typical can) and nun (conical top like a rocket) buoys were introduced in 1900. On several charts in this book, I have identified some buoys that are associated with nearby lighthouses.

Lighthouses and lightships are linked in history as aids to navigation. The first lightships, more than 150 years ago, were placed "on station" at a location where it was not possible to construct a lighthouse. This image shows Palmers Island Light in New Bedford and the lightship *LV 114 / WAL 536*, which was scrapped in 2007, moored to a pier in the background.

One of the interesting aspects of doing research is discovering missing documents and images, found archived and preserved for future generations. This image from the National Archives has, I believe, been mislabeled (not the first I've discovered). Identified as 2nd Dist. West Chop (Holmes Hole), Mass., the image fits no description of a lighthouse built at that location. I have showed the image to several lighthouse authorities, and they could not specifically identify the structure as being Holmes Hole. If any reader has a possible identification, please feel free to contact me. *(Courtesy of NA)*

Centuries ago, the earliest "lighthouses" were nothing more than signaling fires on a hill. Through the years towers would be built. As an aid to navigation, during the day wet wood would be burned to form a smoke signal; at night, dry wood would be burned to produce a light signal. Nearly two millennia in the past, this Pharos was built in what is now Dover, England. Its date of construction has been estimated to be as early as 50 CE or 80 CE, but was more likely built about 140 CE. The height of the original Pharos may be in question, but what you see in this image is most likely close to that of the earliest tower. A second tower was built nearby, but no longer exists. In any case, it is the oldest standing building in England. The tower, on the grounds of Dover Castle, now houses the bells for the nearby castle church (installed sometime in the mid-1400s). The interior of the Pharos has been altered through the centuries.

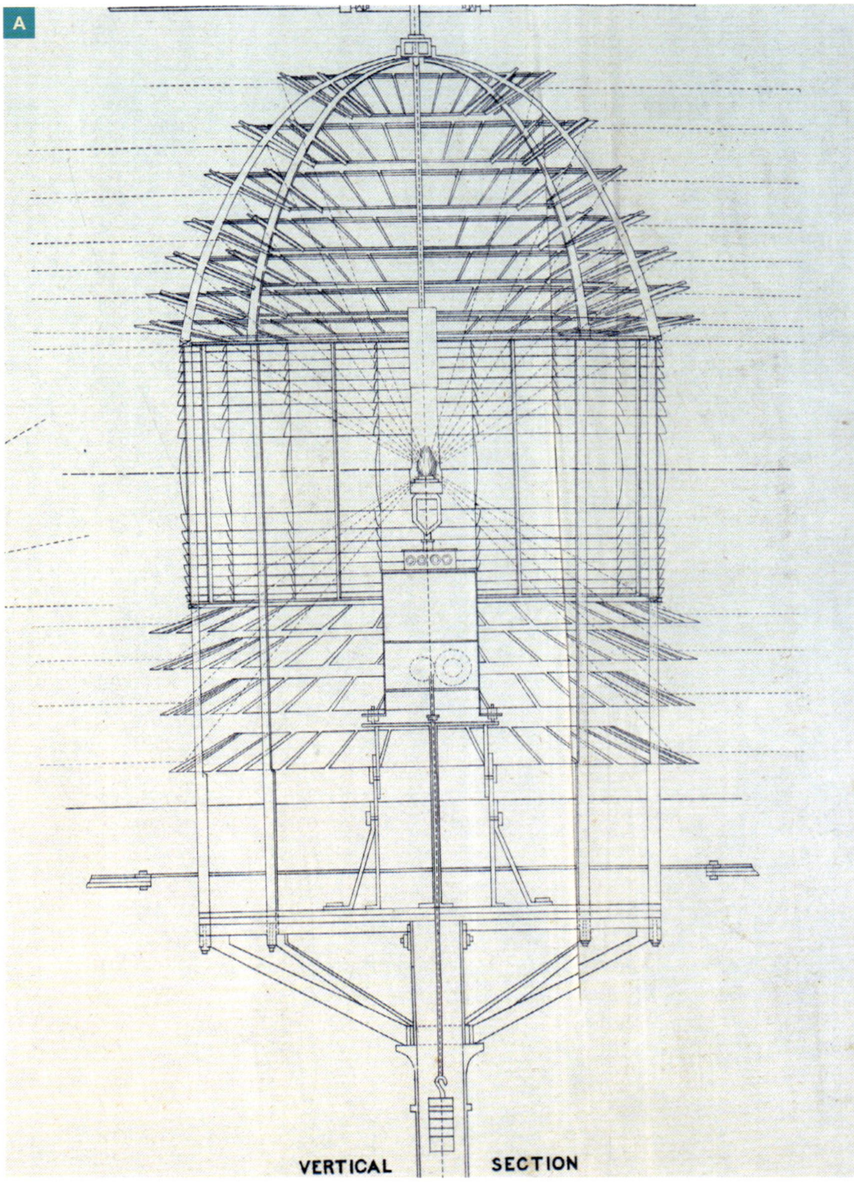

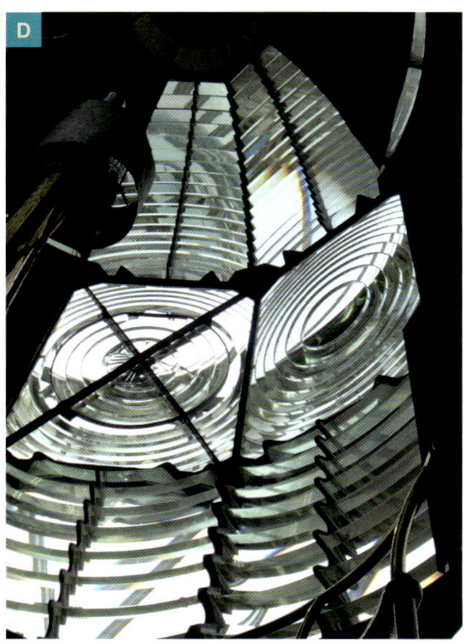

With the development of the Fresnel lens in the 1820s, lighthouses could now provide a bright, powerful beam to guide vessels. Made of curved prisms of glass, the lenses were classified according to their size, and consequently, their usage. The largest, First (1st) Order lenses were designed to be used in the major lighthouses, such as Gay Head and Highland Light in this area. At twelve feet high, nine feet in diameter, and over 2,000 pounds in weight, the 1st order lens was, and is, an awesome piece of glass. **A)** The diagram illustrates a vertical section through a lens, while the color image demonstrates the incredible quality of an actual lens. **B)** This lens was used at the Key West Lighthouse in Florida and is presently on display at their museum. **C)** This image is a sepia print of the 1st order lens from Highland Light, Truro, Cape Cod. Notice the differences in the glass prisms that make up the lens. The lens at Highland Light was damaged when it was removed in the early 1900s, but some pieces are on display at the Truro Historical Society. **D)** The interior view of a 1st order lens was captured at Jupiter Inlet Lighthouse in Florida, which has a range of twenty-five nautical miles. Sankaty Head Light in Nantucket was the first lighthouse on the Cape and Islands to be equipped with a slightly smaller 2nd order Fresnel lens. *(Diagram courtesy of NA)*

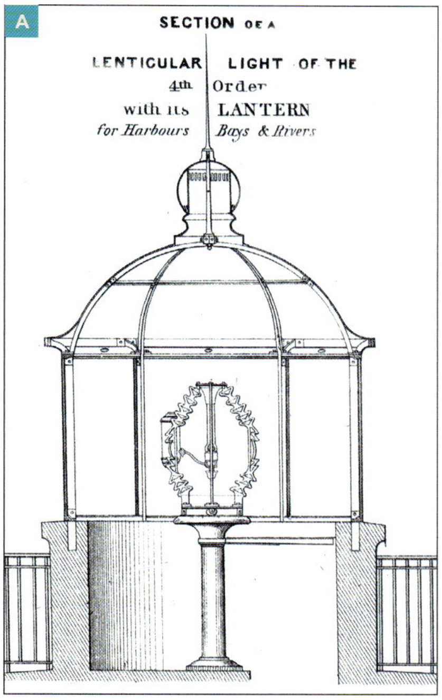

Smaller-order Fresnel lenses were designed for harbors, bays, and rivers, and the most common of those were of the 4th order. In 1884, there were 221 lighthouses throughout America using a 4th order lens, but by 1920, there were 350. **A)** The diagram shows the design of the lantern room and how a 4th order lens might appear in an actual lighthouse. **B and C)** Nobska Light, in Woods Hole, still has an operational 4th order lens. Only about thirty inches tall, the lens could weigh anywhere between 440 pounds and nearly 700 pounds and burned less than 6 ounces of fuel per hour. Note the close-up of the light source. There are many maritime museums that have 4th and 5th order lenses on display, as they were relatively common and small enough to handle without damaging them. **D)** A 4th order lens on display at a museum. **E)** A 5th order lens on display at a museum. *(Diagram courtesy of LOC)*

LIGHTHOUSE TOWER DESIGN

The tradionalist, when thinking of a lighthouse, may conjure up an image of a white tower, a black lantern room at the top, and a flashing light. But as we will find out, there are numerous different styles and designs for these aids to navigation. Although there is no specific classification system for the different kinds of beacons, after observation it is relatively easy to identify the different varieties. With each new Lighthouse Administration, improvements were made in the design, engineering, and technology available to be used in aids to navigation. (More specific details regarding lighthouse construction will be discussed with individual lighthouses.)

The first distinction that is made is whether the lighthouse is built on land, "on shore," or whether it is built in the water, "off shore." In my previous book, *Cape Cod Lighthouses and Lightships,* all the present-day lighthouses on Cape Cod are considered on-shore "stand alone"—that is, they may be constructed of timber frame, stone, or brick, but the beacon, whatever height, sits by itself with a keeper's house nearby. Although they may have been moved, these lights are found on solid ground.

Another variation of "on shore" lighthouse construction is the integral light, where the beacon was found on the roof of the keeper's house. Several early-eighteenth-century Cape lights—Long Point, Mayo Beach, and Nobska Point—were built using this lighthouse design. Relatively low in height, these beacons were usually found in bays and at entrances to harbors. There were several advantages to this plan; the keeper lived in the same building as the light, the house/beacon minimized the land use in a congested area, and—probably the most important in the early eighteenth century—they were cheap to build. Unfortunately, it was not a good design, as the lantern room–roof connection developed leaks and many flooded.

Another variation that is found both "on shore" and "off shore" is the steel skeleton, which is more commonly found down south, particularly in the Florida Keys, but there are two examples in New England. Still standing is the Marblehead Light. Another more somber example is the original "off shore" Minot's Ledge Light that was built in 1850. One supposed advantage of this design was that it would be less affected by storms and waves, but on April 16–17, 1851, a severe storm destroyed the Minot's Ledge tower killing the two keepers. Although not found in New England, another "on shore" and more recent lighthouse design is the reinforced concrete tower that is used where earthquakes may be an issue.

Several "off shore" lighthouse designs are found in Massachusetts and these include the rock foundation (Minot's Ledge Light) that was built of dovetailed or interlocking granite blocks that fit together so a light, with keeper's quarters included, could be built on a rocky wave-swept ledge. A second type of "off shore" lighthouse design is the caisson, coffee-pot, or sparkplug plan (Borden Flats, Butler Flats,and Duxbury Pier). An open-ended cast-iron or steel cylinder was towed to its designated location, filled with stone and concrete, and the lighthouse was constructed on top of it. A variation in the Great Lakes used cribs or cofferdams as support for the tower. A third type was the pile foundation (Boston Narrows, Bug Light) where the light, including the keeper's quarters, was on a platform supported by timbers, or metal piles attached to the seabed. There are no existing lighthouses in Massachusetts of this design. Two other "off shore" designs, neither of which is found in Massachusetts, are the screw-pile and exposed screw-pile (also called reef lighthouses). Both styles used threaded piles that could be "screwed" into the seabed for support. There are only eight remaining cottage-style, screw-pile lighthouses in existence, three of which are in Maryland; and only one of those is still an active aid to navigation, the Thomas Point Shoal Light in Chesapeake Bay, while two are integral parts of museums. The Seven Foot Knoll Light is on display in Baltimore's Inner Harbor as part of the Baltimore Maritime Museum. The Hopper Strait Light is located in St Michael's, Maryland, as part of the Chesapeake Bay Maritime Museum. The latter type, the exposed screw-pile, several of which are still found on Florida reefs, added a large metal plate to the bottom of the pile for additional support. Both would have the light built on a platform at the top of the tower.

A

B

C

D

E

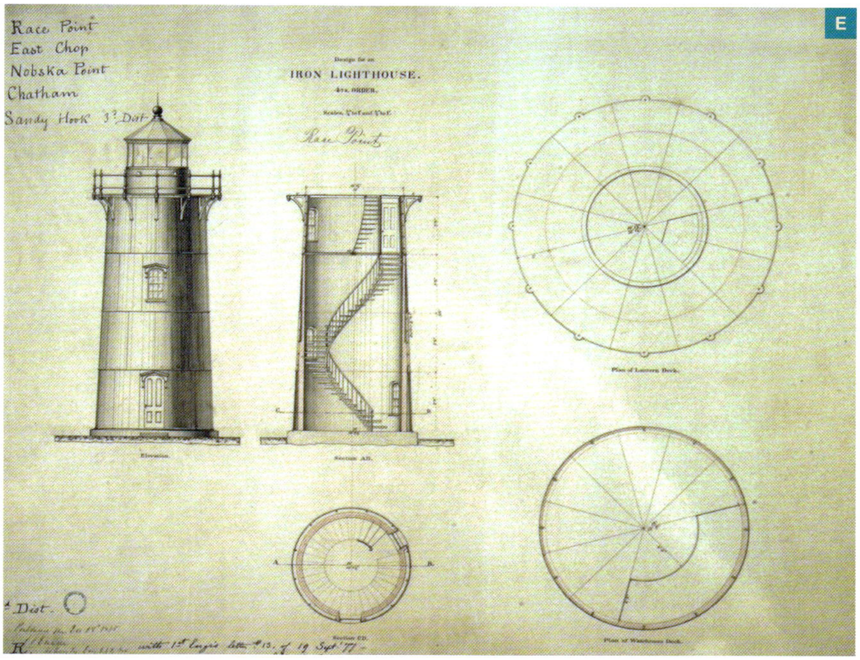
Race Point
East Chop
Nobska Point
Chatham
Sandy Hook 3rd Dist.
Design for an
IRON LIGHTHOUSE.
Race Point

F

G

H

I

J

Beginning from Page 12: The earliest lighthouse towers were constructed by the individual colonies before the American Revolution, having no uniform set of plans and using materials that local builders were familiar with and that were readily available. Wood and rubble stone were commonly used, and several of those towers still stand today. After the Revolution, and with the lighthouse administration in the hands of the Federal Government, there was more organization and coordination. With the development of various technologies, tower construction improved. Plans were implemented to build several towers with the same design. New materials were developed that could be used in a variety of locations, such as cast iron. The following images show the variety of towers that have been built along the coast. **A and B)** Two wooden towers are Plum Island Light and the Gurnet Light in Plymouth. **C)** A typical rubble stone is Bird Island Light in Marion. **D)** Monomoy Light in Chatham was one of the earliest cast-iron towers and was lined with brick. **E)** These plans, dated 1877, are for a cast-iron tower. **F)** One tower built from these plans is East Chop, Martha's Vineyard. Some towers were painted a color other than white; they are all white now. **G)** Originally in Ipswich, this cast-iron tower is now in Edgartown, Martha's Vineyard. **H)** This Thacher Island tower is made of granite blocks. **I)** Minot Light, built offshore on a reef, is also made of granite blocks. **J)** Towers are not necessarily perfectly round; the Scituate Light tower is eight-sided. **K)** Brick was another common material used in towers. This is the rear-range tower in Newburyport. The side facing the water is painted white.

With limited land available, smaller harbor and bay lights would be built into the roof of the keeper's house. They were plagued with problems, and none remain in Massachusetts. **A and B)** Long Point (left) and Nobska (right) are two examples of this design. **C)** Yaquina Bay, Newport, Oregon, was built in 1871, restored, and is now open for tours. *(Black-and-white images courtesy of NA.)*

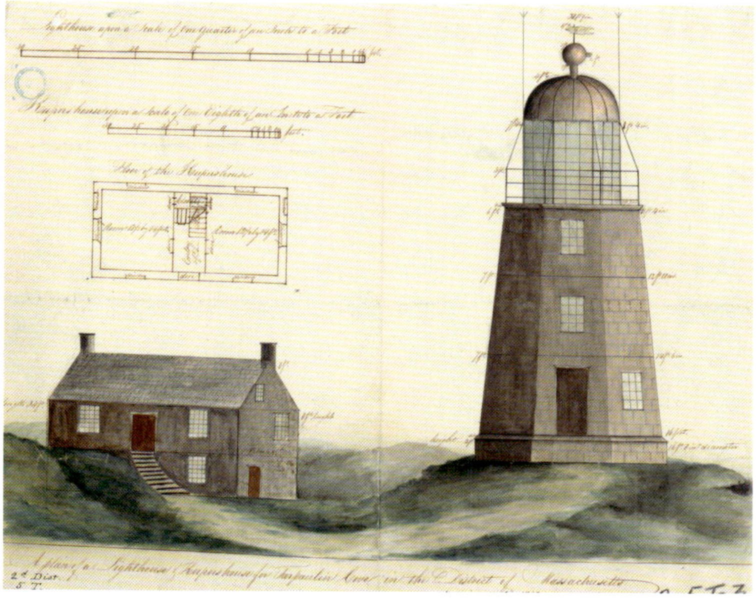

These plans, dated 1818, are for the tower of Tarpaulin Light on Naushon Island.

Screw-pile lighthouses were more common in the mid-Atlantic region, where the towers could be built in shallow, sandy areas. The only one built in Massachusetts was the Narrows Light in Boston Harbor. **D)** The Narrows Light. Two screw-pile lighthouses restored, maintained and open for tours in Maryland are **E)** the Seven Foot Knoll in Baltimore and **F)** the Hooper Strait in St. Michaels, Maryland. *(Black-and-white image courtesy of NA)*

B

To avoid navigation difficulties, sometimes multiple lights would be constructed to aid the ship in determining its location. Several of these were found along the Massachusetts coast. Only one set of twin towers exist today on Thacher Island, just off the coast of Rockport. **A)** The Gurnet in Plymouth used to be twin towers. **B)** This century old postcard shows Baker's Island when it used to have twin towers. **C)** The only lighthouse station to have three towers was the Three Sisters in Eastham on Cape Cod.

C

A

D

E

Skeletal towers were a popular design in the late 1800s and early 1900s because they could be built for half the cost of a traditional tower. Prefabricated, they could be built, transported to remote locations, and erected on site. **D)** Marblehead Light was the only one built in New England. **E)** Sanibel, Florida.

B

C

A

Sparkplug style lighthouses, built between 1871 and 1926, were prefabricated, transported to the location, and built in relatively shallow water. Of the more than thirty towers still in existence, most are found on the Atlantic Coast. **A)** Bug Light, Duxbury, 1871, is the oldest tower of this design. **B)** Butler Flats, New Bedford. **C)** Borden Flats Light, Fall River.

Range lights are two lights (or the same as two day markers) that navigators could use to line up a channel into a harbor. Hospital Point / Congregational Church and Winter Island /Derby Wharf are two examples found in the Salem area. These two images show the cliffs of Nantucket range lights that no longer exist and present-day lights with vertical red day markers that mark the channel into the harbor. The white tower to the right (without a lantern room) is the old (1856) Brant Point Light.

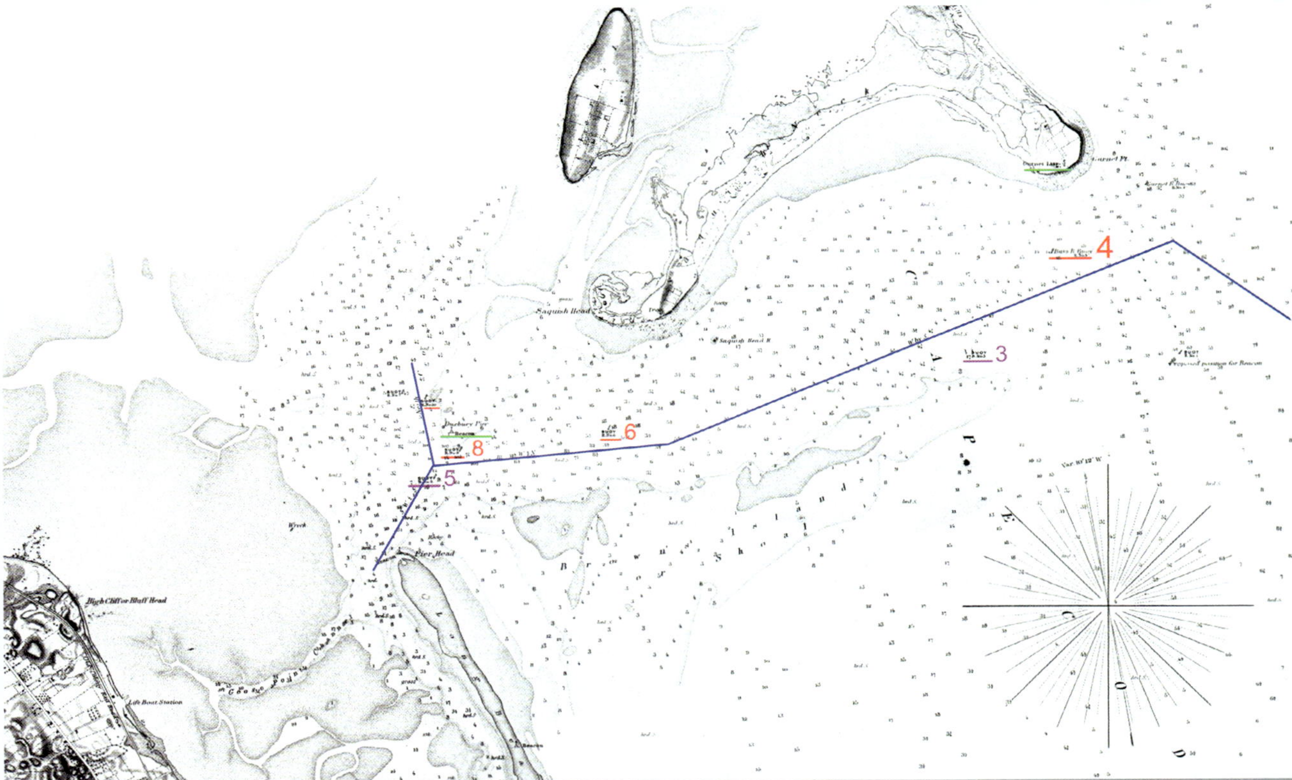

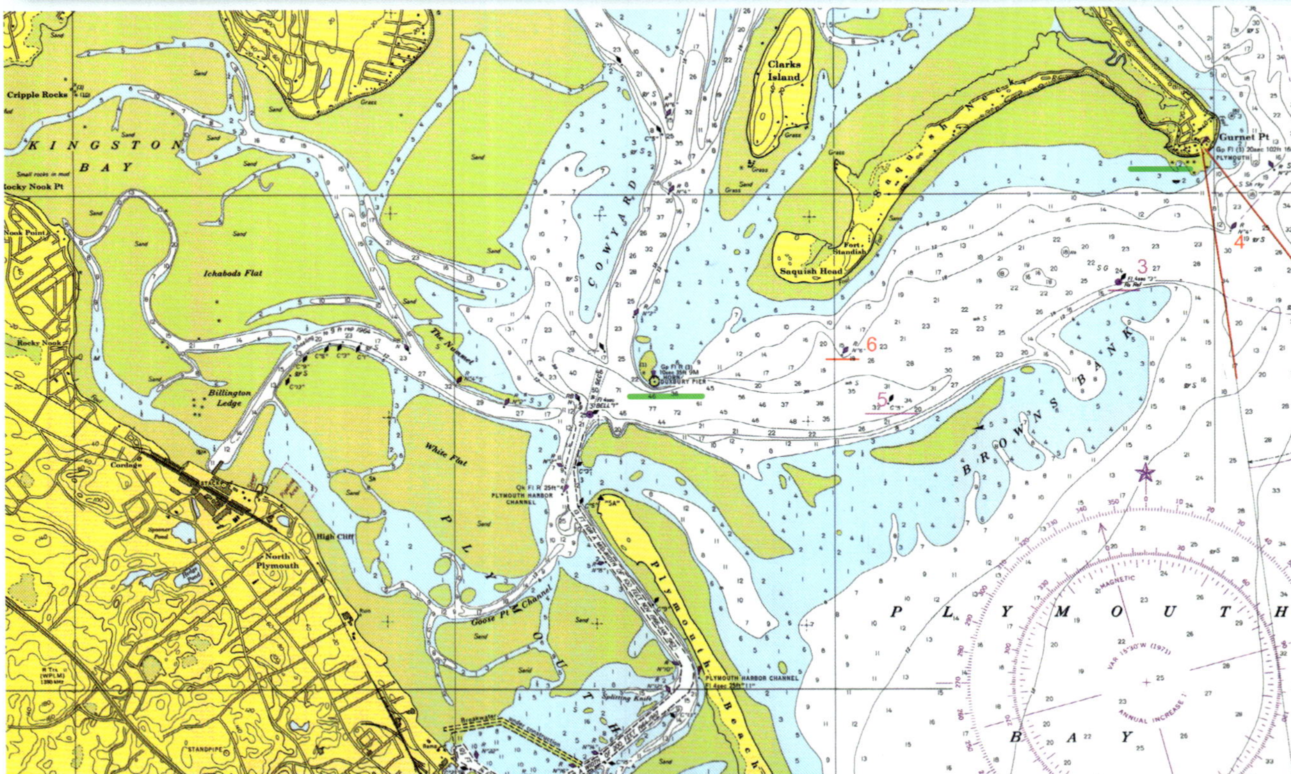

These two navigational charts of Plymouth Harbor are more than a century and a half apart and show the differences that have occurred in cartography. The 1857 chart, noticeably different in its being in black and white, also has several distinctive dissimilarities from the modern chart. The solid blue line represents the sailing course that a ship would take to enter the harbor. On the chart would be written the exact directions showing the bearings in degrees, the distance in nautical miles, and any hazards or significant structures. The even numbers on the red buoys increase as you enter the harbor. The highest number is the last red buoy in the harbor. The left side of the channel with its black buoys is highlighted in violet. *(Courtesy of NOAA)*

BUOYS

Although this book is about the primary aid to navigation—the lighthouse—a brief discussion of buoys is essential, since many are found associated with the nearby lighted towers. (The small unlit harbor aids are the buoys discussed here, not large lit offshore buoys usually with sound.) Many older charts, as seen in this book, would have included as part of their legends sailing instructions that indicated time, distance, and significant features on the land to assist the navigator.

The first mention in the literature involving buoys was in 1767, when the state of Pennsylvania placed two sets of barrels in the Delaware River. Through the years, many colonies and later states would install these minor aids to navigation in harbors, bays, and channels. By 1797, with the country still in its infancy, the Congress authorized and provided sixteen buoys for the waters in and around Boston Harbor. By 1820, spar buoys, tree-trunk-like and preferably made of cedar, replaced the less efficient and not-so-reliable barrels. By the early 1840s more than a thousand were found in America's coastal waters. From twelve to sixty feet in length, the buoys marked the channels and indicated hazards to navigation. Fifty years later there were nearly five thousand. By the 1930s, there were more than fourteen thousand buoys in a variety of shapes, color, size, and location. They were susceptible to problems such as becoming waterlogged and losing buoyancy, or being damaged by maritime traffic. These are some of the reasons wood buoys were replaced in the mid-1800s by iron aids made of boilerplate. The first metal can buoy was placed at Egg Harbor, New Jersey. Compartmentalized, with several airtight sections within, these buoys were more buoyant and easier to maintain.

Anyone who has sailed or boated is aware of the saying "red right returning." Color, as also in the early history of lightships, is important to identify these aids that usually mark channels and underwater hazards. In 1850, Congress systematized buoy characteristics. Upon entering a harbor, the red even-numbered buoys were on the right and the black odd-numbered buoys on the left. The numbers increased as you entered the harbor. In the late 1970s and early 1980s, Coast Guard tests determined that green was more visible than black and the buoy color was changed. Other colors, yellow, white, and stripes, were utilized to indicate specific hazards.

The first bell buoy was placed on station in 1854. Familiar to any boater, the present-day can (shaped like a typical can) and nun (conical top like a rocket) buoys were introduced in 1900. On several charts in this book, I have identified some buoys that are associated with nearby lighthouses.

Our examination of Massachusetts lighthouses will progress from south to north. In contrast to alphabetical structure, this structure lets the reader find their region of interest, and study and observe those aids to navigation. (Cape Cod and the Islands lighthouses are found in a separate volume.)

Buoys are also important aids to navigation. Sailing into this harbor, the red numbered buoy marks the right side of the channel (sailors remember "red right returning"); the green buoy identifies the left side.

MASSACHUSETTS LIGHTHOUSES

FALL RIVER

Fall River is located at the mouth of the Taunton River, which is about twenty miles long with passage through Mount Hope Bay and Narragansett Bay to the open ocean off the coast of Rhode Island. The area was first settled in the mid-1600s, and its early inhabitants were farmers and fishermen. During the mid-1800s a boundary dispute, settled by the Supreme Court, resolved that Fall River was part of Massachusetts and Pawtucket would become part of Rhode Island.

In the early 1800s, the textile industry became established in Fall River and the surrounding towns. The Borden family, most notably Colonel Richard Borden and his nephew Holden Borden, were involved in several ventures including an iron works to produce nails and bar stock, a steamship line to service Boston, Newport, and New York, and a mill that would become the largest in the city. From the 1870s until the 1920s, the textile industry in the city was famous for its production of print cloth—and was the largest source of this material in the United States. The city is also famous for another Borden family member, Lizzie. A children's rhyme repeats her deed: *"Lizzie Borden took an axe and gave her mother forty whacks; when she saw what she had done she gave her father forty-one."*

With increased shipping and maritime traffic, the shoals at the mouth of the Taunton River were a hazard to navigation and a lighthouse was required for safe passage. The flats in the Taunton River and the lighthouse that was built in 1881 were named for the wealthy, famous Borden family so involved in the early development of the textile industry.

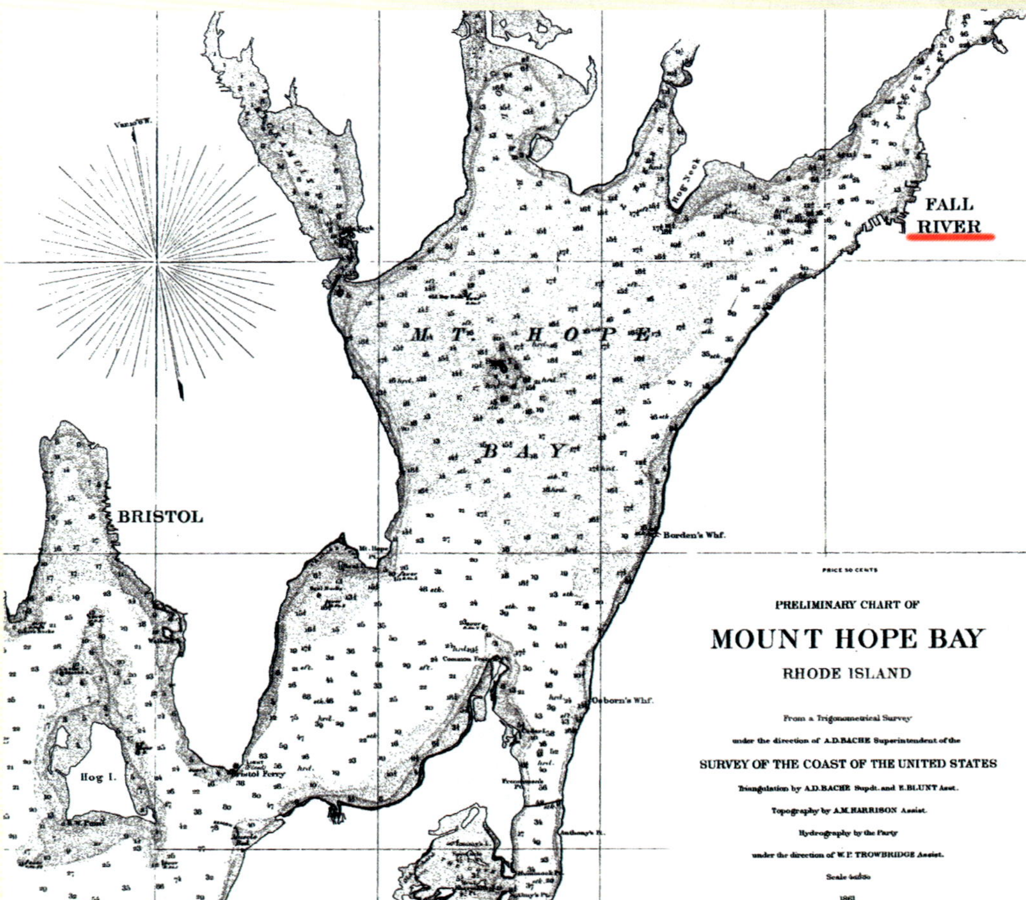

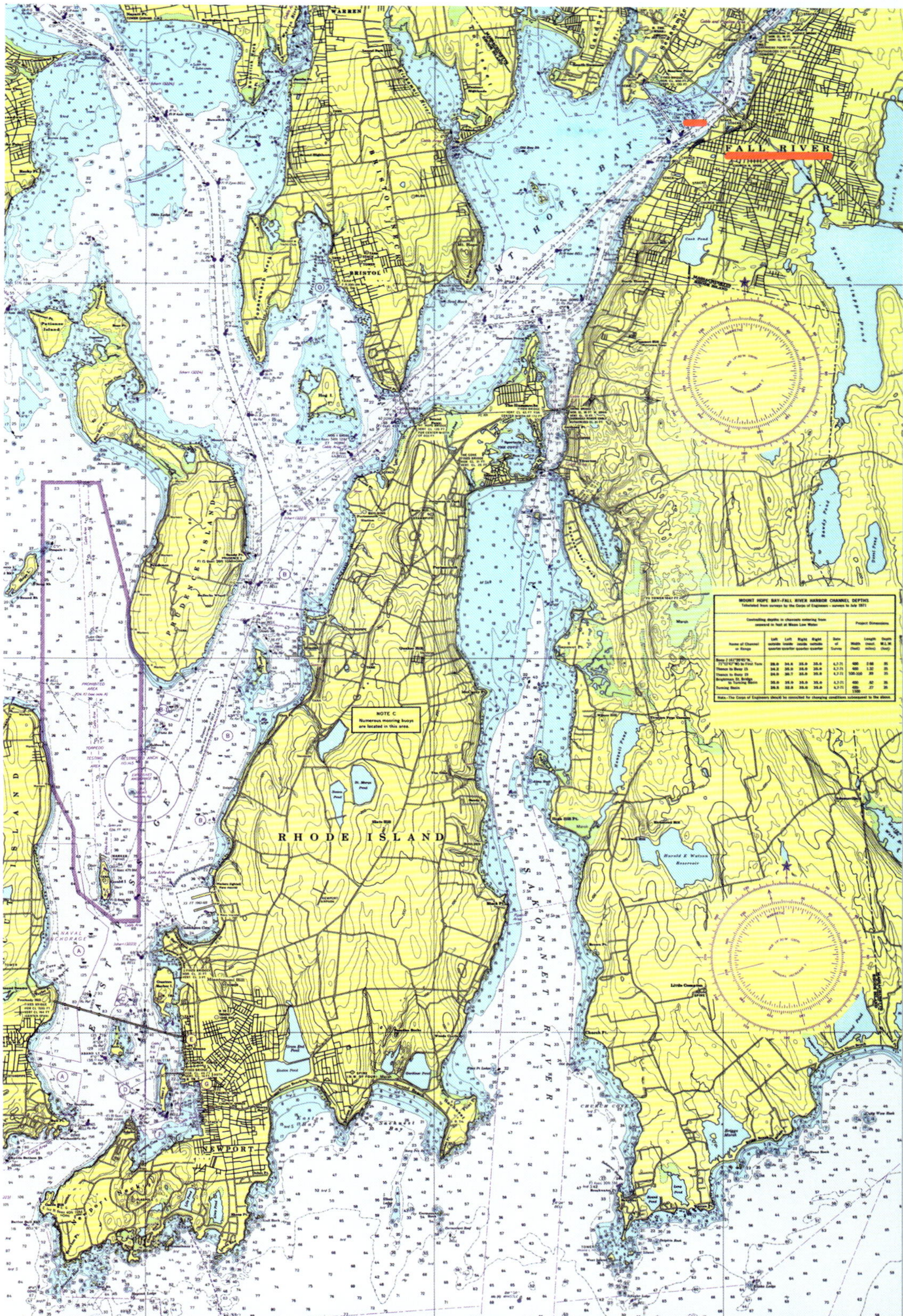

Compare these two charts of the Fall River area. The older black-and-white chart dated 1861 (and available at that time for fifty cents) shows the waterway and Mt. Hope Bay with the City of Fall River on the eastern shore. Not distinctive or identifiable in this image, a beacon is present on the edge of the Borden flats (just to the left of the red-underlined Fall River). The second, present-day chart of the extensive Narragansett Bay waterway indicates the City of Fall River at the far northeast corner. The passage through the waterway is extensive, involves several hazardous channels, and passes numerous navigational aids in Rhode Island. *(Both charts courtesy of NOAA)*

BORDEN FLATS

Located in southeastern Massachusetts on the flats in the Taunton River between Somerset and Fall River, the Borden Flats Lighthouse, first lit in 1881, is one of four caisson-style towers that were erected in Massachusetts. Two, still active aids to navigation, are the Butler Flats Lighthouse (1898) in New Bedford and the Duxbury Pier (Bug) Light (1871) in Duxbury. No longer standing, the first Deer Island Light was also of this design. First developed by the U.S. Lighthouse Board in 1873, this design was a less expensive alternative to the typical masonry construction. They were usually located in wave-washed reefs, shoals, and ledges, sites that posed major engineering challenges. In the northern areas of the east coast of the United States, where ice and ice floes were a problem, screw-pile lighthouses that had been built as the early 1820s were often replaced with the caisson design. Prefabricated, this conical cast-iron light tower was built on a cylindrical cast-iron and concrete foundation to mark submerged hazards. To build this style of lighthouse, the initial construction is the excavation, down to solid ground or rock, of where the base will be located. A cylindrical caisson is then placed in position and filled with rock and concrete. The tower is built on top of this solid foundation. The iron plates would be assembled on shore, then placed on the support base. Although the caisson-style lighthouses may vary slightly in size, the design is basically the same.

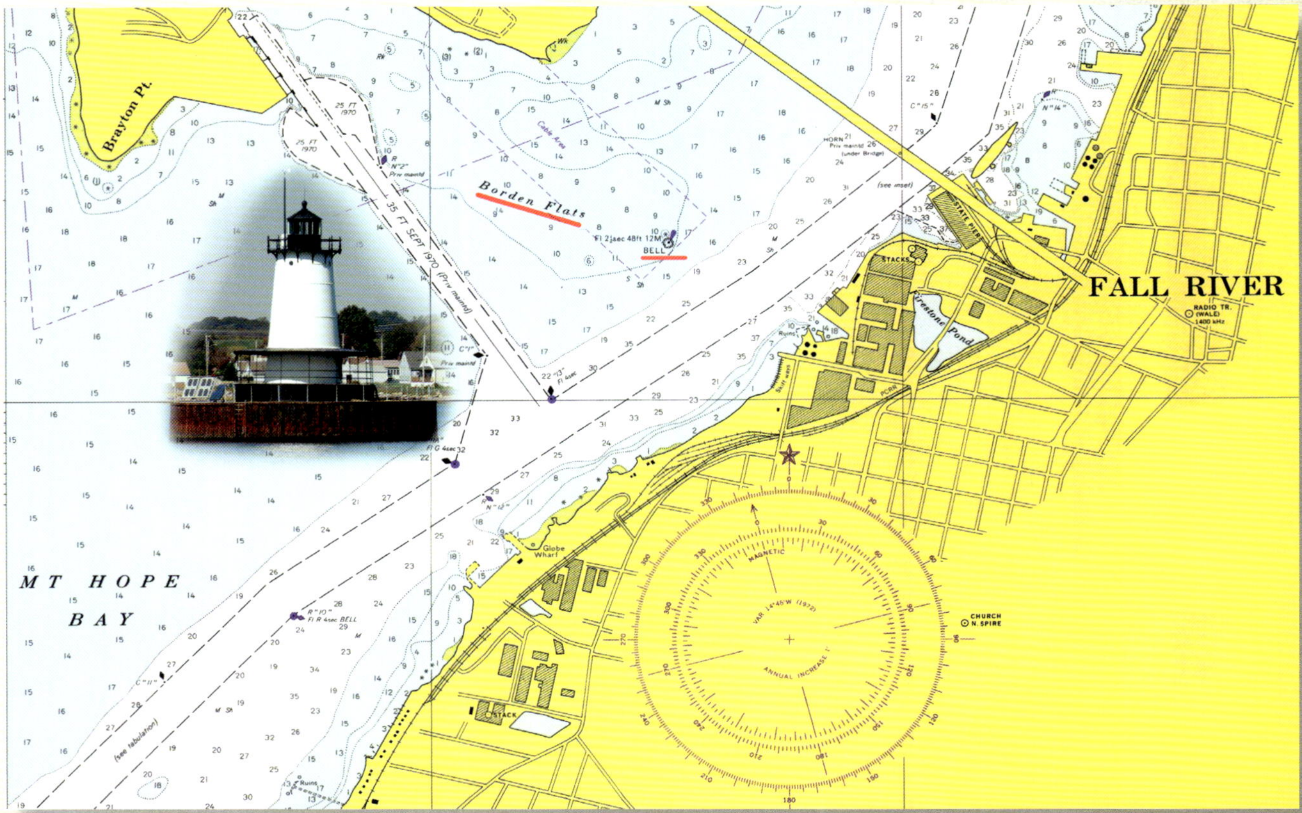

This chart, with an image of the Borden Flats Lighthouse, shows the shallow water navigational hazard, the Borden Flats, and the location of the lighthouse. The designated channel just to the right of the image, leads to a power station. The diagonal yellow line is the Charles S. Braga Bridge (I-195) that now spans the Taunton River. *(Courtesy of NOAA)*

One of the finest steamboats ever built for the Fall River Line at a cost of a million and half dollars, the Priscilla was over four hundred feet long and forty feet wide and could carry 1,500 passengers in luxury. With a crew of over two hundred, she sailed between Boston, Fall River, Newport, and New York. If a person crossed the gangway and walked all the decks, he would have covered more than a mile in returning to his original position. *(Courtesy of LOC)*

This century old image is of Fall River with the mills in the foreground and Mount Hope Bay in the distance. Underlined in red is the Borden Flats Lighthouse. Notice the two black smokestacks to the right, possibly the steamboat Priscilla. *(Courtesy of LOC)*

This image of Borden Light, taken in 1900, shows the original structure. Two sets of davits were used to secure boats above the water. *(Courtesy of USCG)*

Eighty-five years later, the Coast Guard with the tender *White Sage* was in the process of repairing and maintaining the tower. *(Courtesy of USCG)*

Above left: This Coast Guard aerial image was captured sometime in the 1950s. *(Courtesy of USCG)*

Above right: This image, taken several years ago, is from the local marina with the Somerset shore in the background. The tower is now privately owned, but the beacon is maintained by the U.S. Coast Guard as an active aid to navigation. It flashes a white light every two and a half seconds and a foghorn blast once every ten seconds. It was automated in 1963.

Left: A dinghy passes by the light.

In a small craft, it is possible to circle the lighthouse. These two images show different sides of the lighthouse. Compare these images to the charts to put your location in perspective: **Top:** The east side with the Somerset shore in the background. **Bottom:** The south side with the I-195 Bridge and Battleship Park beneath it.

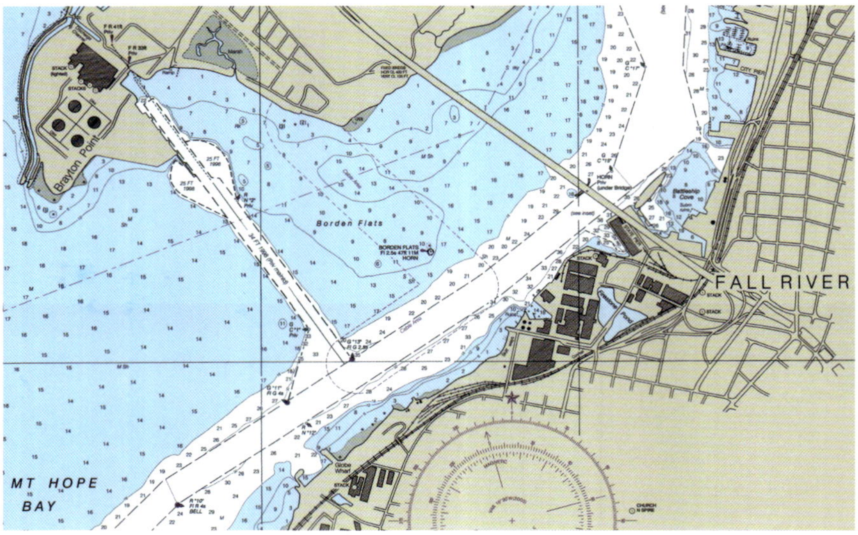

Top: The lighthouse with the power plant in the background.

Center: A relatively recent chart showing not only the lighthouse but the surrounding details on the land. *(Courtesy of NOAA)*

Left: An aerial view of the local marina with the tower just off the shore.

BUZZARDS BAY

Buzzards Bay is a body of water almost thirty miles long and eight miles wide. For more than four hundred years, this waterway has been a popular destination for shipping, fishing, and tourism. Running from southwest to northeast, the bay is bounded on the north by mainland Massachusetts and on the south by the Elizabeth Islands that separate the waterway from Vineyard Sound and the island of Martha's Vineyard. Rhode Island Sound bounds it on the south. Created thousands of years ago by glaciers, the distinctive landscape seen in the charts is the result of the retreating ice shields. Six thousand years ago Buzzards Bay was dry land, and only began to flood when the glaciers began to melt. A significant marine environment, Buzzards Bay was designated an Estuary of National Significance in 1987. It is an extremely viable and productive aquatic ecosystem with numerous economically important organisms, including both shellfish and fish.

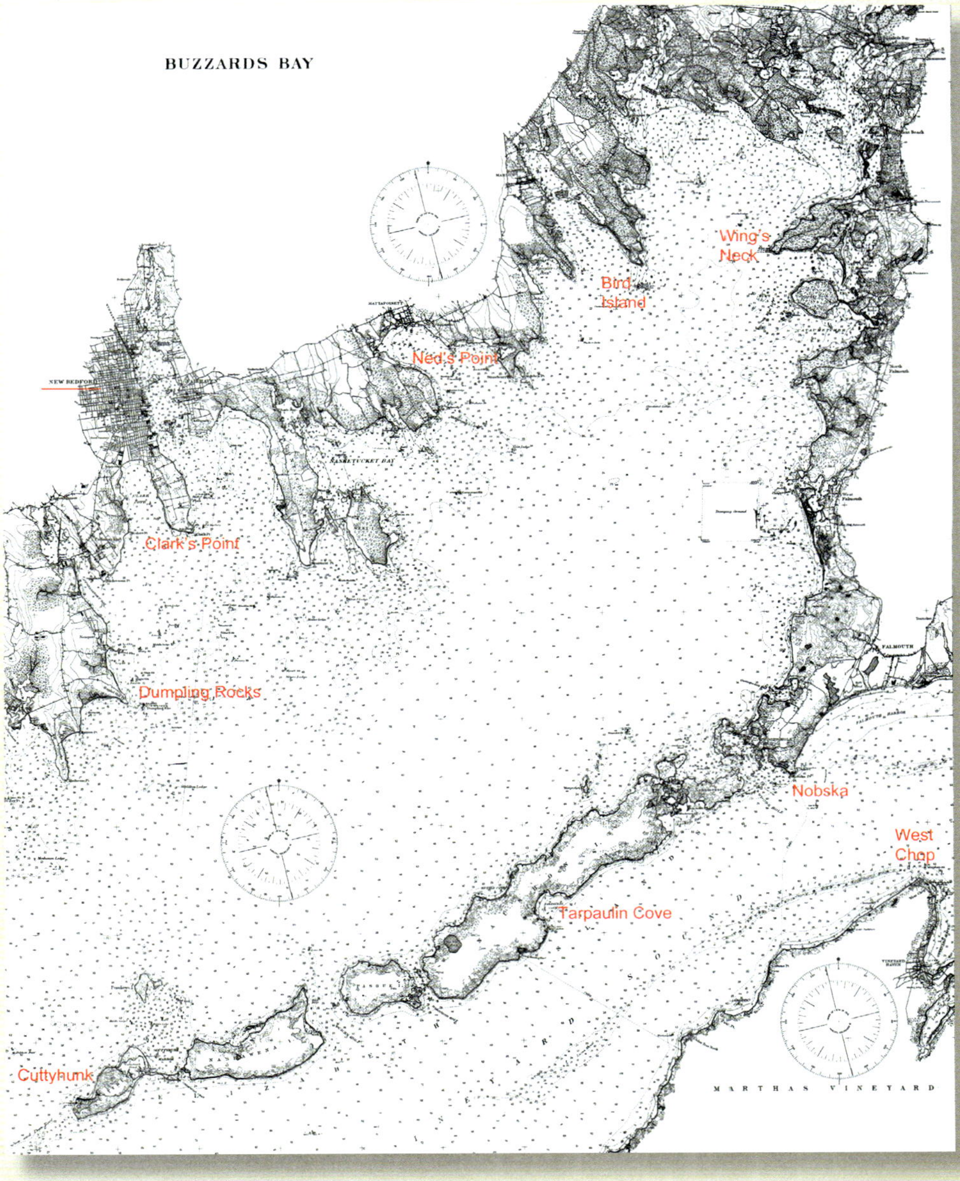

This chart of Buzzards Bay, more than a century and a half old, would have been available and also necessary, along with a *Coast Pilot,* for mariners sailing these waters. Charts of smaller areas, such as New Bedford Harbor, would have included specific sailing directions including specific course lines, bearing, distance, and identifiable structures. Named in red are the lighthouses that navigators would have used to identify their location and determine their correct course. Tarpaulin Cove, Nobska, and West Chop (Martha's Vineyard) would have been used as aids by navigators sailing in Vineyard Sound. Underlined in red (on left side of chart) is the City of New Bedford with its protected harbor. Each lighthouse in Buzzards Bay identified on this chart is described in detail and with numerous images on the following pages. *(Courtesy of NOAA)*

CUTTYHUNK

One of the first settlements in the New World occurred in May 1602 when Bartholomew Gosnold set up camp on what is now Cuttyhunk Island. He named the nearby islands in honor of the Queen of England, Elizabeth. Twenty-five years later, an outpost was set up here by the Plymouth Bay Colony at the headwaters of the bay to establish a trading post to further maritime interest with the Dutch of New Amsterdam (New York). Someone at this time spotted what most likely was an osprey and, thinking it was a buzzard, named this body of water for the bird he had seen. The name has remained.

In May of 1775, the first naval action of the Revolution occurred when two British vessels were captured in Buzzards Bay. Since then, Buzzards Bay has been an active marine environment with numerous activities. With the completion of the Cape Cod Canal in 1914, ships no longer had to sail past the dangerous shoals south of Nantucket, and Buzzards Bay became a more active, dynamic waterway. Lighthouses and lightships were essential guides for mariners as they sailed these waters. As early as the late 1700s, and with more frequency in the early 1800s, lighthouses were being constructed all along the bay, on both north shore and south shore. Lightships were also stationed in these waters to guide vessels. Many of the lighthouses remain today; the lightship stations with their vessels no longer exist.

The Cuttyhunk Lighthouse, no longer in existence, was found on the island on the south side of Buzzards Bay. Cuttyhunk, the last island in the Elizabeth Island chain, was first visited in 1602 by Bartholomew Gosnold for less than a month. It was more than two hundred years later, in 1823, that the first lighthouse station on the island was established. Through the years, three lighthouses were built on the island: in 1823, 1860, and 1891. Damaged by the hurricane of 1944, the light was disestablished in 1947 and a skeleton tower was built nearby. In 1970, all the buildings of the lighthouse were demolished. Only the foundations remain. The present-day steel frame tower, sixty-three feet above sea level, shows a flashing white light.

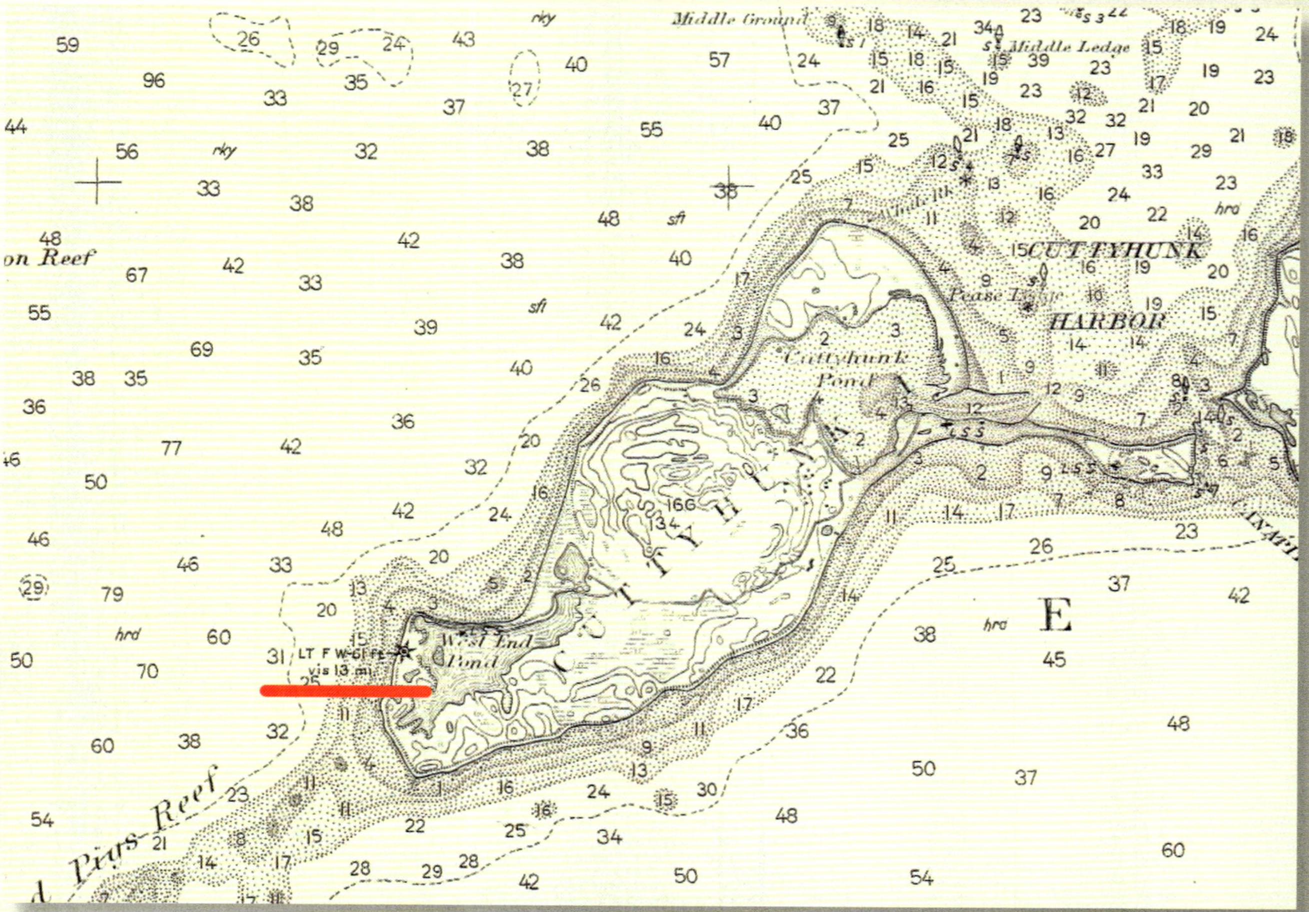

A chart from the 1890s shows the Cuttyhunk Light at the very tip of the last island in the Elizabeth Island chain. It marked the Buzzards Bay channel to the north/west and Vineyard Sound to the south/east. *(Courtesy of NOAA)*

This image in the late 1800s shows the second Cuttyhunk Light. *(Courtesy of USCG)*

The third Cuttyhunk Light was built in 1891. This image was taken shortly after construction. *(Courtesy of NA)*

The present-day steel tower that is the Cuttyhunk aid to navigation. *(Courtesy of J. D'Entremont)*

Above: A recent image of the area with only the Gosnold Tower remaining.

Left: A postcard of the lighthouse and the Gosnold Tower which was dedicated in 1902, the 300th anniversary of Bartholomew Gosnold's landing.

DUMPLING ROCKS

No longer standing, Dumpling Rocks Light was located less than a half mile offshore from Round Point in South Dartmouth, Massachusetts. In 1828, $4,000 was appropriated to build a lighthouse south of the Aponegansett River on a rock ledge barely above sea level. Two stories high, the original lighthouse was of "Cape Cod"–style design with the lantern room located on the center of the roof. Many of the lighthouses built from this plan (Long Point, Provincetown, and Mayo Beach, Wellfleet), whether from poor design or shoddy construction methods, leaked and would eventually need to be replaced. A six-foot wall was built around the early Dumpling Rocks Lighthouse to prevent the sea from entering the building. The 4th order Fresnel lens was added in 1857, and fog horns and signaling devices were added shortly thereafter. The new lighthouse was built in 1890. By 1897, a steam engine was used to operate a Daboll trumpet as a fog signal.

On the fateful day of September 21, 1938, the keeper, his assistant, and four other family members barely survived the hurricane that devastated the area. Water reached as high as the first floor ceiling and, if it weren't for a large rock that crashed into and lodged on the first floor, the house would probably have drifted away. During the storm, wind gusts reached 183 miles per hour, the water rose twelve to sixteen feet in the storm surge, and there were more than six hundred fatalities along the southeastern Massachusetts coast.

The Coast Guard disestablished the lighthouse in 1942 and replaced it with a tower, still standing, that shows a flashing green light.

The following excerpt is from the *American Coast Pilot* (Atlantic Coast, Parts I–II, 1903) that mariners would use when sailing into New Bedford Harbor. Dumpling Rocks Lighthouse was an important aid to navigation for ships transiting these waters. Directions were also included for vessels sailing into Dartmouth Harbor.

> *Approaching and Entering West Channel. 1. For vessels of 20 feet or less draft.—With Hens and Chickens Light-vessel bearing WSW.½ W., steer ENE ½ E until Dumpling Rock Lighthouse bears NE by N., and then steer for the lighthouse on this bearing. When the red bell buoy on the Sandspit is made, steer so as to pass about 200 yards westward and northward of it and about 600 yards southeast of the lighthouse. When passing this buoy, shape the course NE. ½ N., pass about 600 yards eastward of the lighthouse and Middle Ledge buoy. Continue the course until Egg Island beacon and the high water tower in Fair Haven are in range; then stand northward on this range and anchor about ½ mile south of Butler Flats Lighthouse, or follow directions in section 2. (Inner New Bedford Harbor)*

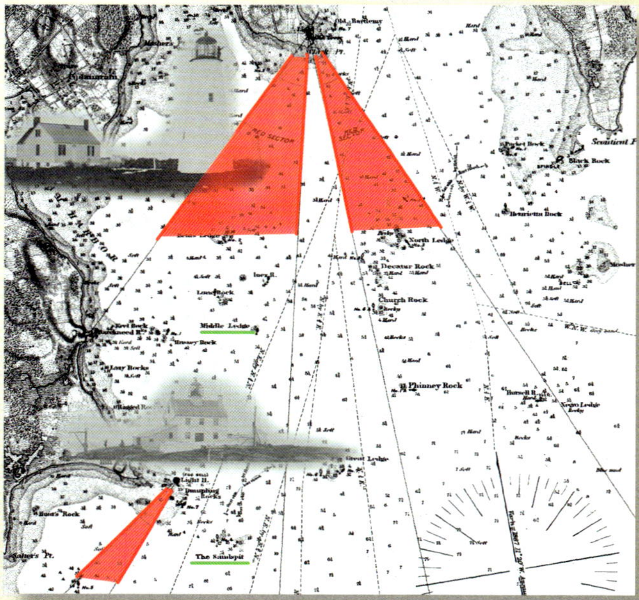

This 1846 chart used by mariners shows the 1829 Dumpling Rocks Lighthouse with its one red sector at the bottom and the 1804 Clark's Point Lighthouse with its two red sectors at the top. Each lighthouse with its distinctive signals would guide mariners into Dartmouth and New Bedford Harbors. Note the green lines which indicate the Sandspit and Middle Ledge that are described in the excerpt from the American Coast Pilot. *(Courtesy of NOAA)*

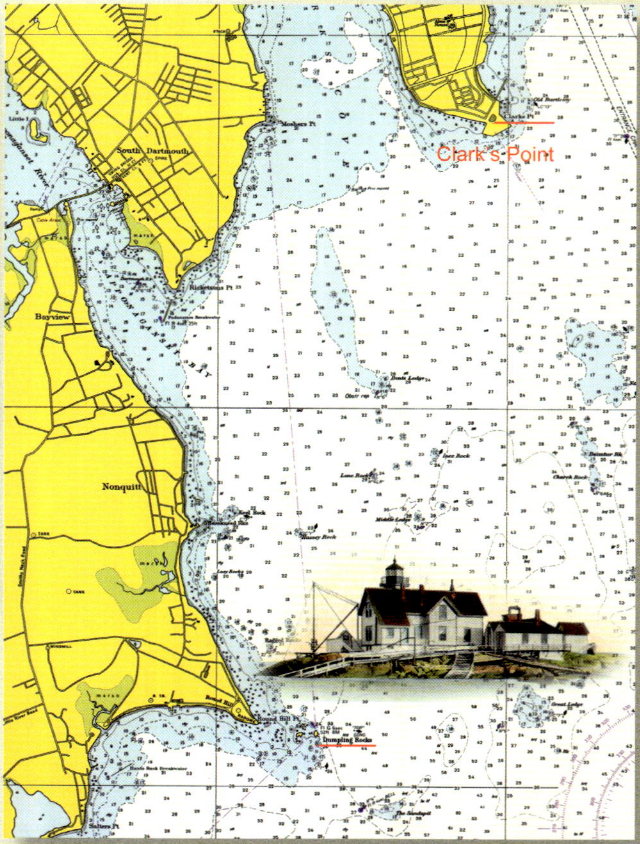

A modern-day chart showing the 1890 lighthouse at Dumpling Rocks and Clark's Point at the top, which is on the west side of the entrance to New Bedford Harbor. *(Courtesy of NOAA)*

The 1890 lighthouse seen in this image replaced the original one that had been built sixty years before. The wood framed keeper's dwelling was built in 1890 with a square white, wooden tower with a 4th order Fresnel lens (fixed white light) that was visible for twelve nautical miles. The ninety foot protective bulkhead can be seen in the foreground. The foghorn is on the other side of the island. *(Courtesy of USCG)*

This is an image of the 1829 Dumpling Rocks Lighthouse. The actual lantern was determined to be forty -three feet above sea level. A system of lamps and reflectors exhibited a fixed white light visible for ten nautical miles. Unfortunately, at extremely high tides or during storms, there would be water in the house. Note the post and bar to the left of the house. During the early days when the lighthouse had been built, the keeper would drop the bar to signal the approach of an inward bound vessel. *(Courtesy of NOAA)*

Above: Compare this undated image with the postcard. Is that the keeper on the walkway on the left? *(Courtesy of USCG)*

Right: A colorized postcard, more than a century old, of the 1890 lighthouse. *(Courtesy of NA)*

Dumpling Rocks (underlined in red) today, as seen from a nearby beach. The closest land is now a private and exclusive golf course.

A present-day aerial image of Dumpling Rocks. The steel tower is the current aid to navigation.

NEW BEDFORD

Along the southeastern coast of Massachusetts, several natural harbors exist and the busiest of these is New Bedford. Probably first discovered and visited in 1602 by Bartholomew Gosnold, the area was not settled until 1652, when colonists from the Plymouth Bay Colony purchased land from Massasoit, a Wampanoag Indian Chief who had aided the Pilgrims. Named Old Dartmouth (which included present-day Dartmouth, Fairhaven, New Bedford, and Westport), the land on the west side of the Acushnet River was incorporated as the town of New Bedford in 1787. It became a city in 1847.

In 1765, Nantucket whaling merchant Joseph Rotch moved to New Bedford, revolutionized the whaling industry, and made the city the leader in this maritime activity. Because of its mainland location, whale products could be more easily transported to other locations. On the Islands Martha's Vineyard and Nantucket, the whale products would still have to be moved by ship again. The famous whaler *Charles W. Morgan* was built and launched in 1841 and is the oldest surviving merchant vessel and the only wooden whaling ship still in existence. Listed in the National Register of Historic Places/Landmarks, she is on display at the Mystic Seaport Museum, Mystic, Connecticut.

The first lighthouse in the area was built in 1797 by local merchants to aid mariners transiting the harbor. For years New Bedford, with whaling in the eighteenth and nineteenth centuries, has been active in a variety of fishing and maritime activities. Throughout the years four lighthouses have been located in the nearby waters. The previously mentioned Dumpling Rocks Light, South Dartmouth (1829–1942), would have been the first lit aid that ships would have seen when they sailed into the harbor. Clark's Point Light (1797–deactivated 1898, relit 2001) is located on the west side on the harbor and was deemed obsolete in 1898. The light is now part of Fort Taber. The Butler Flats Light (1898–present-day) is located in the Acushnet River channel; nearby Clark's Point was deactivated when this light was built. The fourth lighthouse, Palmers Island Light in the inner harbor, was built in 1849, deactivated in 1963, and relit in 1999.

With an interest in lighthouse restoration and the maintenance of these historical maritime properties, the City of New Bedford has been and is actively attempting to preserve these landmarks. The three active New Bedford lighthouses are listed on the National Register of Historic Places. The fourth lighthouse, previously mentioned, was Dumpling Rocks, which no longer exists. It was located just southwest of New Bedford harbor.

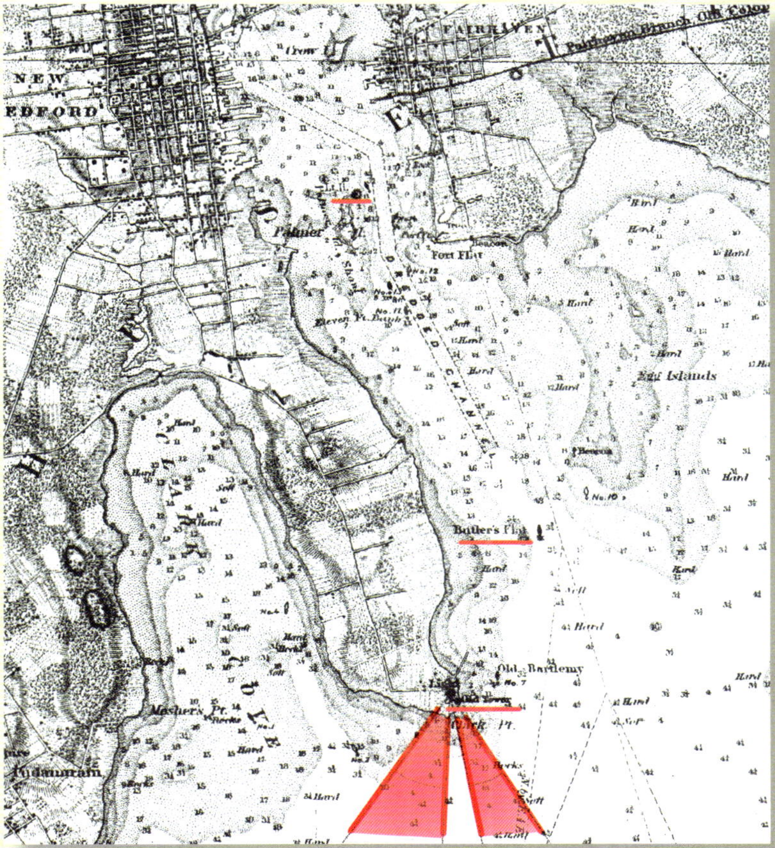

This mid-nineteenth-century chart (1846) of New Bedford Harbor shows the Clark's Point Light with its two red sectors. This chart was published before Fort Taber construction had begun (1857) and Butler Flats Light (1898) and Palmers Island Light (1849) had been built. Navigational aids, some privately maintained, were present in the area where the future lighthouses would be erected. *(Courtesy of NOAA)*

CLARK'S POINT

Many early lighthouses (Brant Point, Nantucket, for one) were built and maintained by local merchants who were concerned with the safety of their ships upon entering the harbor. The tip of land extending from the harbor on the west side of the Acushnet River and known as Clark's Point made an excellent location for a lighthouse. Some signaling devices may have been located here earlier, but the first lighthouse, built by the locals, was erected in 1797. As was also the case in many of these earliest lights (Brant Point, Nantucket, included), only a year later it was destroyed by fire. Rebuilt, the second Clark's Point Light was destroyed in 1803, this time by a possible lightning strike. Then, the U.S. Congress appropriated funds to build a rubble stone tower (see image) in 1804. Major renovations were done less than twenty years later that added four feet to the height and a new lantern. By 1865, the lantern and lamps were replaced. By 1869, the tower was obsolete.

As important as Clark's Point was for a lighthouse, it was presumably more important for defensive fortifications to protect the harbor and New Bedford. In 1778, the British landed at nearby Clark's Cove, marched inland, and burned New Bedford. During the War of 1812, local citizens set up a system of earthworks with muzzle-loading cannons. In 1840 Clark's Point was added to the nation's coastal defense system, and by 1846 several engineers, including Captain Robert E. Lee, designed a granite Fort at Clark's Point. Construction began in 1858 and continued through the Civil War until work was terminated in 1871. Isaac Taber, the mayor of New Bedford during the war, ordered additional construction of artillery batteries and defensive positions; the fort was later named in his honor. With the height of the fort's wall increasing, the light from the lighthouse was masked and not visible through certain sectors. The beacon was moved to the north wall of the fort where a one-story building was constructed and a hip-roofed lantern room added. The light was reestablished at Fort Taber and re-lit on June 15, 1869. Almost thirty years later, the light was discontinued when the Butler Flats Light was built. The original 1804 tower remained on the grounds of the fort until it was torn down in 1906. The light was restored and relit in June 2001. The grounds of the fort are open, with walking and bicycle trails that offer good views of the lighthouse. Fort Taber and the lighthouse are not open to the public at this time.

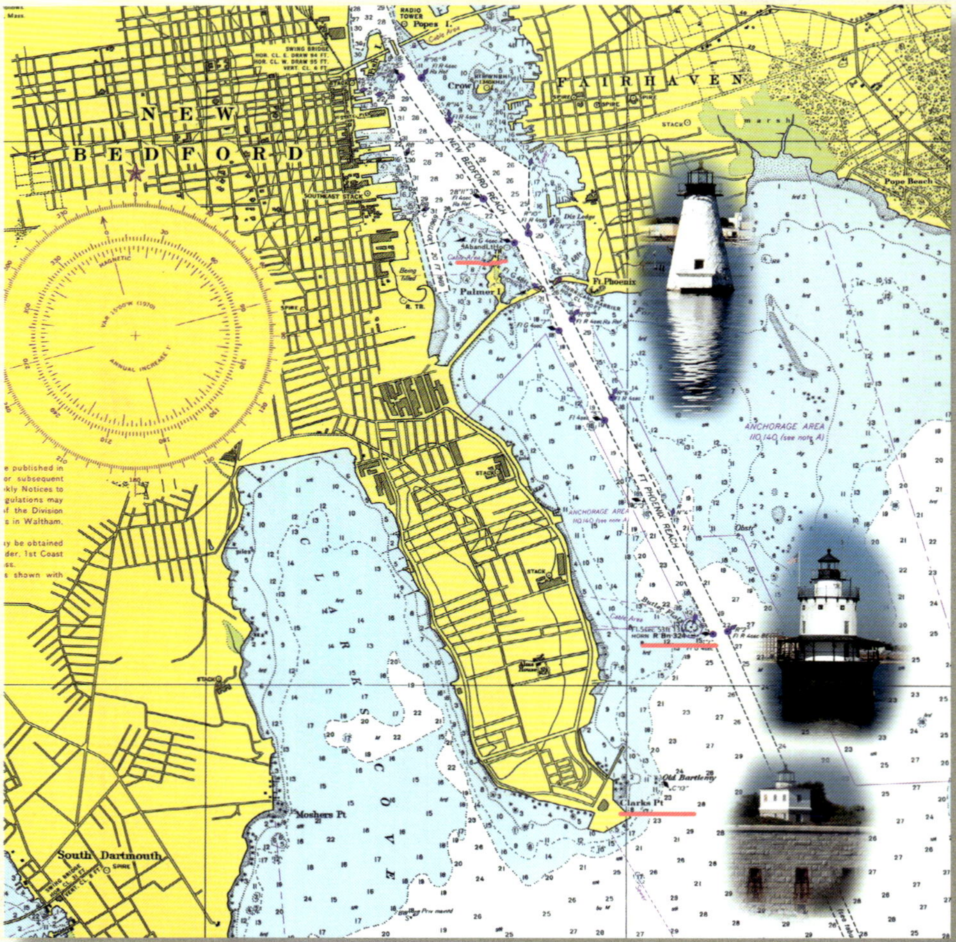

A modern chart of New Bedford Harbor showing the three present-day lighthouses. The red lines indicate their locations. From top to bottom, the lights are Palmers Island, Butler Flats, and Clark's Point. Compare this chart to the previous one. *(Courtesy of NOAA)*

Top left: A view of the keeper's house only. *(Courtesy of NA)*

Top right: Both the original light, on the left, and the light first lit in 1869, on the top of one corner of Fort Taber, can be seen in this image. The original tower was demolished in 1906. *(Courtesy of NA)*

Left: This view, from the water toward the south, also shows both lights. *(Courtesy of NA)*

Two lighthouses at Clark's Point were destroyed by fire (1798 and 1803) before the tower in this image was built in 1804. The original octagonal tower was thirty-eight feet tall with the typical lantern room. Note that the photographer has placed the keeper outside the lantern room looking for a ship and an assistant near the stone wall. *(Courtesy of NA)*

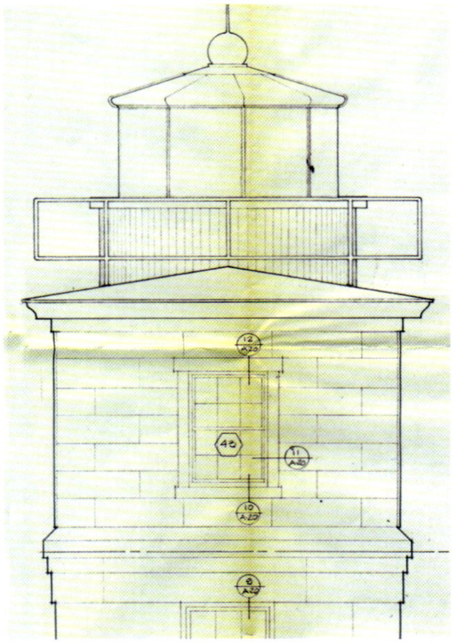

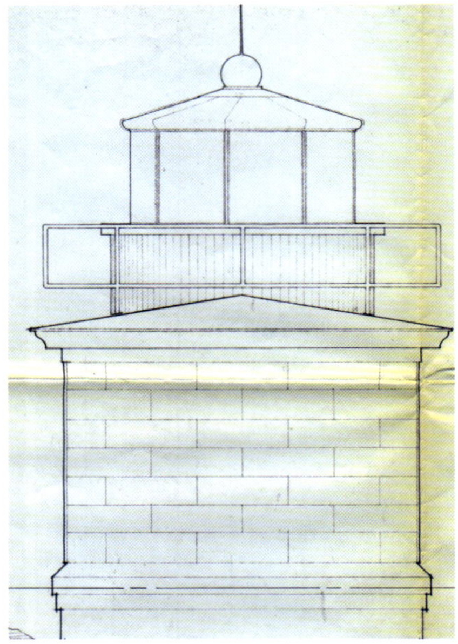

Compare these two sets of restoration plans, on file at the Massachusetts Archives, with the below modern-day image and note the location of the windows on the east side. The north wall has no windows. *(Courtesy of MHC)*

Two exterior views of the lantern room. The black-and-white photo was taken during restoration in the 1970s and the color image is present-day. *(Black-and-white image courtesy of MHC)*

Present day Fort Taber is part of a waterfront park in New Bedford. The main gate is at the center of the back wall of the fort.

Top: A view inside the fort. The lighthouse is located on the northeast corner of the fort.

Center: The two-story Clark's Point Light on top of the fort wall; the City of New Bedford, to the north, is in the distance.

Bottom: A view from the lantern room looking east. In the foreground is a section of the park with the pier. Butler Flats Light, which made this light obsolete, can be seen in the distance in the center.

A short flight of wooden stairs leads from the first floor of the light to the lantern room. Not shown, several sets of traditional metal stairs lead to this floor.

Two views of the modern aerobeacon that was re-lit in June 2001. The funnel on top collects moisture that drips from the roof.

A vessel motors past Fort Taber and Clark's Point Light is in the background.

Two aerials show Fort Taber with Clark's Point Lighthouse on its wall.

BUTLER FLATS

The newest lighthouse in New Bedford Harbor is the caisson-style Butler Flats Light, which was built in 1898 and replaced the Clark's Point Light at Fort Taber. Although the whaling industry had disappeared nearly a half century before, mariners complained of having to navigate past the flats upon entering the harbor. Commercial shipping, fishing, and ferries to the Islands—Martha's Vineyard and Nantucket—still made this a very busy waterway. $32,000 was appropriated, five feet of mud was dredged from the flats, and a thirty-five-foot-diameter cast-iron cylinder was put in place. (F. Hopkinson Smith, who designed this lighthouse, also designed the foundation for the Statue of Liberty.) Once the cylinder was in place, it was filled with stone and concrete. Then the four-floor brick lighthouse was built. More opulent than other lighthouses of this period, the tower contains brick windowsills, Italianate cast-iron brackets, fancy arches, and an unusual balcony balustrade. There are four decks, from bottom to top, they contain first floor office space, living quarters, a galley, and the watch room at the top. The fifty-three-foot-tall lighthouse first used a kerosene-powered 5th order Fresnel lens that was first lit in April 1898. By 1978, the light was automated, unmanned, and turned over to the City of New Bedford by the Coast Guard. In the 1990s, an electrical cable was run to the beacon, a new optic installed, the tower repainted, and security measures installed to prevent vandalism. Good views of the light can be had from ferries leaving the harbor. It can also be seen from East Rodney French Boulevard while driving to Fort Taber.

An early 1900s postcard view of the lighthouse.

Top left & center: Two aerial images: the black-and-white image was taken in the 1950s by the Coast Guard; the color image is present-day and shows the channel in the background. *(Black-and-white image courtesy of USCG)*

Left: Taken from the mainland, this view is of the tower and one of the vessels that use this aid.

Above: These two views in different directions were taken from the first floor deck which circles the tower and is covered by a protective roof.

Above: Taken several years ago from a ferry heading to Cuttyhunk, this image shows not only Butler Flats Light but Fort Taber and Clark's Point Light, which it replaced, in the background. Note the location of the American flag. **Top left:** Looking back into the harbor, this is the south side of the tower. The flag is now on the other side of the tower. Because of its location, maintenance is a major problem for this style lighthouse.

Top: A view through a missing porthole, is located just below the first floor deck.

Left: The lower level, when the tower was occupied, provided the heat and electricity to maintain living conditions in the lighthouse. Now, only electricity is available. Below this level are cisterns to store fresh water.

Unoccupied for many years, the second floor had the sleeping quarters and bathroom facilities. A door leads out to the stairs. No longer used, a radiator is under the window.

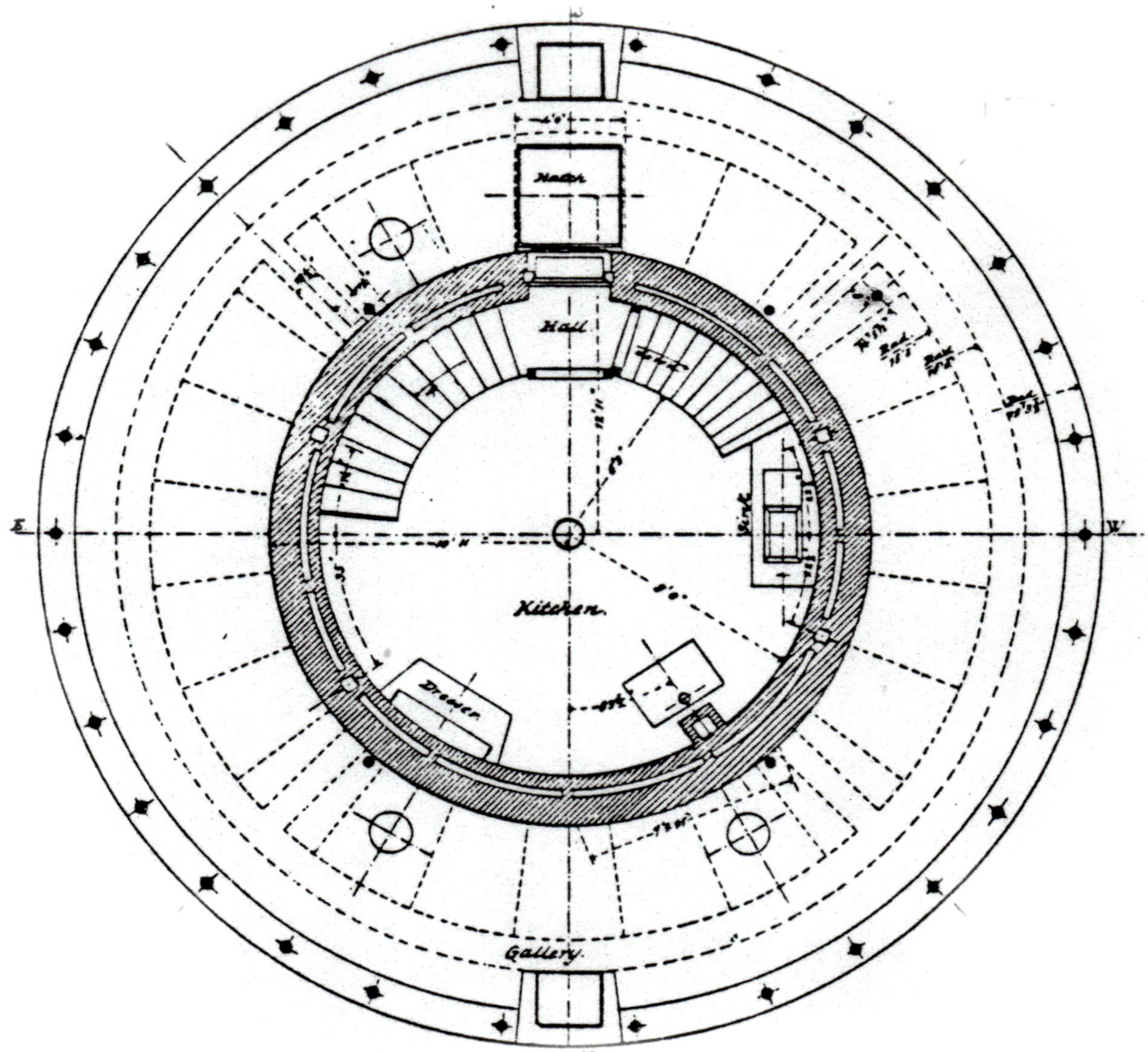

North

Compare this first floor plan to the image and note the location of the different structures.

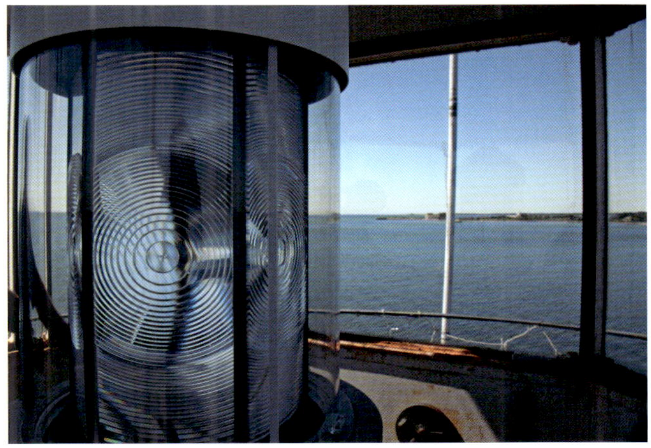

A view of the modern solar-powered beacon with Fort Tabor and Clark's Point in the distance.

The stairs circle the tower and lead to the lantern room; this view is looking down.

A short flight of stairs leads up to the lantern room.

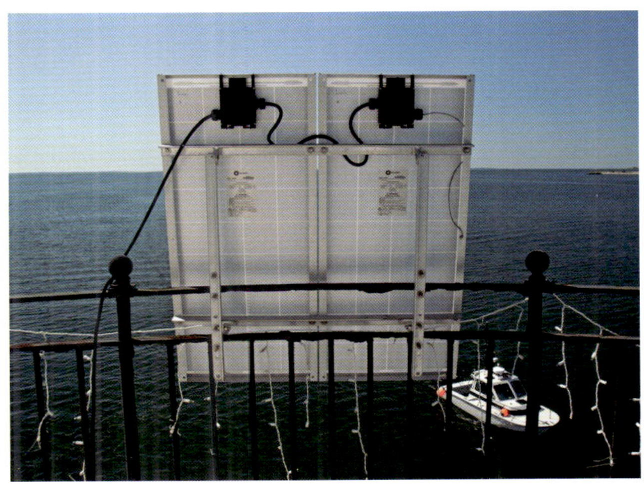

Looking south, on the tower wall is a foghorn with solar panels on the railing.

Cover the photo sensor (black tube in center) located just below the beacon, and the lamp will light.

Looking from the upper deck of the tower, a fishing vessel heads out the channel. The smaller vessel in the foreground provided access to the tower.

In this old lamp mechanism, the bulbs would be automatically turned to a new bulb if one of them burned out.

PALMERS ISLAND

The third New Bedford lighthouse, Palmers Island Light, is found in the inner harbor on an island named for one of the original settlers of Old Dartmouth in the mid-1600s. Constructed like many early lighthouses of rubble stone (rough quarry stone), the tower was built in 1849 for less than two thousand dollars. Palmers Island Light is an excellent example of the Colonial Revival style. Only twenty-four feet tall, the tower walls are thicker at the base (three feet) and taper to the top (eighteen inches) of the structure. The original lantern room was replaced in 1863. Through the years a keeper's house, covered walkway, wooden bell tower, and fog-signaling hut were built on the grounds. Most of these structures, except for the tower, were either totally destroyed or damaged by the hurricane of 1938. The light was automated in 1941. In 1966 arsonists torched the interior and severely damaged most of the lighthouse. A short time later, the original 5th order Fresnel lens was replaced by a 4th order Fresnel lens. In 1963 after construction of the seawall and the storm gate (with a beacon and fog signal on top), Palmers Island Light was no longer necessary. After passing through several owners, the lighthouse was acquired in 1978 by the City of New Bedford and through the years there was more than one restoration and repair of the tower. Finally, in 1999, the tower was re-lit—about 150 years after it was first lit. A modern aerobeacon was installed in the tower which flashes white every four seconds. Although the tower is not open to the public, excellent views of it can be seen from island ferries.

Two images, one over a century old, of the Palmers Island Light with the original bird-cage lantern room. The second image is the present-day tower and walkway. The town of Fairhaven is on the distant shore. *(Black-and-white image courtesy of NA)*

Postcard: This century old postcard of New Bedford Harbor at night shows the Palmers Island Light in the distance. Note the keeper's house to the right of it.

Top & center: Compare these two photographs to see similarities in the background buildings. *(Black-and-white image courtesy of NA)*

Left: A colorized postcard, almost a century old, showing the station and all the associated buildings.

Top two images: Compare these two post-hurricane images to the postcard and the present-day photographs. Only the tower remained standing. All the other buildings were totally destroyed. *(Courtesy of USCG)*

Bottom two images: Several attempts have been made to restore and maintain the tower. These two photographs, taken in 1980, show the lantern-less tower and the lantern room being repaired. *(Courtesy of MHC)*

Top & center: Two opposing views of the Palmers Island Light; one looking northwest with New Bedford in the background the other looking south with the breakwater that was built after the hurricane of 1938. A light atop the breakwater made the Butler Flats Lighthouse no longer necessary. In the event of future storms, the gate can be closed, and with the breakwater any storm surge to the inner harbor can be minimized.

Left: Maintenance is an issue with all lighthouses. Palmers Island Light, in addition, sustains damage to the foundation from high water levels.

CLEVELAND LEDGE

Almost two miles offshore and at the upper end of Buzzards Bay, Cleveland Ledge Light has several exceptional characteristics. It was named for the twenty-second and twenty-fourth U.S. President, Grover Cleveland, who summered nearby and fished in the local waters. Cleveland Ledge was the only lighthouse built by the Coast Guard on the Cape and Islands. It was also the last lighthouse to be activated and lit in New England.

Constructed on a ledge, the light is located about eight miles south of the entrance to the Cape Cod Canal. Construction of the tower began in 1940, when a fifty-two-foot caisson was sunk in twenty feet of water and filled with rock and concrete. The project was put on hold during the early years of World War II, but was completed in 1943 and first lit on June 1. The lighthouse consists of a two-story building with a fifty-foot concrete tower. The design is considered to be Art Moderne, which had been popular in the 1930s. The following year, on September 14, 1944, the structure was put to the test when a hurricane struck the Cape. The nearby lightship, LV 73 Vineyard, was lost with no survivors. Cleveland Ledge Light, with nine men present, survived, and except for a damaged skylight that almost caused the loss of power, the light remained lit. Originally installed with a 4th order Fresnel lens, the tower was automated by the Coast Guard in 1978 with a modern aerobeacon. An electric power cable from the mainland now provides energy to the tower. In 1990, the Coast Guard totally refurbished the Cleveland Ledge Lighthouse, which remains an active aid to navigation with a flashing white signal every ten seconds.

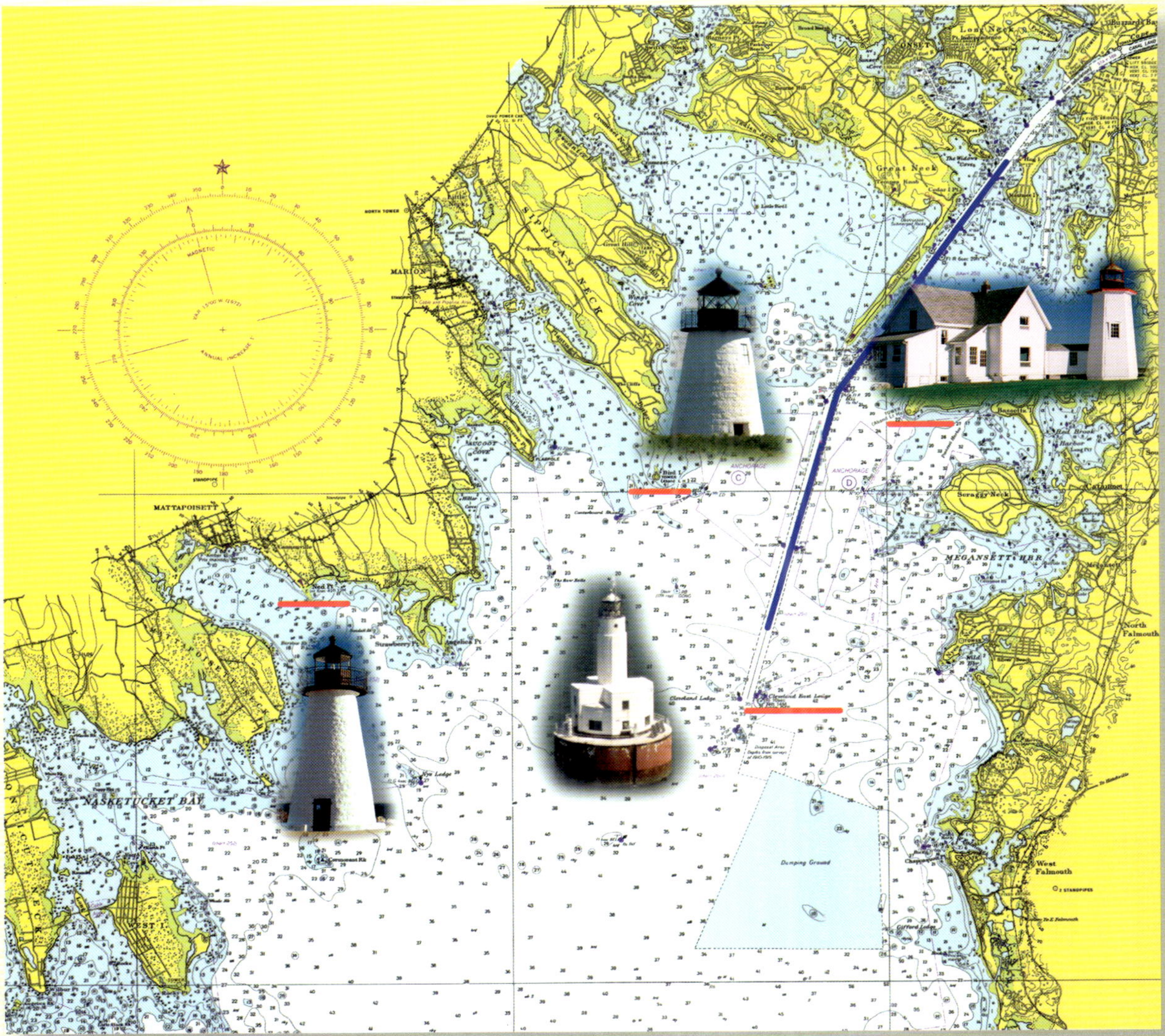

This chart illustrates the four lighthouses and their location in upper Buzzards Bay. Cleveland Ledge in the center of the channel would be the first aid a navigator would see on the approach to the Cape Cod Canal. On the west side of the bay, Ned's Point guides sailors into Mattapoisett Harbor, while Bird Island marks the entrance to Marion and Sippican Harbor. Wing's Neck on the east side of the bay marks Red Brook Harbor to its south and Pocasset River to the north. The dark blue line represents the course a ship would take on its voyage through the Cape Cod Canal. Cleveland Ledge and Ned's Point are still active aids to navigation. *(Courtesy of NOAA)*

Two aerial views of the Art Moderne–designed Cleveland Ledge Light. *(Black-and-white image courtesy of USCG)*

Under full sail, a boat follows the channel towards the lighthouse. *(Courtesy of LOC)*

These three images show the construction of the tower that began in 1940, was halted during the early years of the war, and was finally completed in the spring of 1943. *(Courtesy of NA)*

NED'S POINT

One of the smallest lighthouses on Buzzards Bay, Ned's Point marks the east entrance to Mattapoisett Harbor, which in the 1800s was a bustling waterway involved in shipbuilding, coastal trade, and whaling. The original tower, built in 1838, is still standing and is an active aid to navigation. Edwin "Ned" Dexter was the original owner of the property. In 1837, the U.S. Government paid him $240 for a four-acre site on which to build the lighthouse.

Constructed from rocks from the nearby beach, the original light was fixed white and used eleven lamps and reflectors. Housed in the original bird-cage lantern room, the light was only forty-one feet above the water. In the late 1800s, the present-day lantern room with a 5th order Fresnel lens was installed. In 1923, the light was automated and the keeper's house was moved by barge across the bay to Wing's Neck Light. The light was decommissioned in 1952, and in 1958 the town purchased the grounds, except for the lighthouse. The light was reactivated in 1961 with a modern 250-millimeter lens and a signal that is three seconds light and three seconds dark. In the mid-1990s, the local Coast Guard Auxiliary flotilla renovated and restored the tower. Now, the park is open year round while the lighthouse is open to visitors one day a week during the summer season.

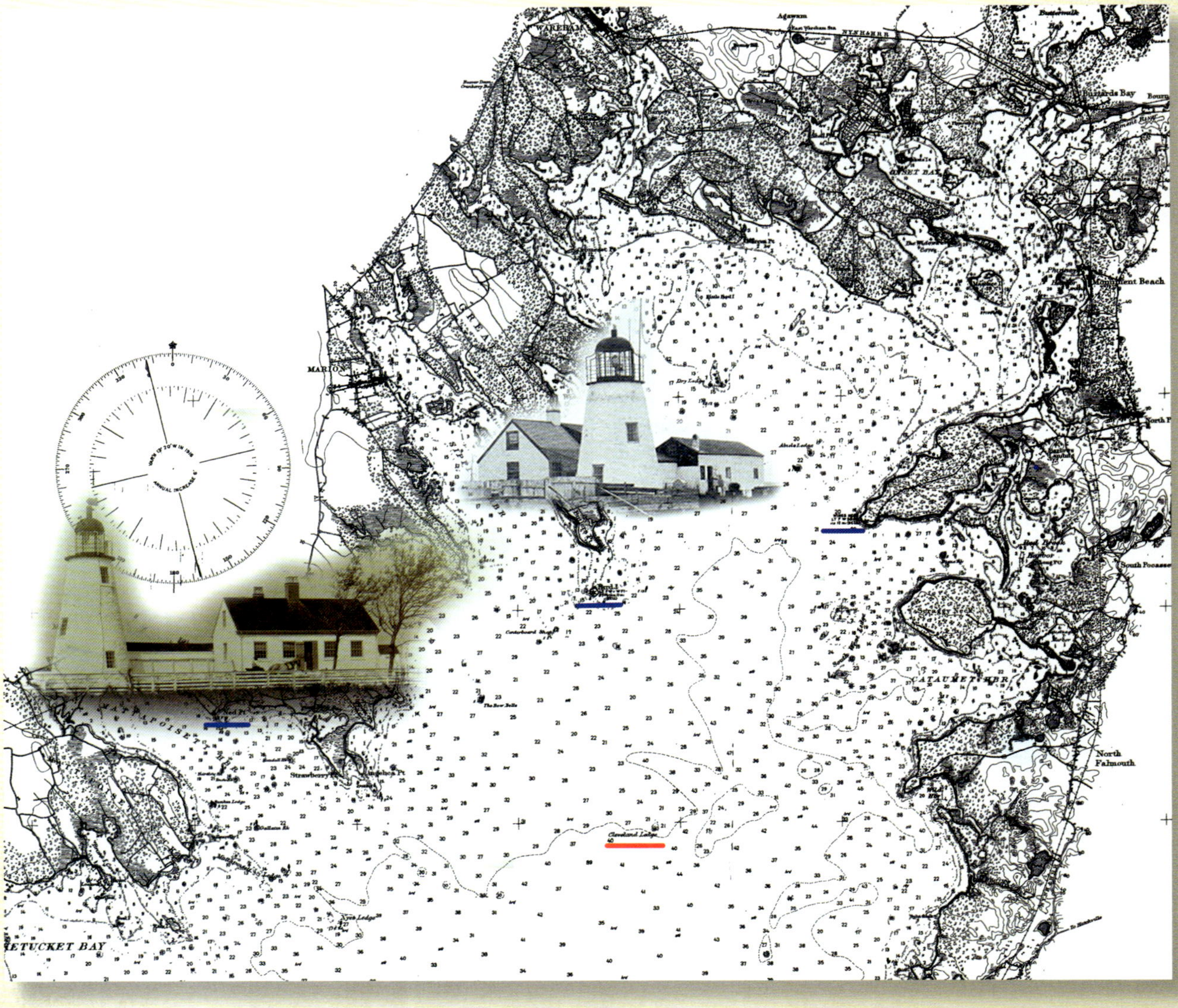

On this mid-nineteenth-century chart, Ned's Point (sepia toned) and Bird Island (black-and-white image) images are superimposed at their location with the original tower and buildings. The blue line on the right side is the location of Wing's Neck Lighthouse. The red line is Cleveland Ledge where the lighthouse would eventually be built. *(Courtesy of NOAA [chart] and NA)*

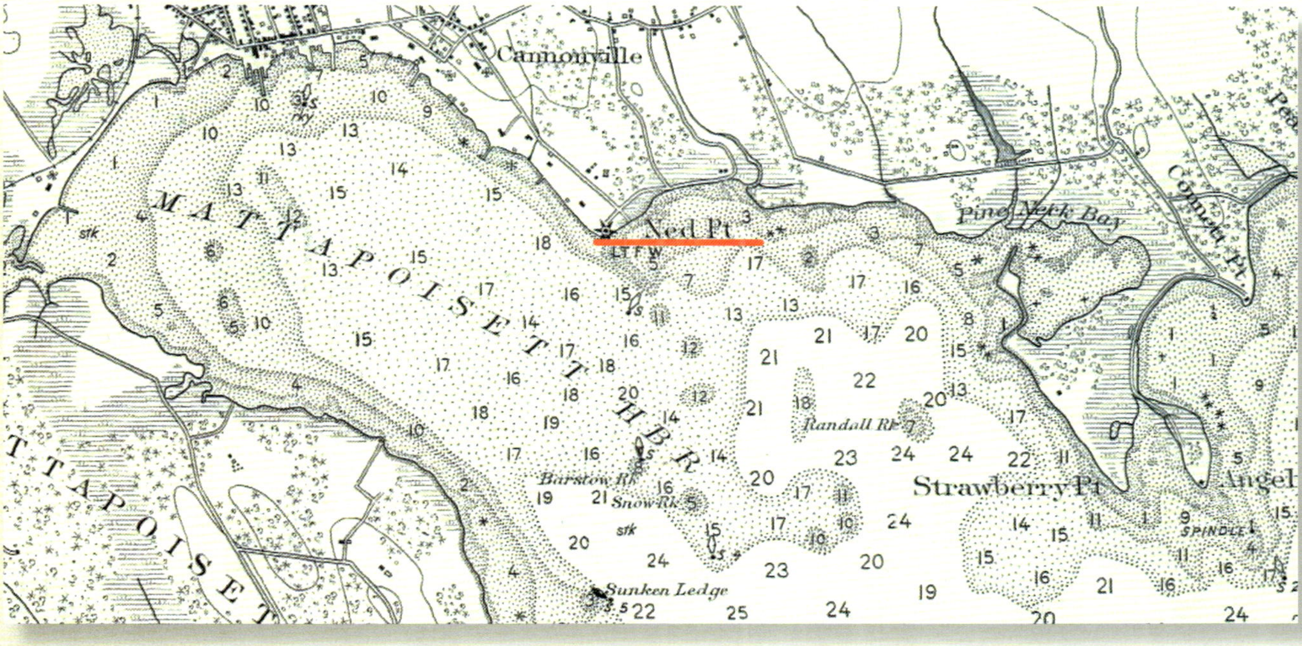

An early 1900s chart indicates Ned's Point Lighthouse on the west side of Mattapoisett Harbor. *(Courtesy of NOAA)*

Two early images captured from opposite sides showing the tower and other buildings. *(Courtesy of NA)*

Early (mid- to late 1800s) lighthouse photographers would produce a sepia-toned oval image of their subject. This is Ned's Point, built in 1838, with its original bird-cage lantern room. *(Courtesy of NA)*

Top: Old images can sometimes be fairly accurately dated by what other subject matter is in the picture. Notice the old car in the foreground of this panorama looking south. *(Courtesy of LOC)*

Center row & left: Three views of the tower. The early black-and-white image still shows windows and a covered entry. *(Courtesy of USCG)*

The door to the light provides location and answers to frequently asked questions. During the summer it is open for visitors. The thickness of the walls are a testament to why the tower survived hurricanes and numerous storms, and is still standing.

A short vertical flight of metal stairs leads to the lantern room.

From the walkway looking west, evidence remains of the location of the keeper's house. The oil house is at the other end of the park.

An aerial image of Ned's Point Lighthouse and the park. Note the location of the oil house.

Two views of the modern aerobeacon. Mattapoisett Harbor is in the background.

Whether it's summer or winter, Ned's Point Lighthouse offers the photographer and lighthouse enthusiast marvelous opportunities to capture this historic beacon.

WING'S NECK

Originally planned to be built in 1837, the Wing's Neck Lighthouse wasn't constructed until 1849, consisting of a six-sided wooden tower atop a stone keeper's house. An oil house was also built in 1849. The first optics were the multiple lamps and reflectors common at the time and used until the late 1850s when a 4th order Fresnel lens was installed. A fire in the ventilator in 1878 destroyed the tower but not the building, which served as a temporary beacon until a new lighthouse could be built. The present-day lighthouse was built in 1890 along with the attached keeper's house. In 1930, the keeper's house from Ned's Point, was floated across Buzzards Bay and now is a house on a nearby street. With the building of the Cleveland Ledge Lighthouse in the early 1940s, this lighthouse was deemed not necessary and it was decommissioned in 1945. Sold to a private party, the property has since changed owners and is now available as a summer rental.

These are two views, taken in the 1920s, of the second Wing's Neck Lighthouse Station from the land and from the water. *(Courtesy of NA)*

With Wing's Neck Lighthouse in the background, the dwelling in the foreground is the keeper's house that was floated across the bay from Ned's Point in Mattapoisett. *(Courtesy of USCG)*

Looking west this is a present-day view of the tower, with Buzzards Bay in the background.

These two aerials show the lighthouse, keeper's house, and the nearby homes at the tip of Wing's Neck in Bourne. Notice the skeletal tower to the north (left, in the above photo) of the lighthouse, which contains instruments used by the Army Corps of Engineers to monitor traffic through the Cape Cod Canal.

Through the seasons, Wing's Neck Lighthouse, decommissioned in 1945, still seems capable of guiding mariners. The keeper's house is available for rental.

BIRD ISLAND

Bird Island Lighthouse (with a stone keeper's house), built in 1819, is one of the oldest towers still in existence after having survived several severe storms, including the hurricane of 1938. Located on a small two-acre island south of Sippican Harbor, Marion, the original optic was a series of lamps with reflectors that produced a fixed white light. In 1899, the light was totally refurbished, and a 4th order Fresnel lens was added to the new lantern room. The hurricane of September 1938, which devastated so much of the east coast, damaged the tower and destroyed all the other buildings on the island. The light was deactivated in 1939 and the Fresnel lens was removed. In the1960s the island was purchased by the town, and the Bird Island Preservation Society began the process of collecting funds to refurbish the tower. By 1997, with a modern new aerobeacon, the tower was relit as a private aid to navigation. It is now maintained by the Marion Marine Department.

Built in 1819, Bird Island Light is one of the oldest extant lighthouses in the area. This image shows the bird cage lantern room. This photograph was probably taken before the 1890s, when the lantern room was replaced. *(Courtesy of USCG)*

Above: A century-old postcard showing the lighthouse and the other buildings; the fog-signaling device was found in the building to the left.

Left: These images, more than one hundred years old, show two different views of the tower, keeper's house, and the other buildings. The pyramidal building housed the foghorn; a bell can also be seen hanging on the outside wall. Except for the tower, which was damaged, all the buildings on the island were destroyed by the hurricane in September 1938. *(Courtesy of USCG)*

The hurricane of September 1938 damaged or destroyed many of the lighthouses on the south coast of Massachusetts. This black-and-white image shows how high the water reached on the tower during the storm. All the other buildings were destroyed. The color image is a similar present-day view. *(Black-and-white image courtesy of MHC)*

Two modern-day views of the thirty-seven-foot Bird Island Lighthouse. Astragal windows (a metal bar separating a triangular piece of glass) can be seen in the lantern room. Roseate terns breed and nest here, and the small two-acre island is off limits for most of the spring and summer.

MASSACHUSETTS BAY SOUTH

The first recorded visit to Plymouth, "America's hometown," was by Samuel de Champlain in 1605/1606, when he observed Native Americans fishing for cod. Later, Captain John Smith, better known for his relationship with the colony in Jamestown, Virginia, explored Cape Cod Bay and is credited with naming the region "New Plimouth."

At the time the first Europeans visited the area, as many as two thousand Wampanoags lived in the region that is now Plymouth. In 1614 and 1617, fishermen and explorers from Europe came to catch the bounty of fish in the nearby waters and brought with them various diseases. When the Pilgrims arrived in December 1620 on the *Mayflower*, as many as 90% of the Native Americans had been killed by plagues brought by the earlier mariners. After the first winter of near starvation, and with the help of the Wampanoags, the Pilgrims were able to farm, fish, and survive in the New World. In the fall of 1621, a celebration was held that is known today as the First Thanksgiving. In the last nearly four hundred years, Plymouth has evolved into a busy fishing and shipping port, and now into a major center of tourism. Nearby, Plimoth Plantation recreates the world of the Pilgrims and Native Americans as they lived in the seventeenth century.

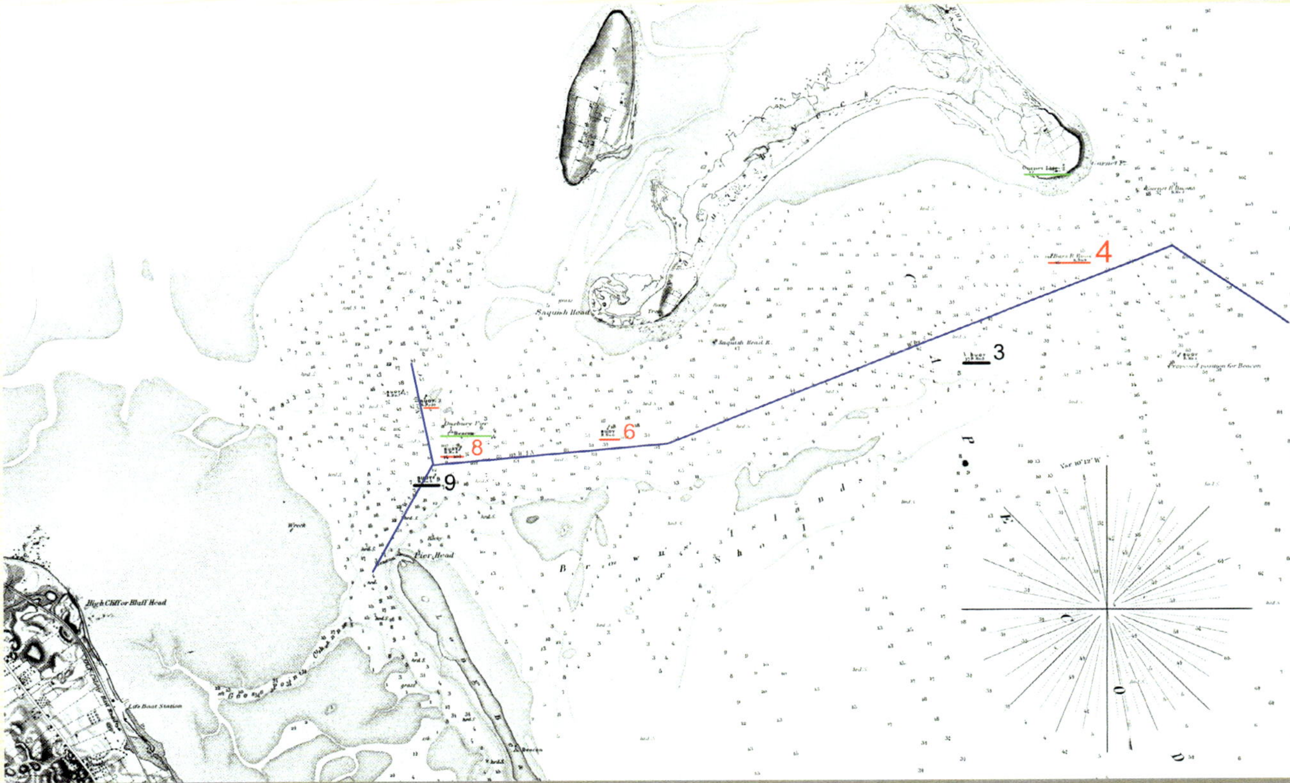

This 1857 chart of Plymouth Harbor shows several interesting aspects of older charts. Not present on modern-day charts, the blue highlighted line represents the course a navigator would steer to bring a ship into port. Also written on the side of the chart would be the information necessary to run that course. Two hundred and more years ago, Plymouth Harbor had a large fleet of fishing vessels. The green line on the right is the location of The Gurnet or Plymouth Light. There is no description written of the lights' characteristics. Mariners would have to go to a publication (Light List) to identify that aid to navigation. The green line to the left indicates a beacon. The Duxbury Pier Light had not yet been built (1871). Notice just to the top of the beacon the shoal off Saquish Head, which was the reason the lighthouse was eventually built. The blue line heading nearly north leads to Duxbury and Kingston Harbor. Numbered buoys mark the sides of the channel. Notice also, how simple the compass rose is and compare it to the ones on the modern charts in the book. *(Courtesy of NOAA)*

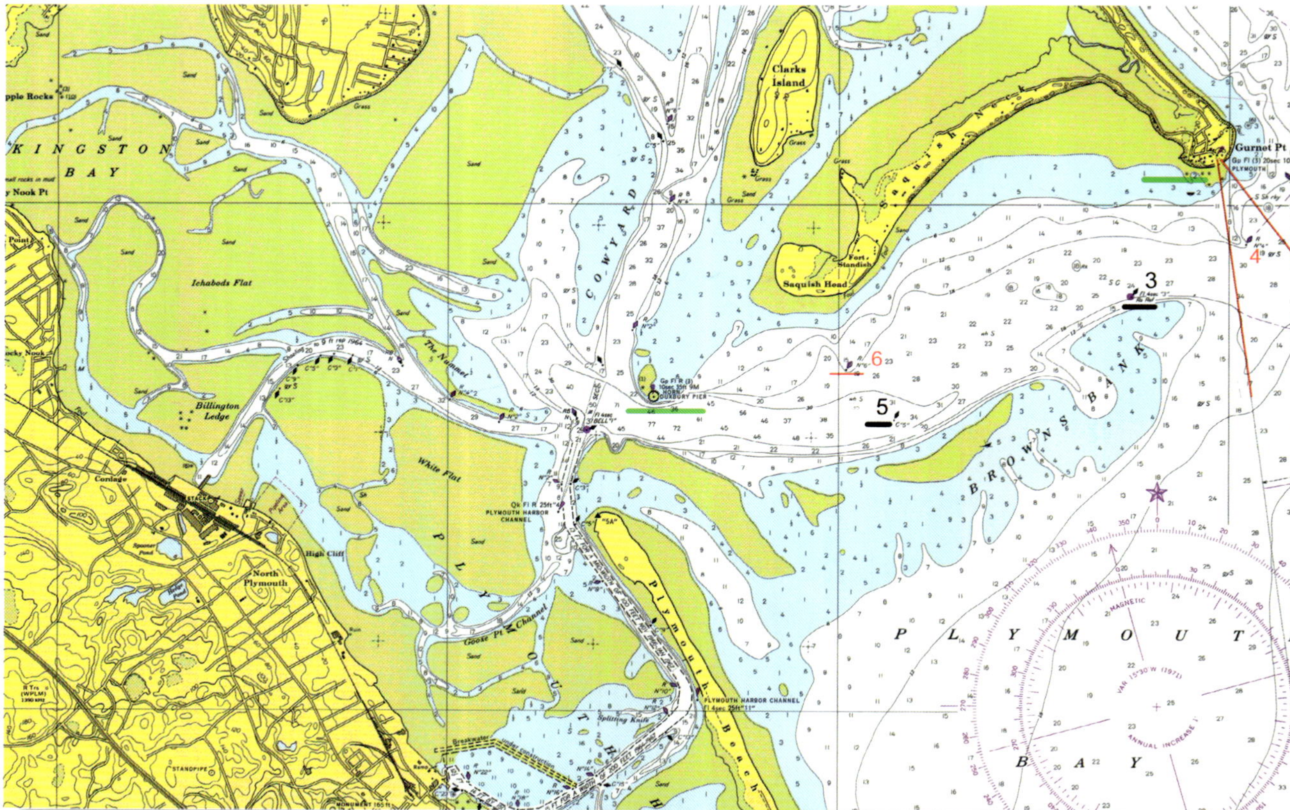

Now compare this modern-day chart of Plymouth Harbor and the identified aids to navigation. For each lighthouse, the specific light characteristics are given. The red numbers represent the red buoys on the right side of the channel when returning to port; the black numbers represent the green buoys (originally painted black, the Coast Guard determined that green buoys were more visible). The green lines identify the two lighthouse discussed in this section, Duxbury Pier Light to the left and Gurnet Light to the right. Navigators can now identify the light while using the chart. Also, red sectors of the light at the Gurnet are identified. *(Courtesy of NOAA)*

Looking eastward from an airplane, this perspective shows the Bug Light in the lower right foreground and the Gurnet with the distinguishing white tower of the lighthouse on the tip of land in the distance.

DUXBURY PIER (BUG LIGHT)

The Duxbury Pier Lighthouse, also referred to as the Bug Light, is important in the annals of lighthouse construction history. It was the first off-shore coffee-pot (spark plug style) caisson lighthouse built in the United States. Located on the north side of the channel that leads to Plymouth, Duxbury and Kingston Harbors, the tower marked a dangerous shoal. The tower, built in 1871 and originally painted brown, is forty-seven feet high and had a 5th order Fresnel lens that exhibited a fixed white light thirty-five feet above mean high water. The caisson was filled with twenty-five feet of concrete (100 tons), and four levels were built on this base. Below the top lantern room, there were two levels of living quarters, as well as an operational level on the bottom. Affectionately, because of its size and shape, the lighthouse is often referred to as the "Bug Light" or simply "The Bug."

In 1900 a water cistern was added that could hold 700 gallons. The light was automated in 1964 and the keepers were removed. Unattended, the tower suffered from vandalism and damage by birds. In the early 1980s, the Coast Guard planned to dismantle the tower and replace it with a beacon similar to the present Deer Island Light (see page 116). A group of concerned residents formed Project Bug Light, and through the years they have restored and maintained the tower. Fundraising for restoration and maintenance, with an active number of supporters, the Project has continued its work with a recent tower restoration. Converted to solar power, a modern 250-millimeter plastic beacon flashes red twice every five seconds and has a range of six nautical miles; the fog signal is one blast every fifteen seconds. This lighthouse is smaller than the Butler Flats and Borden Flats Lighthouses, which were larger in diameter and also had five levels.

Above: One of the earliest images of the Duxbury Pier Light was taken before the decks had been added. Just to the left and behind the dinghy (and not visible in this image) was a stone pier and that was how this aid was named. The pier was not connected to any land, but allowed larger ships to tie up and unload their cargo. *(Courtesy of D. Bicknell)*

Right column: A postcard (top right) and a photograph show the Duxbury Pier Light in the early 1900s. Notice in the background the Gurnet; using the previous chart, identify the location the photographer used to capture the Bug Light. *(Courtesy of NA)*

Two images, including an aerial, show the tower about fifty to sixty years ago. Compare these images with the previous one from the National Archives and see that one of the floors has been removed. Observe the rocks and then determine the different sides of the tower. *(Courtesy of USCG)*

Compare the Coast Guard black-and-white image with these two present-day color images of the tower. Notice the red buoy, which guides mariners further into the harbors (Kingston, Duxbury) in the background. *(Black-and-white image courtesy of USCG; color images courtesy of D. Bicknell)*

Above: Stairs lead to the lantern room; notice the location of the window seen in the exterior views. *(Courtesy of D. Bicknell)*

Top left: A view of the ceiling on the covered walkway. Looking northward, the red buoy marks the channel into Duxbury Harbor. *(Courtesy of D. Bicknell)*

Center & left: Two views of the inside of the tower probably taken sometime in the 1920s. *(Courtesy of D. Bicknell)*

A present-day aerial image of the recently painted Bug Light.

Above & top: This Coast Guard image, taken about the same time as the previous black-and-white photographs, shows the inside of the lens, and upon closer examination the lamp can be seen. Compare this with the present-day beacon. *(Black-and-white image courtesy of USCG; color image courtesy of D. Bicknell)*

PLYMOUTH / THE GURNET

Before the Cape Cod Canal was built in 1914, mariners in these waters would have had two aids to guide them: a light on Sandy Neck in Barnstable to the south, and a light to the west on the north side entrance to Plymouth Harbor. The light on Sandy Neck was first lit in 1827 and has been named in government documents as Beach Point, Barnstable, and as it is known today, Sandy Point Light. The light at the entrance to the harbor, first called Plymouth, is now known as The Gurnet or Gurnet Point. Much the same as Billingsgate Island in Wellfleet, the name for this peninsula was given by the settlers who identified it with both a region and a fish from their homeland, England. It may have had a beacon as early as 1746, but officially the light was established in 1769, making it the sixth or seventh lighthouse built in the colonies. Duxbury, Kingston, and Plymouth built a fort at this location during the American Revolution. The British frigate *Niger* exchanged cannon fire with the fort and the lighthouse was hit by one of these shells. A red flag—legend has it that "Maggie's drawers" were put to the purpose—was run up a pole to indicate that the British had missed the fort with their firing. In 1791 the Commonwealth of Massachusetts ceded the lighthouse station property to the government, and Mrs. Hannah Thomas became America's first female lighthouse keeper. In 1801 the tower burned to the ground and was replaced with a temporary beacon. In 1802, $2,500 was appropriated for twin lights that were 22-foot-tall towers and 30 feet apart; they were first lit in 1803. Equipped with a wheel-shaped optic consisting of six oil lamps and reflectors, the lights were 70 feet above the water and had a range of 19 nautical miles. To the east and that distance away, Race Point Light at the tip of Cape Cod could be seen. By 1843, the towers were rebuilt and 4th Fresnel optics were installed that were 102 feet above the sea. Some concern was expressed by the inspectors that the lights were too close together and that sometimes they were seen by mariners as just one light.

At the end of the nineteenth century, Plymouth maritime traffic drastically declined and the value of the beacon diminished. Later, after the canal had opened, it became an important aid to navigation again. Ships heading north out of the canal would have seen Sandy Neck light to the east and the Gurnet Light to the north along the shore. In 1924 the northeast tower was dismantled; the southern tower remains as an active aid to navigation. In 1994, the light was converted to solar power.

Two images of the twin lights were captured early in the last century. The oval sepia-toned photograph was characteristic of images taken of lighthouses in the nineteenth century. The other image is a postcard. *(Courtesy of NA)*

Popular with photographers, lighthouses were excellent subjects, and most could be shot from an interesting variety of angles. These four postcards more than a century old are different views of the Gurnet and the lighthouse.

Compare this image taken by the Coast Guard in the 1950s with the present-day similar views on page 73. *(Courtesy of USCG)*

As part of a survey of aids to navigation by the Coast Guard in the early 1950s, these two black-and-white aerial images captured the Gurnet and show the surrounding area. Close examination reveals the changes that have occurred to the buildings through the years. Compare these with the two present-day aerial images on the facing page. *(Black-and-white image courtesy of USCG)*

Two present-day aerial images of Gurnet Point, looking east toward Massachusetts Bay and looking north toward Duxbury Beach.

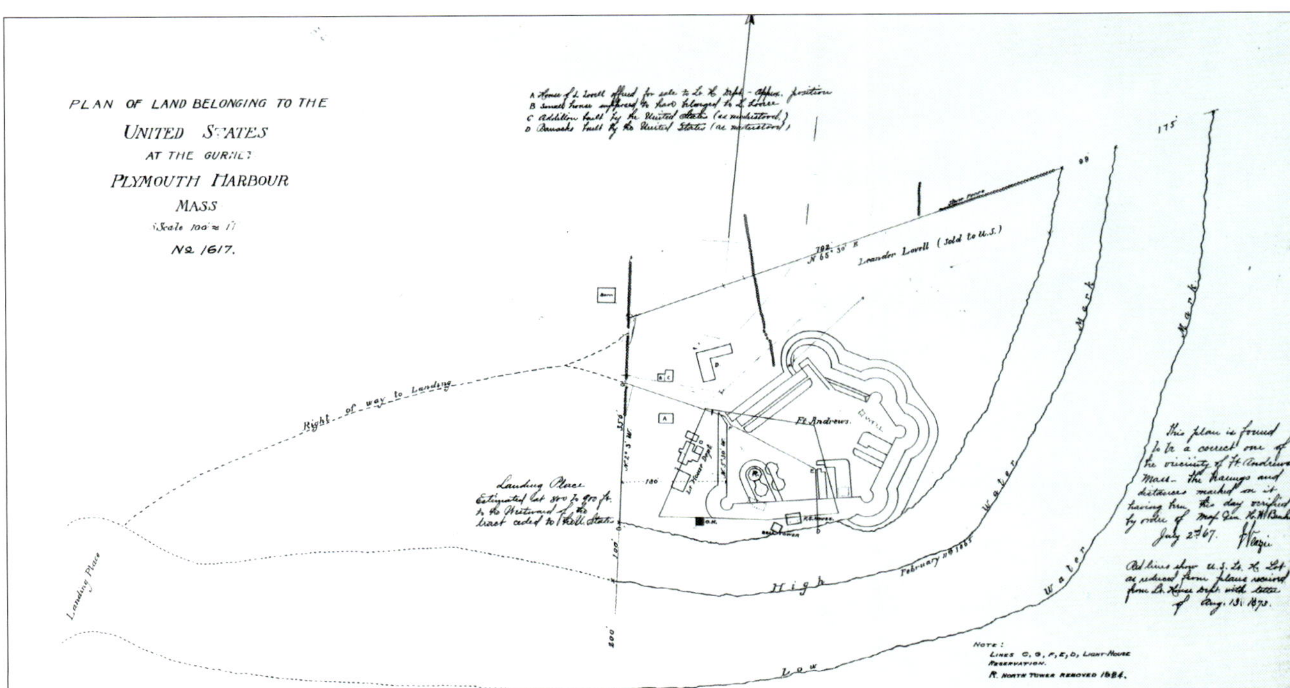

A drawing, dated July 2, 1867, and labeled "Plan of Land Belonging to the United States at the Gurnet, Plymouth Harbor, Mass," was found in historical documents and was included as part of the HABS study of Plymouth Light. Note the design of the fort, and find the protective berms that are visible in the previous aerial images. *(Courtesy of LOC)*

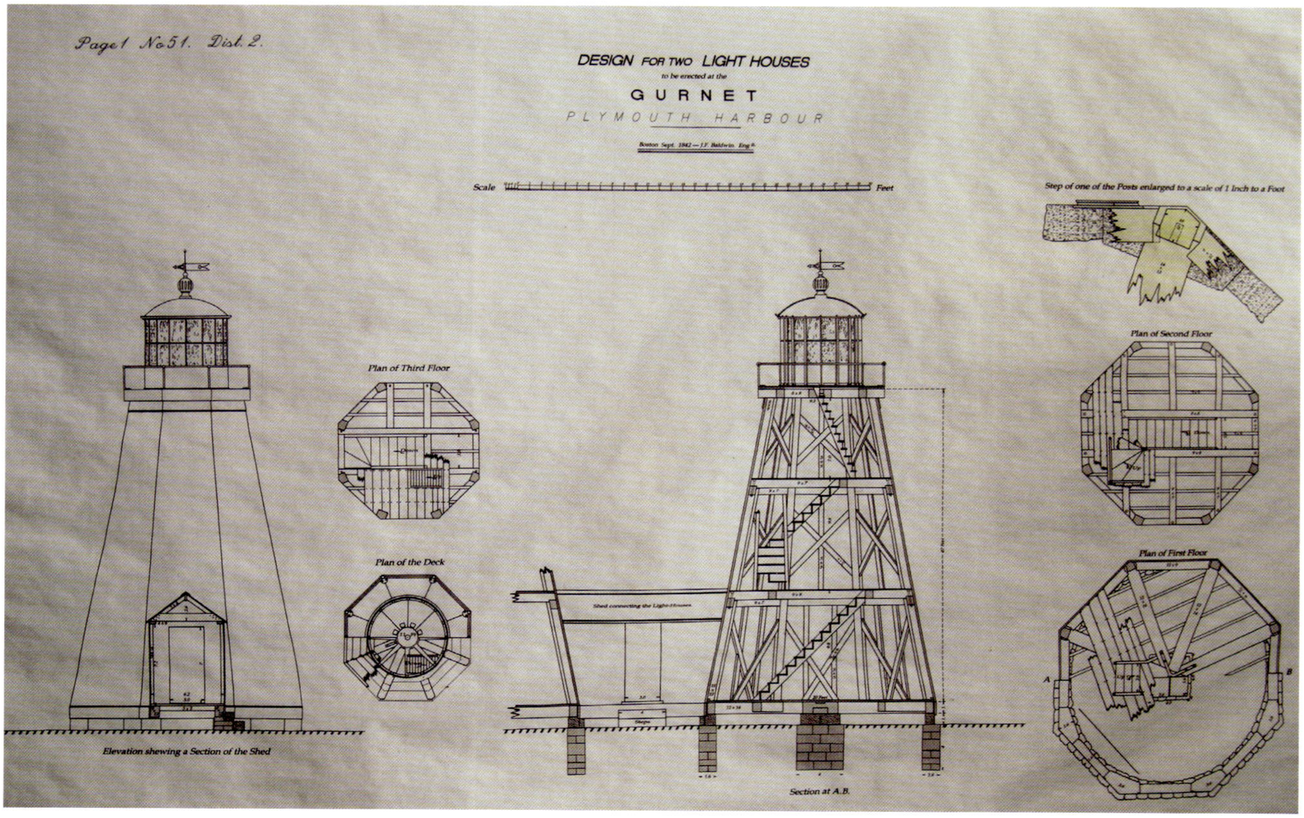

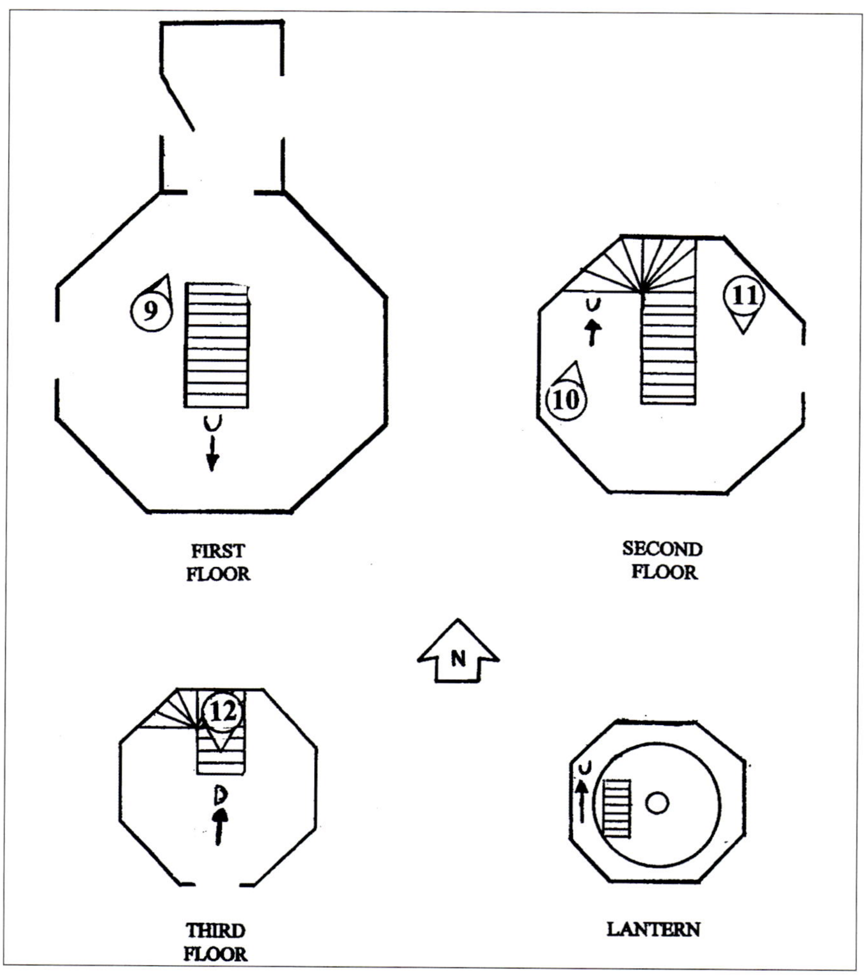

Top: This plan, on display on the first floor of Gurnet Light, shows visitors the tower, floor plans of the four levels, and a cross section showing dimensions of the lumber used in constructing the building. *(Courtesy of NA)*

Bottom: Simplified floor plans showing the arrangement of the stairs; the circles with numbers indicate where the HABS photographs were taken. Some of those images can be seen on the following pages. *(Courtesy of LOC)*

The Library of Congress in conjunction with HABS, HAER, and HALS (Historic American Buildings Surveys, Engineering Records, Landscape Surveys) identifies, examines, photographs, and records the history of a significant property: "Plymouth Light, built in 1843, is significant as the oldest timber-framed lighthouse in the United States. It is located on the Gurnet, a strategic coastal location that has been the site of fortifications manned during the Revolutionary War, the War of 1812, the Civil War, and World War II, and was also the site of U.S. Coast Guard Lifesaving Station." These black-and-white images of the exterior of the tower were captured in the late 1960s by the photographer Robert Brewster and the historical data was collated by Matthew A. Kierstead. Compare them with the present-day color photographs and observe the changes that have occurred in the last fifty years. *(Black-and-white images courtesy of LOC)*

Compare the above three pairs of interior images of the stairs and walls of the tower. The aids to navigation, light and foghorn, are maintained by the U. S. Coast Guard; the tower is maintained, including occasional tours, by the Project Gurnet & Bug Lights. *(Black-and-white images courtesy of LOC)*

Above: An exterior view of the lantern room with the date of construction shown; access to the walkway around the lantern room is only by the ladder on the outside of the tower.

Left: A final flight of stairs leads to the lantern room.

Center: Two views of the lantern room showing the two lamps, which include a back-up if the primary light goes out. The red sector faces south; refer to the present-day chart of Plymouth Bay (page 64) which shows the sector's scope.

Left: This view from the lamp room is looking west into Plymouth Bay. On the third panel from the right, the small red line indicates the location of the Bug Light. The white house, just in front of the tower,is the former keeper's house.

Top: Looking north, the lighthouse with Duxbury Beach in the background.

Center: Located at the highest point on the Gurnet, the signal from the tower can be seen over 360 degrees.

Right: The view from the bedroom of the keeper's house. Rooms are available for seasonal rental.

SCITUATE

In 1810, the Federal government allocated $4,000 for the construction of a lighthouse on the north side of the inlet, land referred to as Cedar Point, leading into Scituate Harbor. A year later, a light tower, wood-framed keeper's house, oil house, and well were built; the light was first lit in September, 1811. One story about the lighthouse is often called "The American Army of Two." During the War of 1812, in September 1814, the British entered the harbor in the naval ship *La Hogue,* and planned to burn the town. The absent keeper's teenage daughters extinguished the light and proceeded to play a fife and drum in the nearby woods. Thinking a force was being mustered, the British withdrew and the town was saved.

The original tower was octagonal, 25 feet tall, and built of split granite blocks lined with rubble stone. The first light was a pan of whale oil with several burning wicks that were placed 35 feet high and visible for six miles. In 1827, the height was increased by adding fifteen feet of bricks and granite. The lamps were also changed at this time; now there were two lamps, the top one fixed white and the bottom one fixed red. They were ineffective as a signal, and it wasn't until 1855 that a Fresnel lens was installed and the problem resolved. When Minot's Ledge Light was built, Scituate Light was deemed unnecessary, and was darkened on November 15, 1860. In 1917, the town paid $2,500 to the federal government for the fifty-foot tower and the surrounding land, with the stipulation that the property be maintained "as an historic landmark."

In one interesting story about the lighthouse, the *Etrusco,* an Italian freighter, ran aground next to the tower during a blizzard in March of 1956. Finally, after rock was removed from the beach, the ship was floated off the following December. The joke making the rounds at that time was that they were waiting for Proctor and Gamble to send a large load of Tide.

Deactivated in 1860, the light was not re-lit until 1990. The first light, blue, was barely visible even from land and it wasn't until 1994 that the light was re-lit as a private aid to navigation. Maintained by the Scituate Historical Society and listed on the National Register of Historic Places, the lighthouse now has a keeper living in the original 1811 house. The tower is open several times a year to visitors. The present 250-millimeter optic flashes white every fifteen seconds. The grounds and breakwaters are open year round, and excellent views can be enjoyed by visitors.

A present-day chart with present-day images showing the two lighthouses just south of Boston, with Minot at the top and Scituate at the bottom. Cohasset Harbor is located to the left of Minot Light; Scituate Harbor and the inlet are located just to the south of the lighthouse image. *(Courtesy of NOAA)*

A present-day aerial image of Scituate Harbor that shows the north side of the inlet with the lighthouse to the left at the end of the land. The red roofed Coast Guard building and dock can be seen on the far left across the harbor.

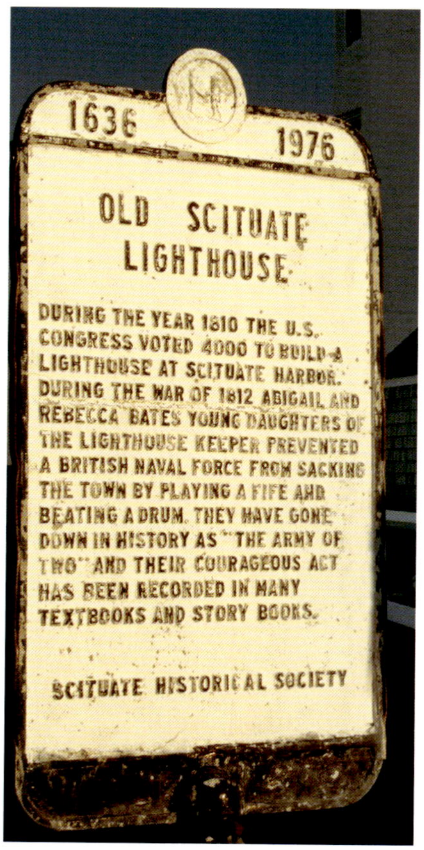

A sign erected by the Scituate Historical Society that briefly explains the history of the light. As noted on the sign, Scituate was incorporated in 1636.

This undated image of Scituate Light and the keeper's house was probably taken before 1885, when the construction of the breakwater began. *(Courtesy of NA)*

This dated image of 1902 shows the end of the breakwater and the spar beacon that was first lit in June, 1901. The spar was destroyed by a storm in 1904 and replaced by a skeleton tower that displayed a fixed red light. The beacon was maintained by a keeper who lived in the nearby house. Note the absence of the lantern room in the tower that was no longer active. *(Courtesy of NA)*

The same vintage as the previous image, this photograph is taken from the north side of the lighthouse compound. Minus a lantern room and not an active aid to navigation, the tower was falling into disrepair. Observe the outhouse just in front of the keeper's house on the right. *(Courtesy of NA)*

An image from the early 1900s. Is the young girl the keeper's daughter?

Postcard: A colorized postcard of the tower when it was falling into disrepair. Evidence of the bricks that were added to increase height can be easily seen.

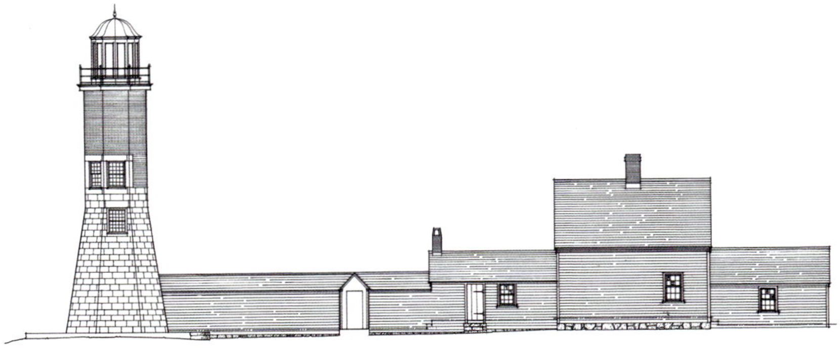

This diagram of Scituate Light was drawn for the Library of Congress HABS study during the 1930s The black-and-white photograph was taken at the same time; the color image is contemporary. *(Plan and black-and-white image courtesy of LOC)*

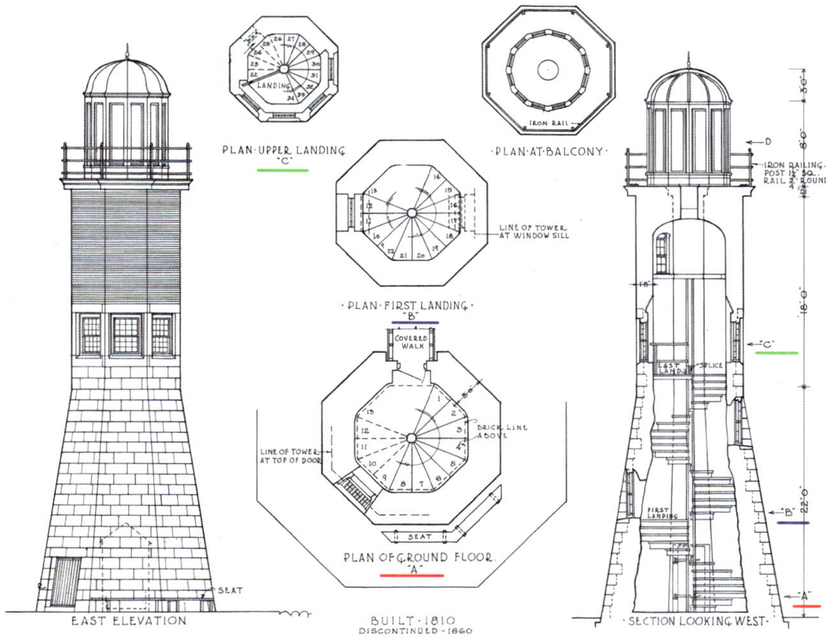

These drawings of the tower, as part of the HABS survey, show numerous details in the structure.

This aerial taken by the Coast Guard in the 1950s is looking northeast towards the inlet and Scituate Light in the distance. The distinctive white building with the pier in the left foreground is part of the Coast Guard Station. It is possible to see the three breakwaters. *(Courtesy of USCG)*

Top row: Two images from the 1950s show a close-up of the tower and view of it from across the harbor. *(Courtesy of LOC and MHS)*

Bottom row: As it looks today, two different sides of the tower.

Decorated for the holidays, this section of the keeper's cottage was built in 1810.

Above: Nearby is the house that was the home of Rebecca and Abigail Bates.

Left: Inside the keeper's house, a painting depicts the story of "the American Army of Two." Below it, in a case, is the fife used during the encounter with the British in 1814. A plaque on the lighthouse commemorates the event.

A short covered walkway leads to the tower.

This image shows a section of the stairs in the tower. The rubble stone near the base changes to brick as you get closer to the lantern room.

Above images: A wooden ladder with six steps leads to a narrow opening and into the lantern room. At the top of the stairs is a small window; locate its position on the previous exterior images.

Two views out the windows in the tower; from the exterior scenes visible in these photos it is possible to identify the tower locations from which they were taken.

Two views out of the lantern room captured in the 1950s. *(Courtesy of MHS)*

Two beacons in the lantern room are unusual; if one lamp burns out, the other one will light. Usually, the lamps would change when one burned out; note the bulbs that used to be used at the Butler Flats Light (page 44). This view is south with a sailboat in the inlet.

A vista looking out the lantern room with the two breakwaters on the north side of the inlet in the foreground. The breakwater, visible in the middle panel, on the south side of the harbor was where the following storm image was captured.

Two panoramas, one at daybreak, and the other during a northeaster.

At sunset, images from around the tower can be captured.

A view of the Italian freighter, *Etrusco*, that was grounded next to the lighthouse in March 1956. The joke at the time was that Proctor and Gamble was going to send a load of Tide to float it off the rocks.

Nearby, Scituate Harbor provides moorings and dockage for a variety of craft.

This present-day aerial image shows Scituate Light at the end of Cedar Point.

MINOT'S LEDGE

Just to the north of Scituate and slightly offshore, rocks and ledges proved hazardous to shipping, and numerous vessels through the years were destroyed. One of these hazards, Outer Minot's Ledge, was picked as the site for an aid to navigation in the form of a skeletal tower. Fraught with problems, work could only occur for a maximum of three hours a day at low tide and then only when conditions allowed. Construction began in 1847 when nine twelve-inch holes five feet deep for the supporting pilings were drilled into the ledge. With its construction hampered by storms, the tower was completed and first lit on January 1, 1850. After completion, storms continued to take their toll on the tower; cross braces had to be removed, repaired and replaced. In March 1851, a violent storm prevented access to the lantern room. Keepers resigned because they felt the tower was unsafe. With two assistant keepers present, a violent storm on April 16, 1851 totally destroyed the tower as each supporting piling failed, tossing the structure into the sea. Both men perished as they tried to reach shore; a monument to their memory can be found overlooking Cohasset Harbor.

Initially a tugboat was placed on station to replace the lighthouse as an aid to navigation; shortly after, a lightship (see page 234) was assigned and remained until the present-day lighthouse was completed.

An engineering marvel, the present-day Minot's Ledge Light took five years to build. The tower consists of 1,079 blocks of Quincy granite and weighs over 2,300 tons; its construction began in 1855. A cofferdam of seven large granite blocks specifically cut to fit together and anchored to the ledge formed the base for the tower. The first tower block was laid in July 1858. The twenty-nine blocks on the second course were dovetail-cut to fit together; each weighed two tons. Storms striking the tower only increase its strength as the blocks are forced together tighter. A 2nd order Fresnel lens was installed and tested in August, 1860 and the light officially restored on November15, 1860. The tower is 114 feet high with the focal plane at 85 feet. In May of 1894, a new optic was installed with a flashing signal of 1 + 4 + 3 (commonly termed "I Love You," from the numbers of letters found in those words) The light was automated in 1947, a 3rd order Fresnel lens installed, which is now on display inside the replica lantern room on the side of Cohasset Harbor. The light was converted to solar power in 1983. An active aid to navigation, the present optic is a modern 300-millimeter beacon; the fog signal is one blast every ten seconds. One of the most restricted access lighthouses, the tower can be seen from the shore at several locations but is best viewed by boat.

This is an image of the first Minot Light. The colorized postcard is probably a good representation of the tower. The wave and ships were added later to the image. We know from historical records that the tower was supported by eight pilings on the outside with a ninth centered on the octagonal framework. A five-ton cast-iron spider at the top of the sixty-foot tower supported a two-story living quarters. The first floor was the bedroom and storeroom; the second floor held the watch room and galley. Atop of this was a sixteen-sided lantern room.

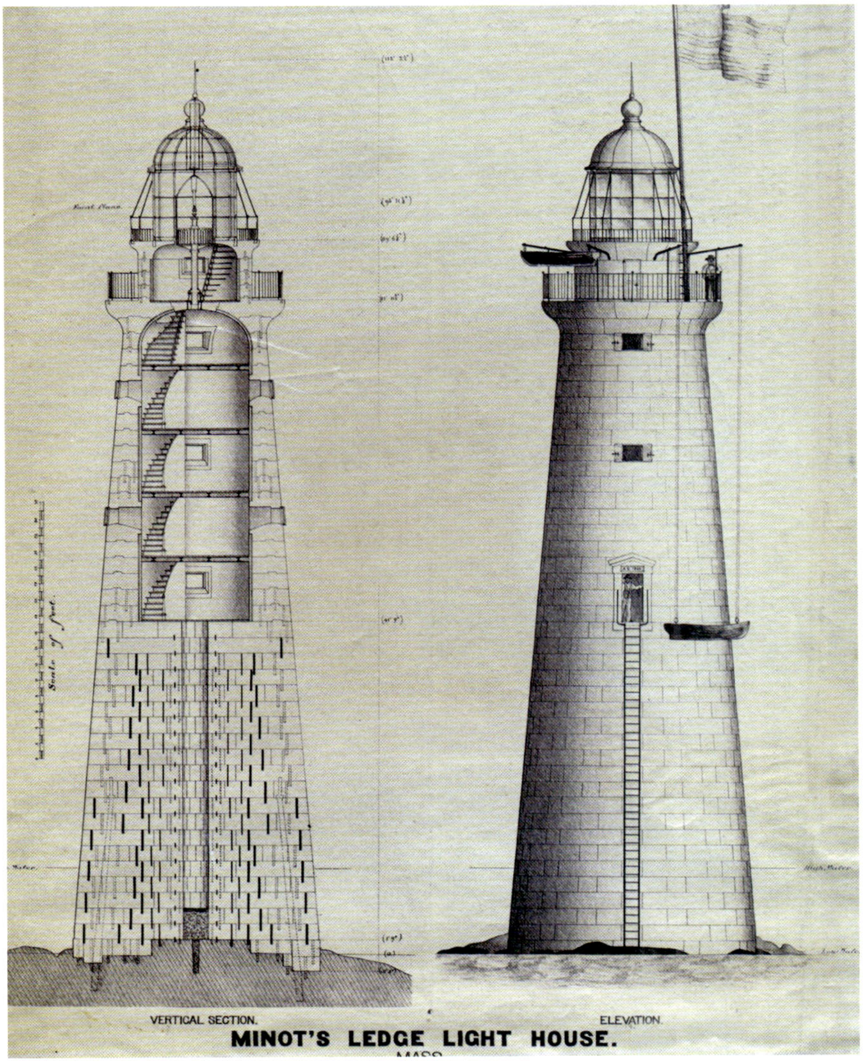

Above: This drawing depicts the first Minot Light falling into the sea on the night of April 16–17, 1851. It is believed that the center support broke first and when the outer pilings could not support the weight, the tower fell into the sea, killing the two assistant keepers. *(Courtesy of NA)*

Left: A plan for the present-day Minot's Ledge Light showing a cross section and the dimensions of the tower. Construction began in 1855; note how it was anchored to the ledge. *(Courtesy of NA)*

Top row & center: A series of photographs taken of the construction of the tower. In the first image, workers are building the base; note the schooner to the right that provided support and supplies to the workers. The second image shows the workers building the twenty-seventh course of granite blocks and starting on twenty-eight. The third image, dated October 1857, shows the site on the shore of Cohasset Harbor where the granite blocks for the tower were prepared. Measured and cut to specific dimensions, the blocks were made to fit precisely together. *(Courtesy of NA)*

Left: Magazines ran articles about the building of the new Minot's Ledge Light, and before photography became a popular form of illustration, drawings would accompany the text. These were probably copied from a photograph, and then details could be added to the scene. *(Courtesy of NA)*

A stereo card and a colorized postcard highlight the severe conditions and the storms that would batter the tower.

A postcard, about seventy to eighty years old, showing the lighthouse during a time when the sea was calm.

This Coast Guard aerial image was taken in the early 1950s; probably unmanned (1947), a lifeboat is attached to the davits near the top of the tower. *(Courtesy of USCG)*

Two more Coast Guard images show the waves hammering the tower; because of its design, the tower actually became stronger as the blocks were forced together. In the righthand photograph, note the ice crusted and covering the tower. *(Courtesy of USCG)*

Far left: Completed in 1989, the tower was renovated and the lantern room repaired. *(Courtesy of USCG)*

Left: A view of the stairs in the tower. *(Courtesy of USCG)*

On a calm, pleasant day, it is a short ride by boat to Minot's Ledge Light. It is possible to carefully circle the ledge and view the different sides of the tower. Close examination of the above image reveals, on the horizon, the skyline of Boston in the distance. Even on calm days, waves break over the ledge.

From along the shore, Sandy Beach on the Cohasset shoreline offers distant views whether it be summer seas or winter storms.

ANTOINE AND WILSON
MEMORIAL
DEDICATED TO THE MEMORY OF
JOSEPH ANTOINE AND JOSEPH WILSON,
KEEPERS OF THE FIRST MINOT LEDGE
LIGHTHOUSE WHO, WHILE MANNING THE
LIGHT ON THE NIGHT OF APRIL 17, 1851,
LOST THEIR LIVES WHEN THE LIGHTHOUSE
WAS SWEPT INTO THE SEA DURING A
VIOLENT NORTHEAST STORM.
"THEY KEPT A GOOD LIGHT"

Above: Overlooking the harbor is this replica of the lantern room at Minot's Ledge Lighthouse. Some of the granite blocks are original from when the tower was renovated in the late 1980s; the original 3rd order lens from the lighthouse is inside the lantern room.

Opposite: Along the shore of Cohasset Harbor, a memorial commemorates the two assistant keepers, John Antoine and Joseph Wilson, who lost their lives when the first lighthouse was destroyed by a storm.

Left: A present-day aerial image; compare it with the previous water views to determine the photographer's location.

BOSTON HARBOR

For nearly four hundred years, Boston and its harbor have been steeped in memorable events. The harbor was first discovered and described by John Smith in 1614. After the Pilgrims settled in Plymouth just to the south in 1620, more colonists arrived from England and began to form communities along the coast. In Boston and in Salem to the north, deep protected harbors offered the colonists a place to live, farm, fish, and develop a community. In 1630, when John Winthrop arrived with his fleet and over seven hundred men, women, and children, the Massachusetts Bay Colony was established as a self-governing entity. Within two decades, more than twenty thousand colonists had arrived to start a new life in the New World.

By 1660, almost all the trade with England came through Boston Harbor. With more ships sailing past these rocky islands and dangerous shoals, it became a necessity to provide navigators with aids to guide vessels into a safe anchorage. Shipwrecks were common in the harbor from the earliest times. The first may have been when an unidentified vessel carrying trade goods wrecked on Peddock's Island sometime in the early 1600s.

Some areas are more dangerous than others, with Deer Island, Point Allerton (Hull), and Harding's Ledge accounting for numerous wrecks. Nantasket Beach also had many wrecks, as vessels trying to reach the safety of the harbor would be blown onto the shore during northeasters.

Beacons, aids, and lighthouses have been part of the rich history of Boston and its harbor from the early 1600s. The following lighthouses, some active and some no longer in existence, are discussed, starting with the outer harbor and then moving to each aid in the inner harbor.

The active aids are The Graves, Boston Light, Deer Island Light, Nix's Mate (albeit a day marker), and Long Island Head Light.

The inactive aids are Lovell's Island Range Lights, The Narrows / Bug Light, Spectacle Island Range Lights, and Broad Sound Channel Range Lights.

AIDS TO NAVIGATION, STILL ACTIVE

This chart, dated 1774, was drawn after a survey of Boston Harbor and shows several interesting aspects of the islands and waterways more than two centuries ago. Castle Island, **1**, was an actual island and was later the site of a fort. Deer Island, **2**, was another actual island and is now the site of a waste water management plant. Spectacle Island, **3**, was the site of a set of range lights; now it is a part of the Boston Harbors Islands National Recreation Area. Long Island, **4**, still has an active aid to navigation. Nix's Mate, **5**, was also an island and now has pretty much disappeared. Lovell's Island, **6**, had a set of range lights and is now part of the Boston Harbors Islands National Recreation Area. Number **7** represents President Roads, the northern waterway that leads into the inner harbor. The Graves, **8**, is a group of ledges and a lighthouse would be built here more than a century later. Little Brewster Island, **9**, was the site of the nation's first lighthouse, Boston, which is still active today. Nantasket Roads, **10**, is the southern waterway that leads into the inner harbor. Compare this chart with the following two that are centuries apart. *(Courtesy of NOAA)*

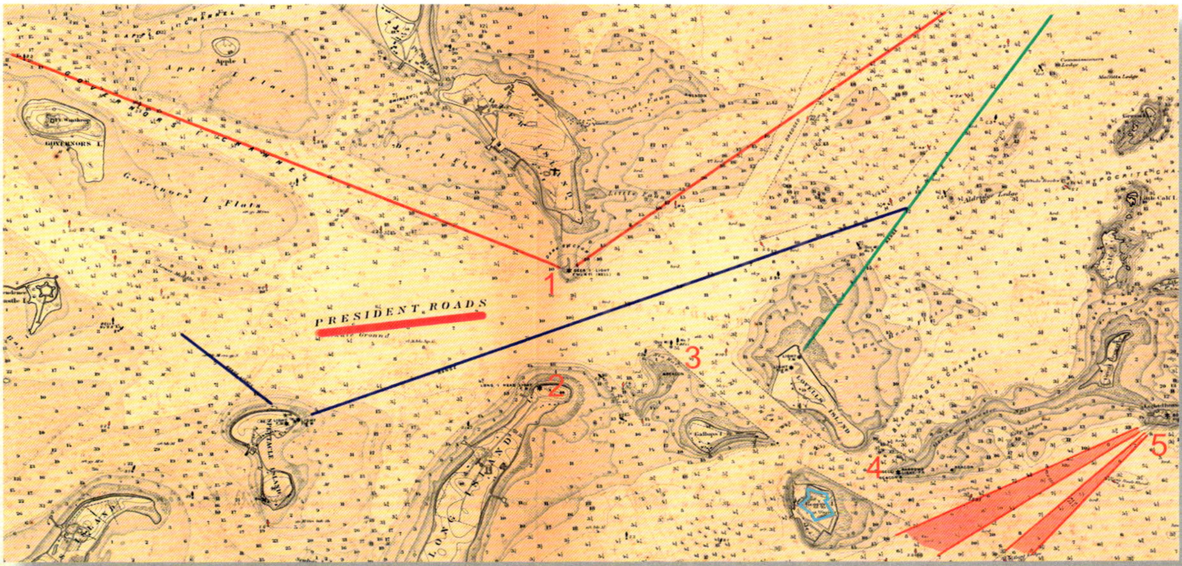

This second chart, dated 1909, shows a smaller section of the harbor and the aids navigators would use to guide their way in and out of the harbor. Deer Island, **1**, was only visible below the two angled red lines; no light could be seen above the red lines, so navigators needed to see this aid to mark the northern boundary of their course. Numbers **2**, Long Island Head Light and number **3**, Nix's Mate identified the southern boundary of the channel, President Roads. The Narrows Light (Bug Light), **4**, no longer standing, (burned down in 1927), guided mariners through the Narrows. Boston Light, **5**, had two red sectors to warn ships of hazards. Not as common today, there were three sets of range lights—two lights that could be lined up to provide a course direction for the vessel—in Boston Harbor; none exist today. The green line is the course navigators would use for the range lights on Lovell's Island. The purple lines represent the two sets of range lights, Broad Channel Range Lights and Spectacle Island range Lights, on Spectacle Island. The aqua colored shape on Georges Island is Fort Warren. *(Courtesy of NOAA)*

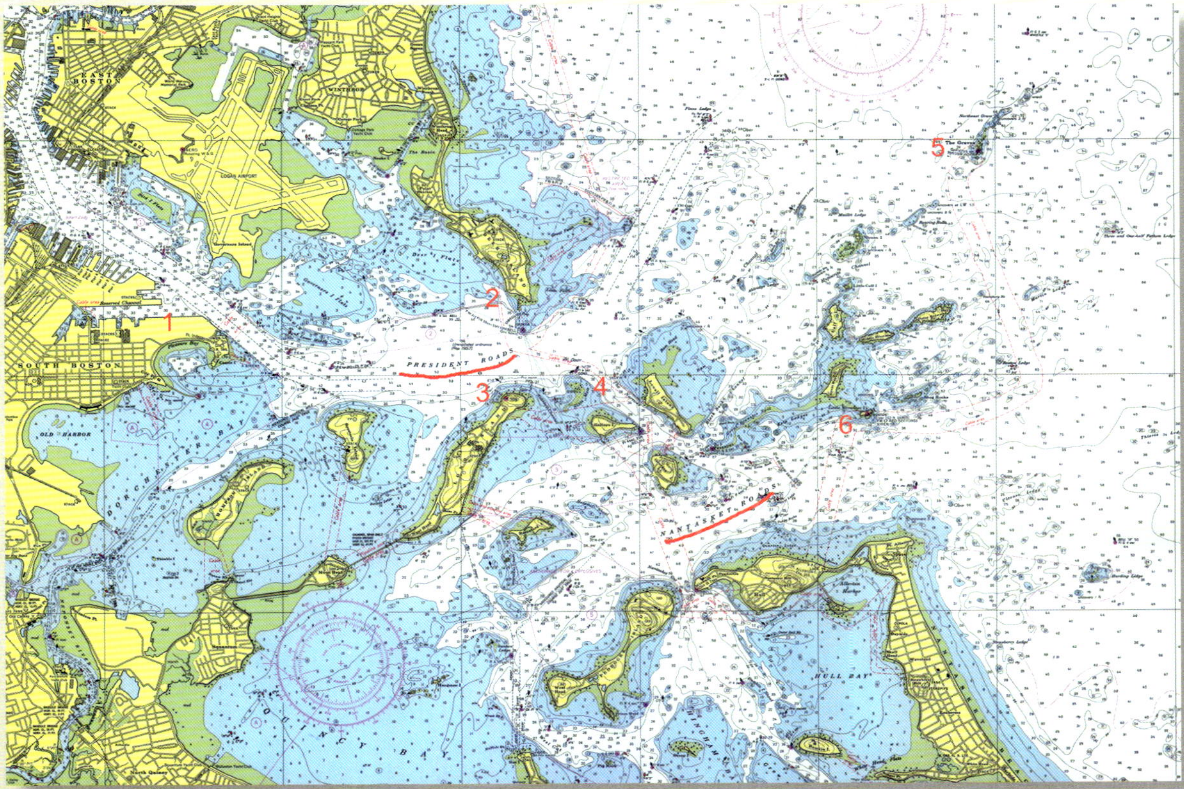

This chart is a present-day plan of Boston Harbor with the active aids to navigation identified. Castle Island, **1**, is now a major recreation area in South Boston. Deer Island, **2**, is now connected to the mainland, Winthrop, and the light is just off the shore. Long Island, **3**, has restricted access; the only section open to the public is the northern end where the lighthouse and a summer camp for kids is present. **4** is the location of Nix's mate. The Graves, **5**, still has an active aid to navigation. Little Brewster Island, **6**, is the location of Boston Light. Underlined in red are the two waterways that lead into the harbor; between 1 and 2, President Roads and to the left of 6, Nantasket Roads. *(Courtesy of NOAA)*

Castle Island, South Boston, past and present. Through the years and with several wars, forts were built on a number of the islands in Boston Harbor. One of the most prominent and easily accessible is Fort Independence on Castle Island. In the shape of a pentagon, it was built starting as early as 1634. In the color image, the monument to the right of the fort is dedicated to Donald McKay, the builder of the famous clipper ship, *Flying Cloud*. Castle Island is in the distance in the century-old image. *(Courtesy of LOC)*

THE GRAVES

One of the most recently built and still active lighthouses in Boston Harbor, The Graves is also the outermost aid and the first lighthouse mariners would see when entering the harbor through the channel called President Roads. Almost two hundred years after Boston Light had been built, the Graves lighthouse was erected on rocky ledges when the Broad Sound Channel leading into Boston Harbor was improved in the early 1900s. The granite to construct the tower was cut in nearby Cape Ann and the project commenced in early 1903. At 113 feet tall, the light with a 1st order Fresnel was first lit on 1 September, 1905. The tower replaced a series of sounding buoys that had been placed on this navigational hazard as early as the 1850s. The light was originally rated at nearly four hundred thousand candlepower and later was improved to more than three million candlepower, making it the brightest and most powerful light in New England.

The tower consists of six decks which start forty feet above the thirty-foot-diameter base. A thirty-five foot water cistern fills the base and provides water for two keepers for six months. The first deck reached by the outside stairs was used for landing and storing supplies; the second deck had two generators for the foghorn and emergency power. The third deck held the crew's quarters, the fourth the galley, and the fifth a library and watchroom. The top deck, the sixth, is twice the size of the lower decks and held the large lens. The original lens was removed when the lighthouse was automated in the mid-1970s. In 2001, the light was converted to solar power. Recently sold at auction by the U. S. Coast Guard, the tower is now privately owned with plans to repair and refurbish the interior rooms. The lantern room and light are still maintained by the Coast Guard.

Above: Undated, this image was probably captured shortly after the tower had been built in 1903. *(Courtesy of NA)*

Left: Taken from a bouncing boat and slightly out of focus, this image of the tower was taken in 1918. *(Courtesy of NA)*

Top & center: These two photographs were shot in 1906 and show not only the lighthouse station but also the tender (unnamed) that delivered supplies. Notice not only the stack from the engine, but the masts that could be rigged with sails. *(Courtesy of LOC)*

Right: An old colorized postcard that shows the tower during the day.

These three aerials were captured more than fifty years ago by the Coast Guard. Compare these images with the present-day shots taken from the water (page 103). *(Courtesy of USCG)*

Another image captured during that survey shows a close-up of the lantern room. Notice the size of the lens and the keepers on the walkway. One is looking through a pair of binoculars. We know this picture was taken before the light was automated in the mid-1970s. *(Courtesy of USCG)*

Top: During a storm, the piers that were connected to the tower were destroyed.

Bottom row: Two recent images captured during repair to the tower. The modern beacon can be seen in the lantern room. *(Courtesy of J. D'Entremont)*

Three views of the present-day tower that were photographed as I rode around it in a boat. The Boston skyline can be seen in the images that were shot of the east side of the tower.

BOSTON

Little Brewster Island, one of the outermost islands in Boston Harbor, has had some form of beacon since the mid-1600s. The earliest was probably a simple pole that had a fire in a basket at the top. Similar to European lights in the 1620s, a fire with wet wood would be burned during the day to produce smoke as a day marker; at night, dry, clean wood would be used to produce a light that could be seen by navigators. As early as 1713, efforts were being made to construct a lighthouse to replace the beacon. After approval from England, construction of Boston Light began in 1715; the light was completed the following year and lit for the first time on September 14. Built from granite blocks and probably about fifty feet tall, the first light in the tower initially burned candles, but this was eventually changed to oil-burning lamps. In 1719, the keeper, John Hayes, requested a deck be built seaward of the tower and a cannon installed to be used as America's first fog-signaling device. The cannon is now on display inside near the tower for visitors to see. At the time of the American Revolution (1775), the British occupied the island and the tower. Twice, American raiding parties attacked the island and were only partially successfully in destroying the keeper's house and several other buildings, but not the tower. That was left to the British when they withdrew from Boston in 1776, and they completely destroyed the tower. By 1783, funds were provided and the tower was rebuilt to a height of seventy-five feet. The walls are more than seven feet thick at the base and nearly three feet thick at the top. In 1790, Boston Light was ceded to the new Federal Government. The first bands for additional support were added to the tower, which started to crack shortly after it was finished. A major overhaul was completed on the tower in 1859 that included lining the inside with brick, repairing outside sections, and adding fifteen feet to the height with a new lantern room. A 2nd order Fresnel was also installed at that time and is still in use today. During World War II, for security reasons, the light was extinguished, but was re-lit in July 1945. The five metal bands you see today were added in the early 1970s. The last lighthouse in the United States to be automated, Boston Light no longer required a keeper in April, 1998. In September 2003, Sally Snowman was appointed as a civilian keeper, the first woman keeper at the lighthouse. Now, from June to October, the island and lighthouse are open for tours by National Park rangers. An active aid to navigation, the light, with a focal plane height at 102 feet, flashes white every ten seconds and is visible for twenty-seven nautical miles. The fog signal is one blast every thirty seconds.

This 1884 sketch shows a British vessel sailing past Boston Light. *(Courtesy of LOC)*

Dated 1897, these two photographs of Boston Light illustrate the station more than a century ago. Close examination reveals the keeper (?) standing on a wooden walkway, a covered walkway that leads to the tower, and cannon just in front of the building to the far right. *(Courtesy of NA)*

These two images were captured in the early 1900s. *(Courtesy of NA)*

Compare these two old postcards of Boston Light not only with each other but with the previous archival images. In some cases there may have been a degree of photographic license.

Two panoramas, the black-and-white one taken sometime about 1906; the color image captured more than a century later. *(Black-and-white image courtesy of LOC)*

To the south of Boston Light and across the channel is the town of Hull. Seen here is the Hotel Pemberton with Boston Light (red underline) in the distance. *(Courtesy of LOC)*

Above: A present-day view of the same perspective of Little Brewster Island.

Left: A relatively recent aerial image of Boston Light and Little Brewster Island. *(Courtesy of USCG)*

A view from a boat looking east; from right to left, Little Brewster Island with Boston Light, Greater Brewster Island, and Graves Light on the horizon.

Top left: The first stop for visitors to the island is the boathouse (1899). No longer used for its original purpose, the building has displays and information about the lighthouse and the island.

Left: Welcoming visitors to the island is Sally Snowman, a civilian keeper. She is the first female keeper at Boston Light. Coast Guard personnel are available for repair and maintenance.

Left: A view of the keeper's house (1884) that is still used as a residence. Cement walkways have replaced the wooden boardwalks that were in place a century ago.

Below left: At the base of the tower, there is a small room with artifacts. The fog-signaling building is to the right.

Below right: In 1964, Boston Light was designated a Registered National Historic Landmark.

Built on this rocky island, Boston Light is not without erosion problems as storms and weathering attack the island. Blocks of granite tumble into the sea with increasing frequency. The oil house (1889) is just in front of the tower. Looking along a pathway, this is the west side of the tower. The fog-signaling building (1876) is to the east or seaward side of the tower.

Past and present: the black-and-white image shows the Daboll fog trumpet, the color image is of the present-day foghorn. *(Black-and-white image courtesy of NA)*

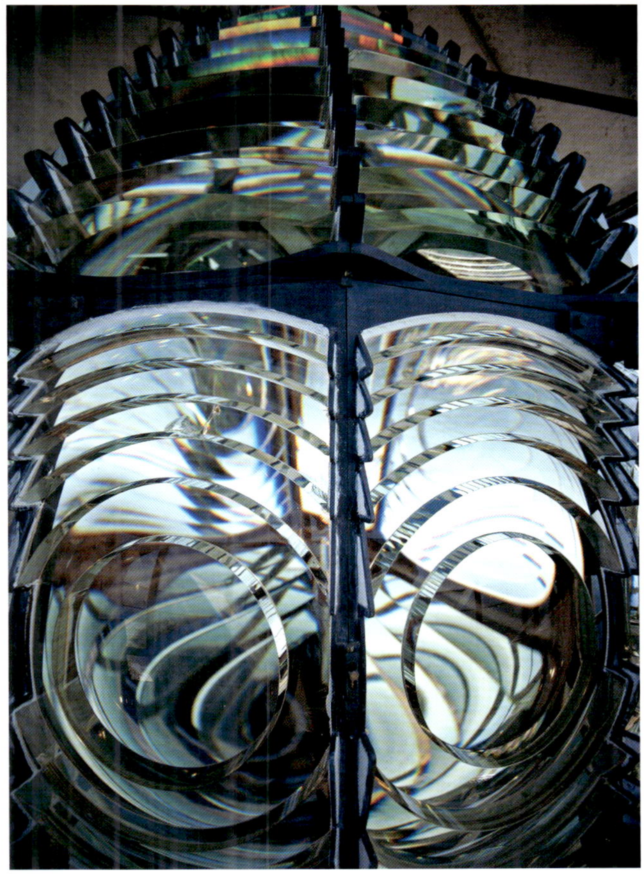

Two images of the 2nd order Fresnel lens. The lens, made up of multiple prisms, has a lamp that produces a light with 1.8 million candlepower.

Above: A window view; note the composition and thickness of the walls

Left: At the base of the tower, cast-iron stairs, built in 1844, lead to the lantern room. They replaced rickety wooden stairs..

Looking west from the lantern room, the island and buildings are in the foreground with the Boston skyline in the distance.

Looking east from the lantern room, outer Boston Harbor is in the distance.

Above: This windmill in nearby Hull provides power for the Boston Light Station.

Left: On display in the room next to the tower is a 5th order Fresnel lens. Other artifacts are also present that have been collected by a previous keeper.

DEER ISLAND

Originally named for the deer that would swim to the island to escape the wolves, the early history of the island is macabre. Through the years, Native Americans (many of whom died) were exiled there during King Philip's War; it became a quarantine location for immigrants; an almshouse was built in 1853 that was later converted to a prison that remained open until 1991; and its present-day occupant is a wastewater treatment plant.

The first aid to navigation, in 1832, was a stone beacon painted red, built at the very end of the island that marked the northern side of the channel. Later, in 1886, at the request of mariners, Congress appropriated funds for a lighthouse that would also include a fog-signaling device. The first Deer Island Light consisted of a cast-iron caisson thirty-three feet in diameter and thirty feet high that was placed on a shoal six feet below low tide. A tower was built on this base with the 5th order Fresnel lens thirty-seven feet above the base. The original signal was fixed white with a red signal every twenty-eight seconds that shone through an arc of 237½ degrees.

Exposure to waves, storms, and ice flows damaged the caisson; repairs were made in the early 1900s, and by the late 1930s a protective wall was constructed around the base. The tower continued to deteriorate through the years and by the late '70s and early '80s it became obvious that it was necessary to dismantle the tower. It was replaced with a white buoy, built in England, that could withstand winds up to 110 miles an hour. Because the white tower blended with the buildings and background on Deer Island, it was replaced with a thirty-three foot brown fiberglass tower in September 1984. The white tower was going to replace Great Point on Nantucket, which had recently been destroyed by a storm, but a replica of the original tower was built on the same site. The present Deer Island Light, because of its distinctive shape, is classified as a matchstick design. It is thought to be the first fiberglass lighthouse in the United States. The light exhibits an alternating red and white flash every five seconds at fifty-three feet above the water level.

Three images, one a colorized postcard, of Deer Island Light, at the turn of the twentieth century. Note the two boats hanging from davits in the photograph at left. *(Black-and-white image courtesy of NA)*

Top right: This Coast Guard aerial view shows the rocks that had been added in the late 1930s to protect the tower. *(Courtesy of USCG)*

In 1938, repairs were made to the tower and these three photographs show some of the details of the repair. Note the additional iron braces added to the base. *(Courtesy of USCG)*

Top: When it became necessary to dismantle the light tower in the early 1980s, it was replaced with this original matchstick design that was painted white. Because it was confused with the Deer Island Treatment Plant, the color was changed to a rusty brown. *(Courtesy of USCG)*

Center: Looking north, behind the tower is the Deer Island Wastewater Treatment Plant. In this view, it becomes obvious why the color of the tower had to be changed.

Left: A present-day view of the Deer Island Light, now solar powered; the most common visitors are cormorants.

NIX'S MATE DAYBEACON

This aid to navigation, located near the outer limits of Boston Harbor, marks a dangerous shoal near three of the major channels in and out of the harbor. Nix's Mate daybeacon now stands on a rocky one-acre shoal, once an island, near Long, Deer, Lovell and Gallop's Islands. In 1636, the island was twelve acres and sheep were grazed on it. Unsubstantiated, the naming of the island may have occurred in the 1630s when a Captain Nix was murdered by the first mate, who was convicted of the crime and hanged on the Island. Supposedly, he stated "God, show that I am innocent. Let this island sink and prove to these people that I have never stained my hands with human blood."

In 1726, after a pirate was executed in Boston, he was hung on Nix's Island to warn other sailors to avoid piracy. Mining for gravel, used as ballast in ships that were being built locally, was probably the reason the island was reduced in size. In the early 1800s when the island was slowly disappearing, the U.S. Congress failed to respond to pleas for assistance. Instead, Massachusetts appropriated three thousand dollars to build the wall and beacon. By the early 1830s, the U.S. government built a stone platform topped by a wooden pyramidal beacon. In 1841 after being struck by lightning, the tower burned to the ground but was quickly rebuilt.

Presently, the eight-sided wooden tower, about twenty feet above the waterline, is covered in a thin layer of concrete. Hollow, the interior can be visited from an opening in the south wall. A white band separates two black bands. The Coast Guard, which was going to replace the beacon, rebuilt the aid in 2003 after public outcry. Nix's Mate Daybeacon was added to the National Register of Historic Places in 2004.

This undated image from the National Archives was probably taken sometime early in the last century. *(Courtesy of NA)*

An early 1900s color postcard of Nix's Mate at almost high tide. Note the differences in the top of the structure.

A present-day photograph of the beacon, which is frequently visited by cormorants.

With Nix's Mate in the foreground, this view shows the Boston skyline in the distance welcoming maritime visitors.

Looking south, these two views include Nix's Mate and Gallop's Island in the background. The bui ding to the left is on Lovell's Island, which is a part of the Boston Harbor Islands Park.

LONG ISLAND HEAD

There are thirty-four islands in Boston Harbor; Long Island is the longest (1.75 miles long) and the largest (214 acres). Long Island Head, at the northeast corner, has for more than two hundred years been the site of lighthouses and fortifications. It is the closest point on the island that faces the channel leading into the harbor and is well suited for an aid to navigation and a fort. There have been four lighthouses on the island. The first was a rubble stone tower, twenty feet tall, with a seven foot lantern room. In October 1819, the light, fixed white, was first lit with a series of lamps and reflectors. By 1843, wood decay in the structure and damage caused by severe winter weather necessitated that the tower be replaced.

The second lighthouse, a cast-iron design, the first of its type in America, was built and first lit in 1844. The sections were seven feet tall and twelve feet in diameter at the base, with a diameter of six feet at the top of its thirty-four foot height. A twenty-inch-wide deck circled the lantern room that had sixteen panels of glass, each measuring four feet wide by sixteen inches tall. In 1857, a 4th order Fresnel lens was installed that replaced the lamps and reflectors. Storms continued to take their toll and, by 1881, the tower, now the third Long Island Head Lighthouse, had been rebuilt, the keeper's house replaced, and a 3rd order Fresnel lens installed. An oil house was built in 1892. The fourth and present-day tower was built in 1901 in a new location. With Fort Strong nearby, it was decided that the new tower should be in a position that would not be affected by the firing of the guns.

Originally unpainted, the 1901 tower was built of brick fifty-two feet high. The keeper's house was moved to the new location. In 1902, the tower was painted white, its present color. In 1929, the light, now using acetylene gas, was automated; nearby Fort Strong was abandoned. In 1982, the Coast Guard discontinued the light, but by 1985 the tower was renovated and relit using solar power. Located on what is now a restricted island, the lighthouse is not open for visits. Several times during the summer, Friends of Boston Harbor offer cruises to the island.

Compare these two images of two cast-iron design lighthouse towers. The black-and-white photo shows the second Long Island Head Lighthouse that was built in 1844, the first type of this style in America. The color image is Monomoy Light, another tower of that original design, on that island off the coast of Chatham. It was built in 1849 and is no longer active. *(Black-and-white image courtesy of USCG)*

The 1881 tower as seen from the water. Compare the vegetation with present-day images. Note the other buildings. Fort Strong is on the back side of this drumlin (glacial hill). *(Courtesy of NA)*

These two archival images show the third (1881) tower built on Long Island. This popular cast-iron design is similar to other lighthouses along the Massachusetts coast (pages 157 and 185). *(Courtesy of NA)*

This is an image of the 1901 brick tower before it was painted white. *(Courtesy of USCG)*

Compare these two postcards to the archival and present-day images.

Taken in the mid-1940s; note the covered walkway that connected the tower and the house. *(Courtesy of USCG)*

By the mid-1950s, only the tower and oil house remained. *(Courtesy of USCG)*

In the early 1980s, the Massachusetts Historical Commission did a survey of lighthouses, and that was when these images were captured. Images include the entryway, a close-up of the tower, the modern 250-mm aerobeacon, and a view from the lantern room looking south (now the site of a summer camp for children of Boston). *(Courtesy of MHC)*

Above: Now encircled by trees, two views of the tower.

Left: The tower taken several years ago from a ship; the roof of the entry way is barely visible.

A spiral flight of stairs leads to the top of the tower; a short metal flight of stairs leads to the lantern room. *(Courtesy of J. D'Entremont)*

Above: Now nearly hidden by trees, the lighthouse is found south of the channel that leads through the harbor.

Left: Named in 1899 for a Civil War Hero, Major General George Crockett Strong, the fort was active from the 1867 until the 1960s. The fort is located to the south of the lighthouse, and as can be seen in this photograph, empty gun emplacements are hidden in the woods.

LOVELL'S ISLAND RANGE

A little more than a mile from Boston Light, Lovell's Island was close to the original main channel into Boston, and landmarks (a large tree) aided mariners as early as the 1700s. With the opening of the new northern channel (Broad Sound) in the early 1900s, additional aids became a necessity. Money was appropriated and the two towers were built in 1902–1903. They were first lit in April 1903. The front tower was about thirty feet tall with a 4th order Fresnel lens that was fixed red; the rear tower was forty feet tall and also had a 4th order lens that flashed red every five seconds. Mariners who lined up the two lights knew that they were in the center of the channel. As on many of the other islands in the harbor that had fortifications, Lovell's had Fort Standish. When the fort expanded, the lighthouses were discontinued. They were dismantled in 1939; all that remains is the oil house. Now the island is part of the National Park-Boston Harbor Islands. A variety of activities including camping, hiking, and exploring the old fort are available to the visitor.

A view of the range lights showing their differences in height; note the boardwalk that connects the two towers. *(Courtesy of NA)*

A present-day set of range lights and markers guide mariners into Nantucket Harbor.

Top: Compare this aerial view to the land water vistas. *(Courtesy of D. Bicknell)*

Center: This view has the front range light in the foreground. *(Courtesy of NA)*

Bottom left: This image of one of the keepers' houses was taken at the time when it was being moved from the island in the 1920s. *(Courtesy of NA).*

Bottom right: A black-and-white postcard of the Lovell's Island Range Lights.

Presently, the dock at Lovell's Island welcomes visitors during the busy summer season.

The red-roofed oil house is all that remains of the lighthouses on Lovell's Island.

THE NARROWS (BUG LIGHT)

Early in the history of Boston Harbor, mariners would sail through The Narrows, the main shipping channel into the city. Charts in the late 1700s showed an unlit beacon at the end of this tide-covered piece of land. Money was finally appropriated in the 1850s, and a cottage style screw-pile lighthouse was built. Seven pilings supported a six sided wooden tower covered by a galvanized roof. The optic was a 6th order Fresnel lens, fixed red, which was visible for seven miles. These smaller Fresnel lenses, used primarily in bays and harbors, were not required to produce a signal much more than ten miles. Larger Fresnel lenses, used along the coast, required longer distance lights. Some light beams may reach close to thirty miles.

Through the years, several shipwrecks occurred in the vicinity and the keepers were involved in rescuing numerous crewmen. Ice was a problem, but although the pilings may have been damaged, the tower survived. On June 7, 1929, the real problem was fire. After a project to remove paint, the keeper, Tom Small, was using a blowtorch and a spark accidently ignited the roof. Within fifteen minutes, the tower was engulfed, the keeper barely survived, and before the fireboat arrived, the tower was totally destroyed. It was never rebuilt.

Close examination of this image of the Narrows Light reveals a bell on the facing wall. Also, the keeper can be seen working on the deck. In times of limited visibility, the bell would be struck every twenty seconds. *(Courtesy of USCG)*

Two old photographs show The Narrows Light. A ramp allowed access; note the boat hanging on the davits. The iron legs and wooden tower do give the impression of a bug, hence the idiosyncratic name "The Bug Light." *(Courtesy of NA)*

Left column: Over a century old, these three postcards provide different views of the Bug Light.

Top right: The present-day aid to navigation is located near where the original Narrows Light was built.

BOSTON, SATURDAY MORNING, JUNE 8, 1929—TWENTY-TWO PAG

FIREBOAT 44 PLAYING ON WHAT'S LEFT OF BUG LIGHT

"BUG LIGHT" IS DESTROYED BY FIRE

Paint Burner Machine Spark the Cause

Gas and Bell Buoy Placed There as Temporary Warning

HULL, June 7—The Narrows Light, known more familiarly as "Bug Light," situated at the east end of Lovells Island at the entrance of Boston Harbor, was destroyed because of a spark from a paint burner machine, it was disclosed tonight by Capt George E. Eaton of Melrose, superintendent of the 2nd Lighthouse District, to whom Keeper Thomas Small submitted his report.

Capt Eaton also announced that at 5 o'clock this afternoon, four hours after the fire at the lighthouse, a temporary gas and bell buoy was placed in the water at the site. The buoy flashes a red light every three seconds, being 3-10 light and 2 and 7-10 eclipse. The lighthouse that is now only a memory also flashed a red light.

Mariners Notified

The buoy was placed in position by the lighthouse tender Mayflower which brought it from the Chelsea buoy station. Capt Eaton said the buoy will remain in service pending action by the authorities at Washington. Capt Eaton notified all mariners' agencies.

According to the report made by Keeper Small, he was engaged in removing the paint from the outside walls of the lighthouse with a paint burning machine this morning. Suddenly, according to the keeper's report, he noticed a portion of the wall over his head, where the paint burning machine had not yet been used, had caught fire, presumably from a spark. A fresh wind fanned the flames.

Continued on the Fourth Page

"BUG LIGHT" IS DESTROYED BY FIRE

Continued From the First Page

So rapidly did the fire spread he only had time to gather a few valuables and take to his rowboat to save himself. The keeper lost all his personal possessions and furniture.

Was Alone at Lighthouse

During the Summer months the keeper's wife and 8-year-old son live with him on the lighthouse. He was alone on the lighthouse today, as his wife and son were visiting the family of Cornelius J. Collins of 769 Broadwny, South Boston. Keeper Small rejoined his family at the Collins home tonight. He will remain there temporarily until assigned to another lighthouse.

The lighthouse was left a twisted mass of iron. The wooden construction furnished such fine fodder for the flames that Engine 44, the Boston fireboat, and the Hull Coast Guard crew, in their power surf boat, were unable to save it. Keeper Small was taken on board the Coast Guard boat and carried to Chelsea to file his report.

Several barrels of oil located in the base room, near the bulkhead, were the object of attention by the firemen, who feared they would explode. They tumbled into the water and this danger was averted.

"BUG LIGHT" STOOD UPON SPIDERY LEGS

"Bug Light," as it is familiarly known to everybody who has ever gone out of Boston Harbor by the way of the main ship channel instead of out Broad Sound, was what might be called an amphibian lighthouse. At low water it stood on its spidery legs on the

mission, addressed the closing session of the organization's 52d annual convention here today.

"I believe therefore," he continued, "that the American people and editors have confidence in you, and will suspend final judgment upon the right or wrong of the matters involved until we can present our doings and reasons therefore and until the Federal Trade

LIGHTSHIP RETIRED 1930 AFTER 74 YEARS

WASHINGTON, Aug. 18 (UP) — A weather-beaten veteran of three-quarters of a century of safely guiding thousands of ocean liners into port, lightship No. 1 has been retired from the lighthouse service, according to an announcement by the commerce department.

With no motive power but sails, this trim little 103-foot vessel, constructed entirely of wood, spent 37 years showing the way to ocean-going steamships off Nantucket shoals, the most exposed but important station in the lighthouse service.

After breaking her moorings twice in 1892 during violent storms, No. 1 was replaced by a propeller-driven ship and sent to duty at Savannah harbor, where she served for 37 years.

Lightship No. 1 has been replaced at Savannah by No. 94, a steel vessel built in 1911, which has been serving at Frying Pan shoals, N. C. A new ship has taken over Frying Pan shoals.

GLOUCESTER BOAT SINKS IN STORM 1931

Crew of Nine Marooned on Nantucket Lightship

NEW BEDFORD, Feb. 9 (UP)—Nine fishermen were reported safe aboard the Nantucket Shoals lightship today, after the sinking of the Gloucester fishing schooner Aloma in a snow storm early yesterday morning.

First word of the loss of the Aloma came here today in the form of meagre reports indicating that Capt. Wallace Walker and all eight members of his crew were aboard the lightship.

Efforts of coastguard craft to reach the lightship and bring the marooned fishermen ashore were frustrated temporarily by high seas.

Above: The headlines in the Boston paper on Saturday June 8, 1929, described the loss of the Bug Light. Other recent items of maritime interest were also included in this saved document. *(Courtesy of NA)*

Right column: After the fire and at low tide, a photographer captured the remains of the lighthouse. *(Courtesy of NA)*

HOOPER STRAIT

The Bug Light was the only screw-pile lighthouse ever built in New England. Two were built on Long Island, New York, but most were built in the relatively protected areas of the Mid-Atlantic of the Chesapeake region, Florida, and Texas. If they were replaced, and some never were, the caisson, sparkplug, coffee-pot design was the most common alternative. Since the Bug Light was destroyed more than eighty years ago, Hooper Strait Lighthouse on the grounds of the Chesapeake Bay Maritime Museum, St. Michael's, Maryland, allows enthusiasts to visit a screw-pile design beacon. Although there may have been regional variations, walking through the two levels with the numerous rooms suggests how the keeper (no family allowed here) would have passed his time. Examine the images here and assess what the Bug Light may have looked like when it was an active lighthouse.

Above: Located on the grounds of the Chesapeake Bay Maritime Museum, the Hooper Strait Lighthouse offers lighthouse enthusiasts the opportunity to visit this style design. Restored, this is the way the Narrows Light may have looked. Nighttime stays are also available through the museum.

Left: A sign explains how the ends of the seven pilings, screw-shaped, would be augured into the soft sand to support the building. More difficult to construct than straight piles that would be driven into the sand and mud, screw-piles would hold better during the winter months. Ice would build up on the pilings and with the tides moving the ice, damage would occur to the supports. It hardly seems possible nowadays, but several of the lighthouses actually broke up and floated away because of ice damage.

The first floor had a partially covered deck on the outside and windows/door that allowed views in all directions. The Museum has restored and refurbished the interior to its probable original condition. Walk through the door and step back 130 years. Some of these images overlap so it is possible to develop an idea of the floor plan. **Clockwise from top left:** A pot-bellied stove provided heat in the winter; the keeper conducted business at the desk in the background. Weights, on a line, provided the fog signal with power. A second wood stove was used for cooking; a pantry was located just off the kitchen. There was a tool room with a water cistern. On the second floor, the main rooms are bedrooms with their closets.

Top: As technology and engineering techniques improved the design of lighthouses, old towers would be replaced with newer more efficient versions. In this image, the screw-pile Brandywine Shoal Lighthouse, Delaware (built and first lit in October, 1850) is being replaced by a caisson-style tower which was first lit in October 1914. Although the original tower was still in serviceable condition, the living situation for the keeper was cramped and daily chores difficult. The decision was made to replace it, in the same location, with the new tower. Riprap was built around the base to protect it from ice floes.

Left: A flight of spiral stairs leads to the lantern room.

Above right: This 3rd order Fresnel lens is on display in the tower.

SPECTACLE ISLAND RANGE & BROAD SOUND RANGE

Most locations for lighthouses have only one tower; several sites may have (or have had) twin towers—for example, Thacher's Island, Baker's Island, and The Gurnet—and only one had three beacons—The Three Sisters of Nauset (Eastham). Spectacle Island, in inner Boston Harbor, is unique. It had not only one set of range lights, but two. They were identified as the Spectacle Island Range Lights and the Broad Sound Range Lights. No evidence remains of these four towers. Through the years and like many of the harbor islands, Spectacle Island has had a myriad of activities. A quarantine station for smallpox in the 1700s, summer hotels in the 1800s, and a variety of garbage- related operations until the late 1950s were some of these activities. With fill from the "Big Dig," the island is now larger and higher than it was four hundred years ago.

The Spectacle Island Range Lights were the first pair constructed, when almost $10,000 was appropriated in 1895. By June 1897, the new station was described in the Notice to Mariners:

> *On May 20 a fixed red reflector light was established in each of the two towers recently erected on the north side and easterly point of the northerly part of Spectacle Island, south side of President Roads, Boston Harbor. Each tower is a white, octagonal, pyramidal, shingled structure with a small window on the northwesterly side, from which the light is shown. The focal plane of the front light is 29 feet above the water and 13.3 feet above the base of the tower and of the rear light 54 feet above the water and 23 feet above the base of the tower. The rear tower stands 379 feet SE. ½ S. in rear of the front tower. ... The lights mark a range line to guide NW. ½ N. from the line marked by the South Boston Range Lights up the main channel to Boston.*

When the Broad Sound Channel Inner Range Lights were built in 1903, confusion reigned. Not only were the lights on the same island, but the towers were close together. Changes were made in 1904 to the Spectacle Island Range Lights by moving the towers to new base a very short distance from their original location. In addition their colors were changed from total white to three equal divisions, the top and bottom white, the middle section red. When the shipping channel changed, these range lights were discontinued in July 1913, after only sixteen years.

In the early 1900s, money was appropriated for several aids to navigation that were to be built in Boston Harbor, The Graves in the outer harbor, and two sets of range lights: the first set on Lovell's Island and the second set on Spectacle Island. This second set of range lights on the island was called Broad Range Channel Inner Range Lights. They were first lit in April 1903. The two wooden, originally red, towers were about three hundred fifty feet apart and both had 4th order Fresnel lenses. In 1904, they were painted white. The front tower flashed white every five seconds; the rear tower was fixed red. The towers were decommissioned in the 1950s. Spectacle Island is now part of the Boston Harbor National Recreation area and offers a visitor center, marina, café, and over five miles of hiking trails. Little remains of its storied past.

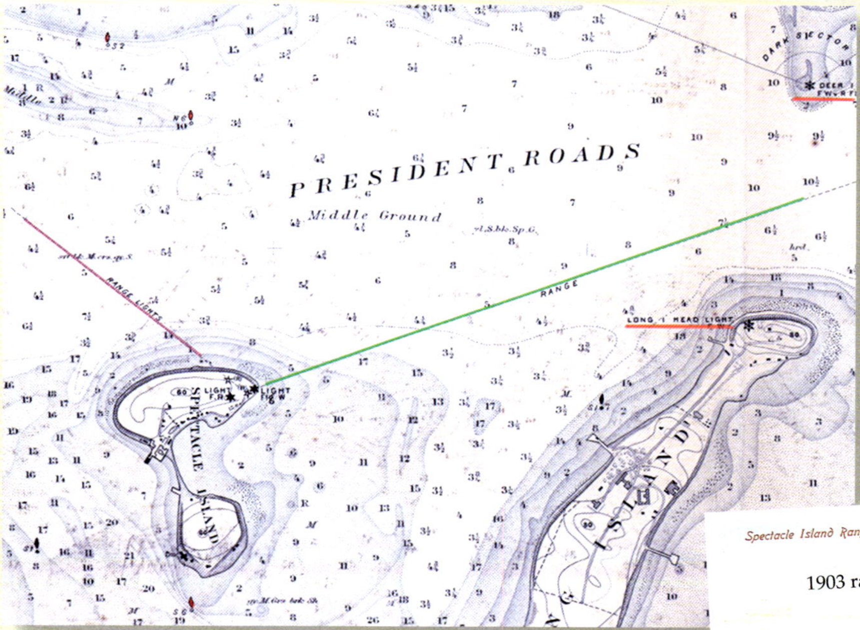

Sometimes a picture as a historical document is worth more than a thousand words. In the case of the range lights on Spectacle Island, this chart, dated 1909, and this postcard of the same vintage allows us to identify them and determine their location. Knowing the characteristics of the light (on the chart) with the range line indicated, the towers arrangement can be assessed. The Spectacle Island Range Lights are indicated by the pinkish line; the Broad Sound Channel Inner Harbor Range Lights are indicated by the greenish line. Compare the chart to the postcard. Note also, two other aids to navigation, Long Island Head Lighthouse and Deer Island Lighthouse. *(Chart courtesy of NOAA; postcard courtesy of J. D'Entremont)*

The photographer of these images is lost to history, but because they are dated, July 23, 1897, we know these are the first set of range lights built on the island. From the photographs, we can observe the actual structure of the rear tower, several views of the keeper's house, and the boat house and ramp (low tide?). Notice Long Island Head in the distance; this gives us the direction (east) the image was captured from. *(Courtesy of NA)*

Postcard: Another vintage postcard that shows, although not very well, the two sets of range lights on the island.

The same date, July 23, 1897, these two images were taken from the water. Probably the same photograph, the second close-up of the tower and keeper's house is probably an enlargement of the first island view. Note the location of the two towers. Close examination of the rear tower shows no lantern room, but a window near the roof eave; this is where the fixed red light was located. *(Courtesy of NA)*

Two slightly different water views of the Broad Sound Channel Inner Range Lights. Note the keeper's house that was built for the first set of range lights. *(Courtesy of USCG and NA)*

This aerial of the island gives a different perspective of the range lights. *(Courtesy of Harriet Jennings)*

Top & center: These two images, looking east and seaward, provide a view of the channel ships would use to enter the harbor. Long Island Head Light can be seen in the distance. *(Courtesy of NA and Dolly Bicknell)*

Left: The rear tower sometime after the station had been deactivated (1950s). Notice there is no lamp in the lantern room. *(Courtesy of NA)*

MASSACHUSETTS BAY NORTH

EGG ROCK

No longer in existence, Egg Rock Lighthouse, off the coast of Nahant, would be the first beacon a mariner would have seen as he headed north out of Boston Harbor. Named for the bird breeding ground, the first lighthouse was built on this three-acre island in 1856. After several wrecks and concerns from the fishing fleet in nearby Swampscott Harbor, funds were finally, after several attempts, appropriated to construct this aid. The fleet in 1855 had forty schooners with more than 200 fishermen bringing home more than five million pounds of cod. The original light was fixed white using a 5th order Fresnel lens, but was changed shortly after to fixed red. In the late 1800s, the lighthouse complex was totally rebuilt. A cellar was added to the keeper's house for storage. The tower now had a fixed red light ninety feet above sea level. During World War I, the light was extinguished to prevent enemy submarines from sighting landfall. After the war, the light was automated, but the decline of the fishing fleet no longer necessitated an aid to navigation at Egg Rock. By 1920 when it was no longer required, the keeper's house was put up for auction and finally sold for $160. The light was dismantled in 1922. While trying to move the house to Nahant, cables holding the building snapped and the house slid into the sea. Some materials were salvaged, but the house collapsed into the ocean. In the late 1920s, the tower was dismantled and the island was cleaned up. It is now maintained as a bird sanctuary by the state.

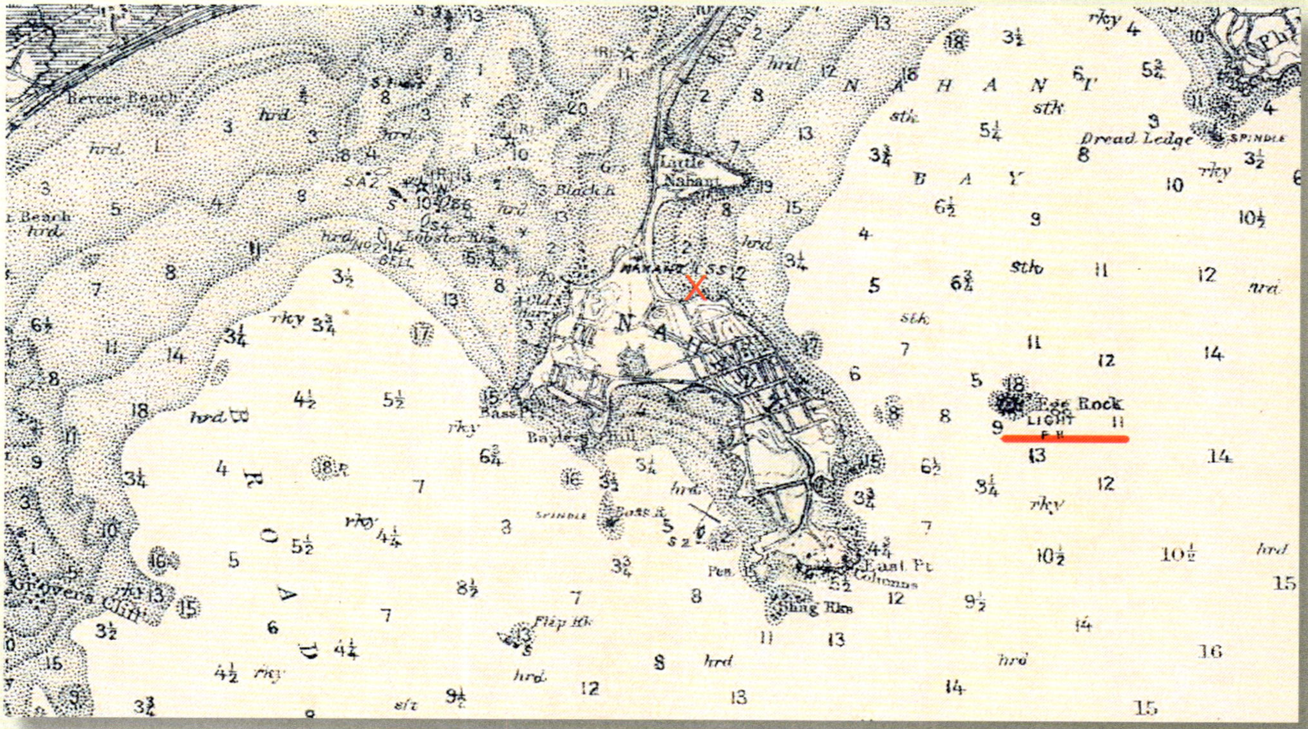

This chart from 1904 shows Egg Rock Lighthouse, which was located just off the coast of Nahant. Usually associated with lighthouses, the red X to the left represents the location of the nearby lifesaving station. *(Courtesy of NOAA)*

Three views of the lighthouse taken more than a century apart and all captured from nearly the same spot. The sepia-toned photograph captured in the late 1800s is on file at the National Archives; the color postcard is from the early 1900s; and the present-day image was taken on a stormy day.

Left: A postcard of the rebuilt (1897) Egg Rock Lighthouse. It was not unusual for people to visit the island on calm summer days.

Three images of the original Egg Rock Lighthouse captured from different locations and during different seasons. Part of the difficulty in identifying images chronologically is that many historical photographs in various archives are undated. These images from the different views also show the other buildings that were necessary for proper operation of the aid. *(Courtesy of NA)*

Along the beach in Nahant is the former and distinctively shaped lifesaving station. Just offshore and to the right in this image is Egg Rock.

MARBLEHEAD

The present-day Marblehead Lighthouse is unique in being the only skeletal tower lighthouse in New England. Lighthouse enthusiasts may be familiar with three other lights of the same design in southern Florida: Sanibel Light (1884) on that same island; Gasparilla Island Light (1881, 1927) formerly known as Boca Grande Entrance Rear Range Light; and Hillsboro Light (1907) in Pompano Beach. It is possible to view all three of these lights closely. Some images and discussion of those three lights are included here for a comparison of this distinctive beacon and tower plan.

The original Marblehead Lighthouse, built and first lit in October 1835, was similar to other aids of that era. The twenty-three foot white tower, with an attached keeper's house connected by a covered walkway, was located on a neck of land north and east of the harbor. Then as now, Marblehead is a safe deepwater port that supports a considerable variety of vessels. Sailing vessels returning from foreign ports and a local fishing fleet from centuries ago have been replaced by a sizeable fleet of recreational sailboats. A fixed white light about fifty feet above the water would guide mariners into the harbor. In 1857, a 6th order Fresnel lens replaced the original lamps. With more large cottages being built around the lighthouse and obscuring the light, in the 1870s a mast (a point of conjecture was its height, reported to be one hundred feet) was erected to hold the light and make it visible. By the 1890s plans were made to construct a larger tower. The distinctive present-day 105-foot cast-iron lighthouse was built in 1895 and first lit in April, 1896; it displayed a fixed white light with a 6th order Fresnel lens. Eight eighty-four foot tall pilings, placed twelve feet apart at ground level, support the tower. Concrete foundations anchor each piling. A lower construction cost (about half the price) than the traditional lighthouse may have been the motivation behind this design. Lighthouses of this design were erected where support was an issue, and by spreading out the base, a tower that reached at least a hundred feet could be built. Besides those in Florida, examples of this plan are also found on the shores of the Great Lakes.

The color of the light was changed twice, once in the early 1920s from white to fixed red (so not to be confused with the lights in town) and then to fixed green (1938). The tower was painted "metallic brown" so it could be easily distinguished from its surroundings. White may have made it look better, but the functionality of the tower as a daymarker was lost. The oil house remains but the keeper's house was torn down in 1959. The light was automated in 1960 and now has a modern plastic lens. The tower now stands in a beautiful park, Chandler Hovey (named after a resident who purchased the land and later donated it to the town), overlooking the harbor and nearby water.

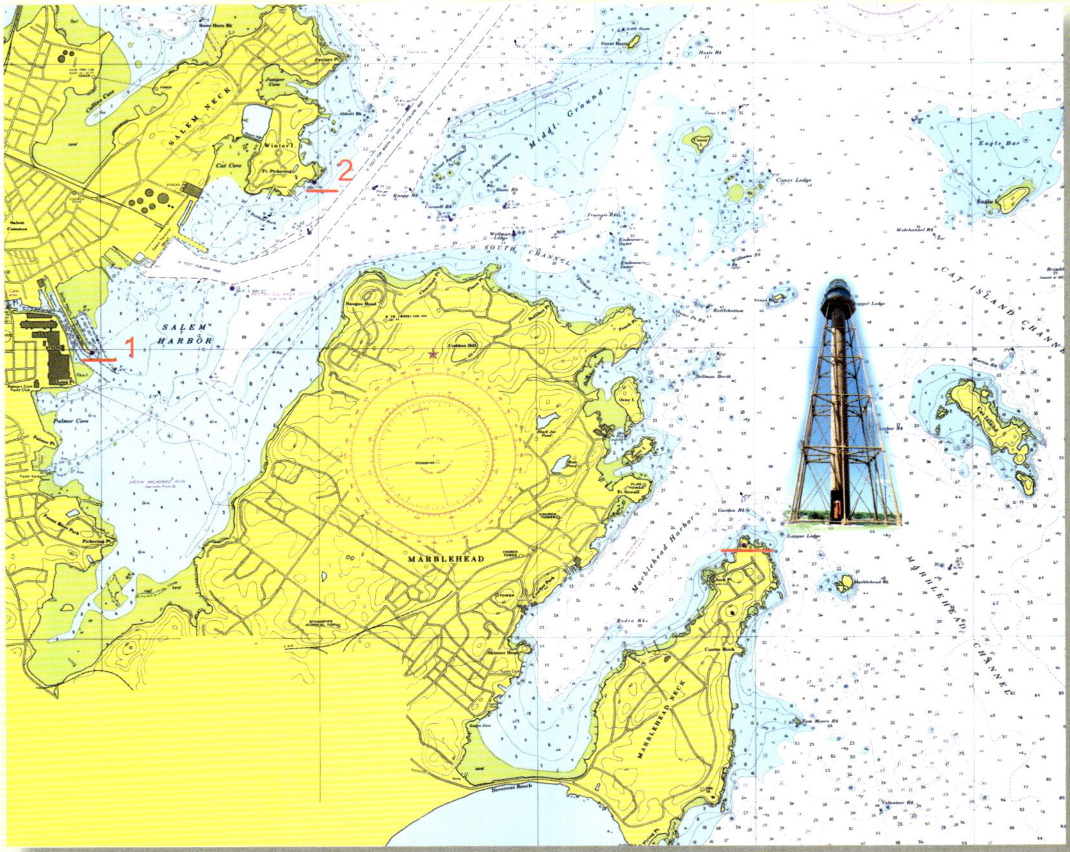

This present-day chart of Marblehead and Salem harbors shows the location of Marblehead Light on the point of land on the east side of the harbor. Located to the north and in Salem Harbor are two lights, **1)** Derby Wharf and **2)** Winter Island (Fort Pickering). *(Courtesy of NOAA)*

Top Images: These two panoramas captured in the late 1800 show Marblehead Harbor from opposing views. The light's location is underlined in red; notice how many of the houses and buildings are the same today. *(Courtesy of LOC)*

Above: Another old image of the original tower captures the covered walkway and the keeper standing at the right corner of his house. *(Courtesy of NA)*

Left: This late-1800s image is of the original Marblehead Light. The pole (100 feet?) was installed when surrounding homes blocked the light from the tower at the left. *(Courtesy of NA)*

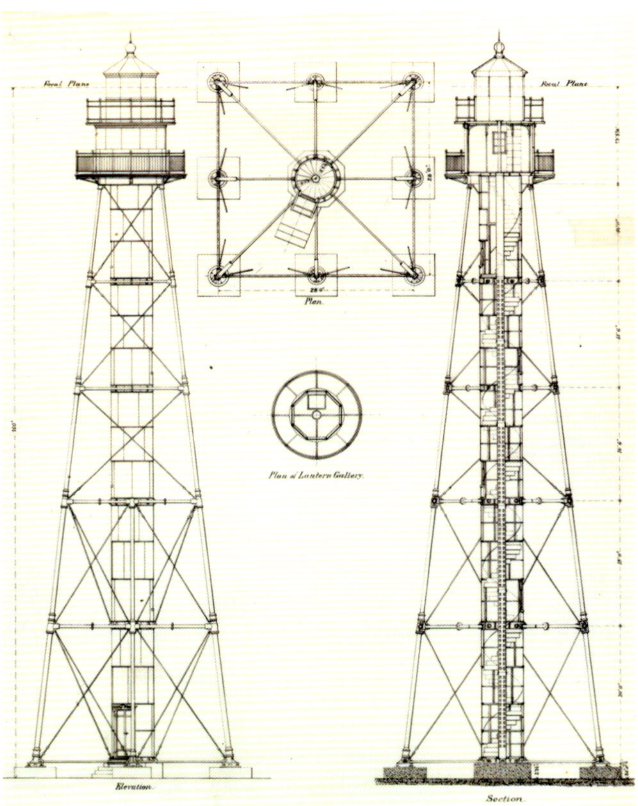

Above: This photograph, undated, was taken from the water to show the tower. *(Courtesy of USCG)*

Left: Plans for the steel skeleton tower at Marblehead; these were also used for other towers, such as Sanibel Light in Florida. *(Courtesy of NA)*

In this view the covered walkway has been removed. *(Courtesy of NA)*

Two century-old postcards show Marblehead Light.

Above: Compare this image of Marblehead Harbor, looking east, to the above postcards; the tower is in the distance.

Left & below: These two black-and-white images of Marblehead Light were taken in the early 1980s when a detailed survey was completed by the Massachusetts Historical Society. *(Courtesy of MHC)*

Sometime in the mid-1930s, these aerial images were captured of Marblehead Light. *(Courtesy of USCG)*

A panorama of Chandler Hovey Park showing the light at the end of a rocky point of land. Marblehead is in the distance behind the tower.

The door in the tower opens to a central supporting post and circular stairs.

Two skeletal tower lighthouses built within a year or two of each other. Sanibel Light in Florida has the palm trees and keeper's house at its base.

Above: Looking up the east side of the tower with its framework of support rods.

Left: An image looking down the stairs that lead to the lantern room.

Looking out one of the windows in the tower. The harbor is in the distance.

A modern beacon, 300 mm and fixed green, is found in the lantern room; the bracket at the bottom left of the lamp is a sensor that activates the light.

Salty Dog enjoys the beach near Sanibel Light in Florida.

Above: From the deck of the lantern room, the harbor in the foreground is filled with recreational craft, and the Boston skyline (overlined in red) is in the distance.

Left: A view out the lantern room looking north.

A view of the harbor from the park.

Two opposing present-day aerial views of Marblehead Light.

SALEM REGION

With its deep protected harbor, Salem appealed to the colonists from Europe and was settled in 1626, shortly after the colonies had been formed at Plymouth, Gloucester, and Boston. Probably best known for its history of witchcraft allegations, Salem at the time was a center of maritime activities. During the American Revolution, Salem Harbor had as many as eight hundred vessels, most of which were privateers that attacked and destroyed British ships. Famous for its trade with China and its large fishing fleet, in 1790 Salem was the sixth largest city in the New World. Walk the streets near the harbor today and find fine architecture representative of a previous era. More Colonial homes built before 1900 are found in Salem than in any other area in America. Remnants of a Federal era coastal community before 1800 can be found in several neighborhoods. As shipping and trade declined, Boston and New York, with their deeper harbors, became the favored ports. Tourism is now a major activity in the city.

After passing Marblehead Light to the south, mariners sailing north would find four lighthouses, three of them in Salem: Baker's Island (1798), Winter Island (1871), and Derby Point (1871). Just to the north in Beverly is Hospital Point (1872). While each light will be discussed in more detail, it is interesting to note that Baker's Island was previously one of the earliest set of twin lights built in America. Although they are independent beacons, both Winter Island and Derby Wharf form a set of range lights into Salem Harbor; Hospital Point is the Front Range light with a local church spire the rear range light.

It is less complicated to discuss these four aids to navigation in Salem Sound waters and how they relate to each other together than trying to deal with each beacon independently. Our discussion of lights starts offshore and then moves into each respective harbor, first Salem and then Beverly.

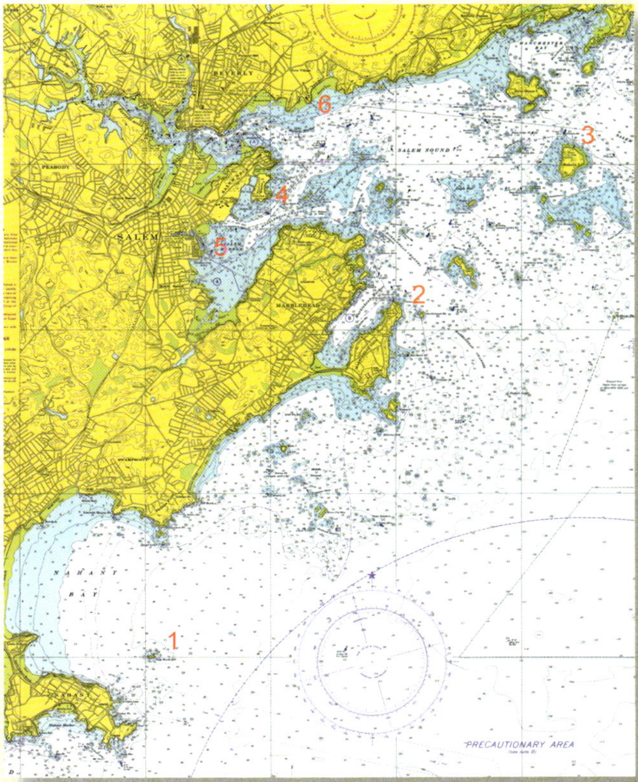

This large-scale present-day chart of the northern coast of Massachusetts from Nahant to Manchester shows the location of six lighthouses. Number 1, previously discussed and no longer in existence is Egg Rock, off Nahant; number 2 is Marblehead; number 3 is Baker's Island; number 4 is Fort Pickering (Winter Island); number 5 is Derby Wharf; and number 6 is Hospital Point. *(Courtesy of NOAA)*

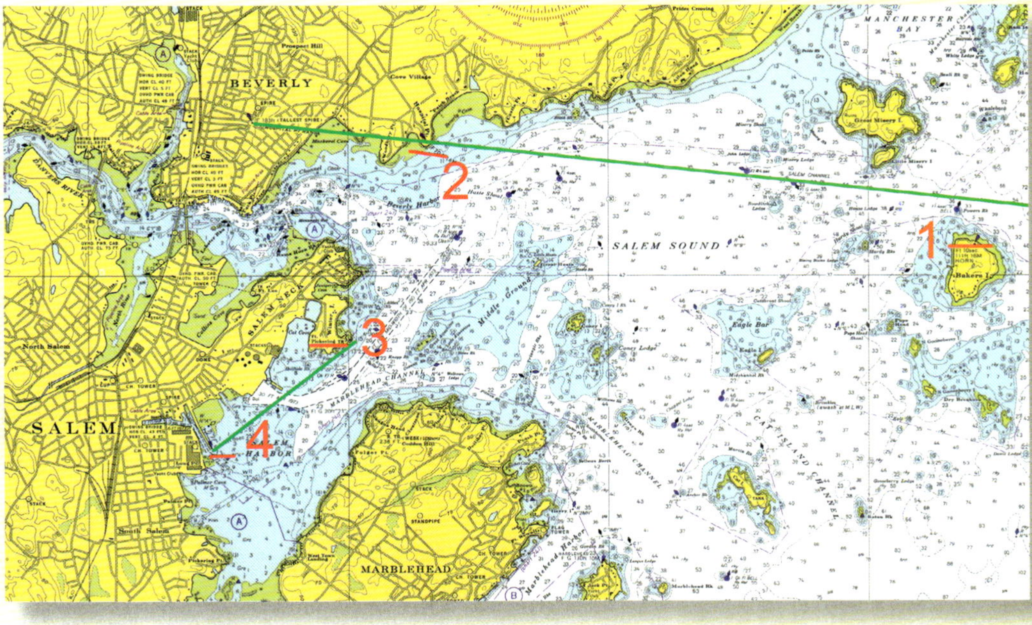

A smaller scale contemporary chart shows the four lighthouses discussed in this section. Underlined in red is the location of the tower: 1 is Baker's Island; 2 is Hospital Point; 3 is Fort Pickering; and 4 is Derby Wharf. The top green line shows the navigation line formed by the Hospital Point range lights. The green line between 3 and 4, which is actually a set of range lights, is the navigation line between Winter Island and Derby Wharf. *(Courtesy of NOAA)*

BAKER'S ISLAND

This sixty-acre island, about three miles from Salem Harbor, was named by Governor John Winthrop in 1630, possibly for John Baker who had been killed while building a ship. Later, in 1660, the island was deeded to the town of Salem, but in 1731 it was sold to a private party; the island is still privately owned. With the maritime activity in nearby Salem Harbor, a daymarker had been erected on the island by 1791. By 1796 and after much lobbying by local merchants and mariners, Congress authorized the construction of twin beacons (wood framed) about forty feet apart with a keeper's house built between them. They were first lit on January 3, 1798. As a result of poor construction materials and methods, one of the lights was discontinued because the tower had deteriorated badly. By 1820 and after numerous nearby wrecks, plans were developed for the reestablishment of twin lights. Two granite and concrete towers were built and lit in 1821. Not the same height because of the sloping land on the island (each light had to be the same height from the water), the two towers were referred to locally as the "Ma and Pa" or "Mr. and Mrs." lighthouses. The shorter tower was torn down in 1926.

The present station includes a fifty-nine-foot-tall lighthouse, two Victorian keepers' cottages (1878), brick oil house (1855), and fog-signaling building (1907). The original optics were a set of multi-lamps and reflectors. A 4th order Fresnel lens was installed in 1855; a modern plastic optic is now present. The light was automated in 1972. The alternating rotating optic flashes red and white every twenty seconds. Listed on the National Register of Historic Places, the lighthouse is not open to the public, but in partnership with the National Park Service and the Essex National Heritage Commission, who are owners of the station, future visits may be possible to the lighthouse.

Above: An aerial view of Baker's Island; the lighthouse can be seen on the far side (north end) at the top.

Left: Probably taken in the late 1800s, this is one of the earliest images of the twin Baker's Island Lights. Close examination reveals at least ten people standing by the house. Compare this image to the color postcard on the opposite page and note the similarity. *(Courtesy of NA)*

Another old image of the lights from a different perspective; note the obvious difference in height between the two towers. *(Courtesy of NA)*

This third image, looking north, with one tower visible in the distance shows the keepers' houses and other buildings. The smaller, Mrs. Tower is hidden from view. *(Courtesy of NA)*

As an aid to navigation, a lighthouse was not only visible as a daymark or as a characteristic and distinctive light at night, but most also had some form of fog-signaling device. Invented in the mid-1800s, the Daboll trumpet used a vibrating column of air to produce an audible sound. Both steam and coal powered, the sound was produced from either vibrating discs or air being forced through holes in revolving discs. Like the light, the fog signal was also distinctive and characteristic of that station. *(Courtesy of USCG)*

Two images, the same vintage, include a color postcard and a dated 1919 black-and-white photograph from the National Archives. Compare the images and note the people included in the postcard, which adds a degree of ambiance. *(Black-and-white image courtesy of NA)*

This aerial image of Baker's Island Light was probably taken about a half-century ago. *(Courtesy of USCG)*

A view of the tower, oil house and solar panels. *(Courtesy of P. Karwowski)*

Compare these two views of Baker's Island Light from the water: the color image is present-day, the century old black-and-white is from the Light List. North is to the right. *(Color image courtesy of P. Karwowski; Black-and-white image Courtesy of USCG)*

One of the keeper's house with the light in the background. *(Courtesy of P. Karwowski)*

Granite stairs lead to the lantern room. *(Courtesy of P. Karwowski)*

A view out one of the windows; note the wall thickness. *(Courtesy of P. Karwowski)*

Looking north from the lantern room with its modern aerobeacon, a VRB-25 that produces an alternating red and white signal every twenty seconds. *(Courtesy of P. Karwowski)*

An aerial view of the Baker's Island Lighthouse Station.

Two vistas from the outside walkway; one looking south with the keeper's houses in the foreground and the other looking west with the Salem power plant towers on the horizon. *(Courtesy of P. Karwowski)*

FORT PICKERING (WINTER ISLAND)

Sailing into Salem Harbor, the first lighthouse one encounters is the Fort Pickering (Winter Island) Light on the right-hand side of the channel. Of the same vintage as Derby Wharf and Hospital Point, this lighthouse was built and first lit in 1871. In 1870 Congress had appropriated thirty thousand dollars to construct three lighthouses: Fort Pickering, Derby Wharf, and Hospital Point. Located on Winter Island and not connected to the mainland, a keeper's house and oil house were also built at that time. Made of a cast-iron outer sheath, the tower is lined with brick on the inside. The original optic was a 5th order Fresnel lens that was only twenty-eight feet above the sea Although not specifically identified as a range light, mariners would line up this light—Fort Pickering—with Derby Light to mark the channel into the harbor. Before the turn of the century (1897), both Fort Pickering and nearby Derby Wharf Lights were discontinued; as an aid to navigation, they were no longer considered necessary. Like many unattended lighthouses, weather and vandals took their toll on this beacon. A group of concerned citizens, with the aid of the City of Salem, restored the lighthouse, now listed on the National Register of Historic Places. A private aid to navigation, Fort Pickering Light is solar-powered and flashes a white light every four seconds with a modern optic. While the tower is not open to the public, the lighthouse can be seen from Winter Island Park.

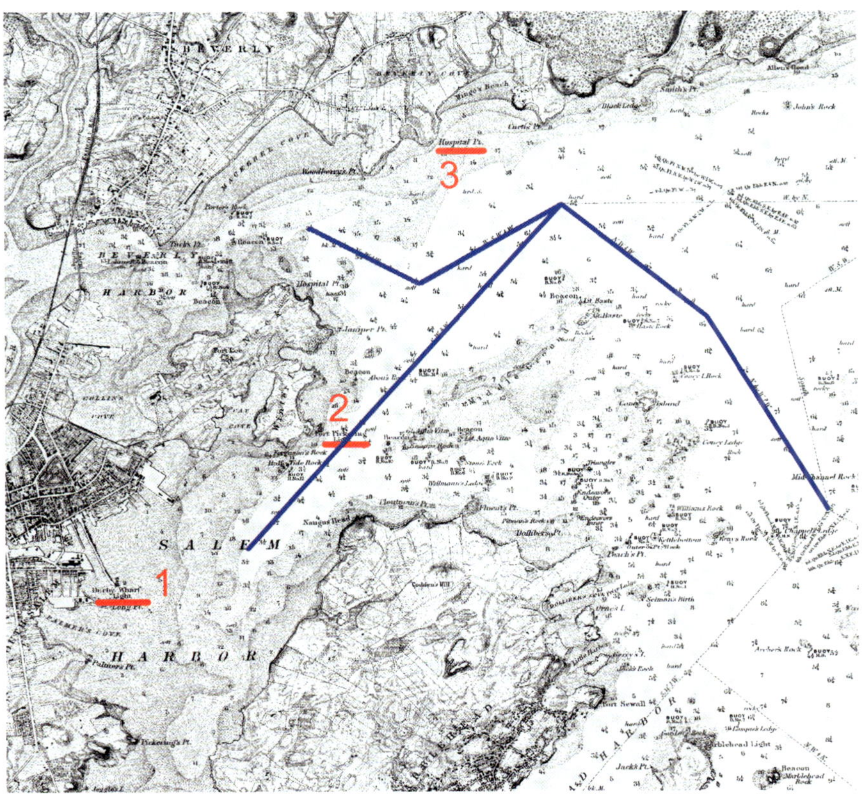

Top: An aerial view of Fort Pickering Light. Salem Harbor lies beyond.

Left: This chart shows an interesting anomaly. A section of Salem Harbor, courtesy of NOAA, and dated 1868, identifies two lighthouses as part of the legend, as you would expect: Marblehead Light and Baker's Island twin lights, both aids to navigation built in the eighteenth century. Yet it shows lights at Fort Pickering **(2)** and Derby Wharf **(1)** also—which were not built by this date. Hospital Point, built in 1872 **(3)**, is not shown as a light. Since all three lights were built about the same time, one would expect to see all three listed and identified as aids to navigation. Maybe this chart was reprinted in 1871 and then not dated. Whatever the explanation, it is a nifty old chart. The blue lines represent navigational channels into Beverly Harbor (top) and Salem Harbor (bottom). *(Courtesy of NOAA)*

Postcard: This old postcard, more than a century old, shows three interesting features about Fort Pickering Light: 1) for many years, the tower wasn't white, but red or brown; 2) a walkway was necessary to gain access to the tower; and 3) the tower was built not on land but slightly offshore.

Top and left: Two undated photos taken from opposite sides of the tower. The tower and walkway were constantly damaged by severe storms. The walkway was destroyed several times: 1879, 1904, and 1978. During the Blizzard of 1878, the door was ripped from the tower. *(Courtesy of NA)*

Left: Two views of the tower from opposite sides at low tide; the only time that the tower can be accessed also requires a ladder. Baker's Island Light can be seen in the distance.

No longer standing, this image of the Winter Island keeper's house was taken in 1916. *(Courtesy of NA)*

Stairs lead to the top of the tower. Because there is no central support, bricks line the walls for addition stability.

A view looking up the stairs with the cast-iron five panel lantern floor.

This vista is looking north out the lantern room; underlined in red is Hospital Point.

Top: Looking southeast, the land in the distance is Marblehead.

Center: This view is looking south out the lantern room; underlined in red is Derby Wharf Light. Mariners would line up these two lights, Winter Island and Derby Wharf, to guide them into the harbor.

Bottom row: A modern plastic lamp produces the light signal; several bulbs can be seen on the inside of the lamp.

In this winter view, Winter Island Light marks the entrance to Salem Harbor.

Now part of a park, the lighthouse is located along a walkway at the end of the land. Notice in the image the foundation of a fort that once occupied this point.

This aerial view, with the lighthouse to the bottom right, shows part of what was once Fort Pickering.

It was once an active Coast Guard station (until 1965) and aircraft were stored in this hangar.

DERBY WHARF

The lighthouse in inner Salem Harbor is Derby Wharf, built in 1871 and first lit only two weeks after Fort Pickering Light had been lit. Located at the end of the half-mile-long wharf that once housed more than a dozen large warehouses and numerous businesses, this fourteen-foot square brick tower had a 5th order Fresnel lens that displayed a fixed red light twenty-five feet above the water. It has one steel door, and there are no windows or exterior adornments. There was also no keeper's house built, as the light was maintained by local caretakers who lived nearby. Through the years, several changes occurred with the optic: in 1906 a 4th order lens was installed; in 1910 a 6th order lens was installed; and a modern plastic optic was installed in 1983. Electrified in 1930, the light was discontinued in 1977. Owned by National Park Service, the tower is not open to the public, but can be walked around at the end of the wharf. With a flashing red light every six seconds, Derby Wharf Light is a private aid to navigation.

A present-day chart of Salem Harbor with the square brick Derby Wharf Light at the bottom and the round cast-iron Fort Pickering Light at the top. The green line represents the navigational channel that these two lights would designate to vessels entering or leaving the harbor. *(Courtesy of NOAA)*

An aerial image of Derby Wharf with the light at the end of the wharf.

Present-day Derby Wharf with the lighthouse barely visible at the end. Centuries ago, buildings that included shops and warehouses would be found on the wharf. Now one ship, the *Friendship*, is tied up where ships that once roamed the world were moored.

This image of Derby Wharf Light, captured in the middle of the last century, was taken when the wharf was being repaired. *(Courtesy of USCG)*

Derby Wharf Light is part of the Salem Maritime National Historic Site.

Look closely at the lantern room windows; special wires in the glass were installed to prevent vandals from breaking windows. *(Courtesy of USCG)*

A view of the light taken more than a century ago; the bricks had not yet been painted white. *(Courtesy of NA)*

A close-up of the lighthouse at the very end of Derby Wharf. There are no windows in the short tower and a door facing the shore side provides access.

Top row: Two different views from the lantern room that include the modern red aerobeacon; one looking down the wharf toward the custom house and the other looking out the harbor with the power station in the distance.

Center row: Two flights of stairs lead to the lantern room; the first set is red and wood, the second set is black and metal. Notice the metal base to the lantern room. Both rooms in the tower are empty.

Left: This is the view looking up the stairs into the lantern room.

A panorama of Derby Wharf Light looking out the harbor.

At the landside end of Derby Wharf, the distinctive Custom House is in the center of the image. Taxes would be collected from ships bringing imported cargo into Salem Harbor. As early as 1649, Salem had a Custom House.

HOSPITAL POINT

With Baker's Island Light in the outer harbor, Hospital Point Light guides mariners into Beverly Harbor. It is also used by vessels to enter Salem Harbor from the north. Originally known as Paul's Point, this rocky point of land on the north side of Beverly Harbor had a signaling apparatus here as early as 1711. A fort, still discernible on the ground, was built on this location previous to 1775. A smallpox hospital was built on the grounds in 1801, which was later used as a barracks during the War of 1812. The building burned to the ground in 1849, but the name remains. In 1871, the town of Beverly gave the land to the U.S. Government for a lighthouse. The first temporary wooden tower was promptly replaced by the present brick tower. Completed in 1872, the station also included a two-story wood-framed keeper's house and a brick oil house. The house was used again during World War II as barracks. After the light was automated in 1947, the house was retained by the Coast Guard as the residence of the Commander of the First Coast Guard District.

The Federal-designed tower still has its original optic, a relatively rare 3½ order Fresnel lens. About halfway in size between a 3rd and a 4th order lens, it has an inside diameter of about thirty inches and is forty-four inches tall. It is considered to be a 750-millimeter optic. For comparison, the 1st order Fresnel lens (the largest) is 1840 millimeters and the 6th order (the most common, and smallest) is 300 millimeters. Common present-day plastic optics are in the 250-to-300-millimeter range. Another interesting aspect of the light is a condensing panel that concentrates the light beam down the center of the channel. As a mariner moves off the center line the light will diminish. The light, at seventy feet above the waterline, is fixed white that shows through 360 degrees.

As mentioned earlier, Hospital Point is the front light in a set of range lights. In May 1927, the lighthouse's name was officially changed to Hospital Point Range Front Light when the First Baptist Church (1801), a nautical mile to the rear, had an optic installed in its spire. It is called the Hospital Point Range Rear Light. Previous to 1927, the church spire, during the day, could be used as a marker for vessels entering the harbor. By installing two 300-millimeter optics that had been used on lightships, the spire with the light at over 180 feet above the waterline could now be used at night. A fixed white light is visible only two degrees to each side of the centerline with the Front Range light. Automated, the beacon is referred to as "the church with the harbor light." Other churches have been used as aids to navigation, but the First Baptist Church in Beverly is the only official aid at the present time.

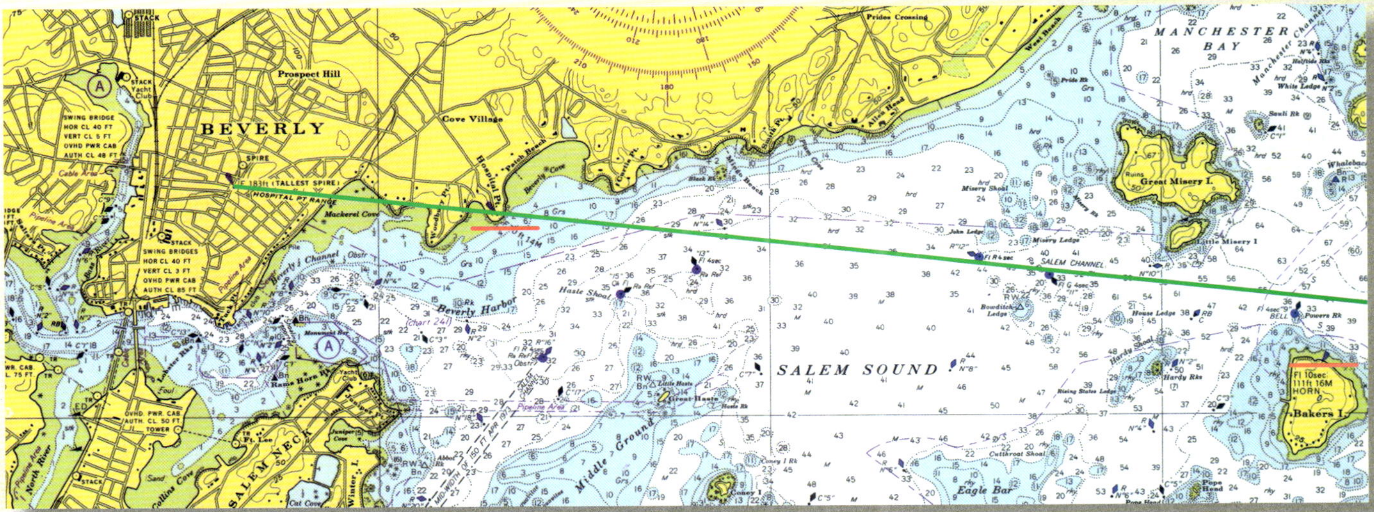

A present-day chart showing two lights underlined in red: Baker's Island on the right and Hospital Point on the left. The green line starts on the left at the First Baptist Church spire, passes through Hospital Point, and on towards Baker's Island. Note the narrow distance between the buoys just to the southwest of Great Misery Island. *(Courtesy of NOAA)*

Two signs at the site explain and describe to the visitor relevant information not only about the lighthouse but the surrounding grounds.

Three postcards, from the early 1900s, show three different views of the lighthouse.

Parlor cards, slightly larger than a postcard and usually not mailed, show the Hospital Point Lighthouse sometime more than a century ago. *(Courtesy of NA)*

The grounds surrounding Hospital Point are private, but in the winter it is possible to get good views of the tower. The tower is open for visitors on selected dates during the summer season.

Three aerials of the Hospital Point Light Station: the first in snow was from the 1950s *(Courtesy of USCG)*. The black-and-white image was captured in the early 1980s *(Courtesy of MHC)*. The present-day color image shows a perspective of the area.

Two views showing the area behind the tower, which includes the oil house with a vista seaward and the grass-covered ramparts that were part of a fort built in 1775.

Two images of the tower taken more than a half-century apart. *(Courtesy of NA)*

Entry to the tower is through a door on the west side; wooden stairs lead to the lantern room.

A window in the tower offer views north and south.

Two close-up views, taken thirty years apart, show the lens. *(Black-and-white image courtesy of MHC)*

Seen in these three photos, the 3½ order Fresnel lens with a light of 12,000 candlepower produces a fixed white beam that is visible up to fourteen miles. The condensing panel that focuses the beam of light can be seen. If you stray from the channel, the light becomes dimmer.

The white line represents the line a navigator would follow when entering or leaving the harbor. Notice the buoys, barely distinguishable, just to either side of the white line.

In downtown Beverly, the First Baptist Church houses the rear-range light used in conjunction with Hospital Point. Notice the small rectangle about halfway up the top section of the steeple; this is the rear-range light.

CAPE ANN REGION

Leaving Salem Harbor to the south and sailing northeast, the navigator and the ship next approach Cape Ann, a rocky peninsula about thirty miles north of Boston, and its six lighthouses. Each will be discussed, including (from south to north) Eastern Point, Gloucester Breakwater Light, Ten Pound Island, Thatcher's Island, Straitsmouth Island, and Annisquam.

First visited by John Smith in 1614 and later occupied by English settlers in 1623 as a fishing and farming colony, Cape Ann was named in honor of the mother of Prince Charles, Anne of Denmark. Many early settlers would move to nearby Salem, which would become the Colonial seat of government. With its natural harbors Gloucester, Rockport, and Pigeon Cove, Cape Ann for centuries has been equated with a rich and storied maritime history. In Gloucester Harbor, world-known for its fishing fleet, there are two lighthouses, Ten Pound Island built in 1821, and Eastern Point built in 1832.

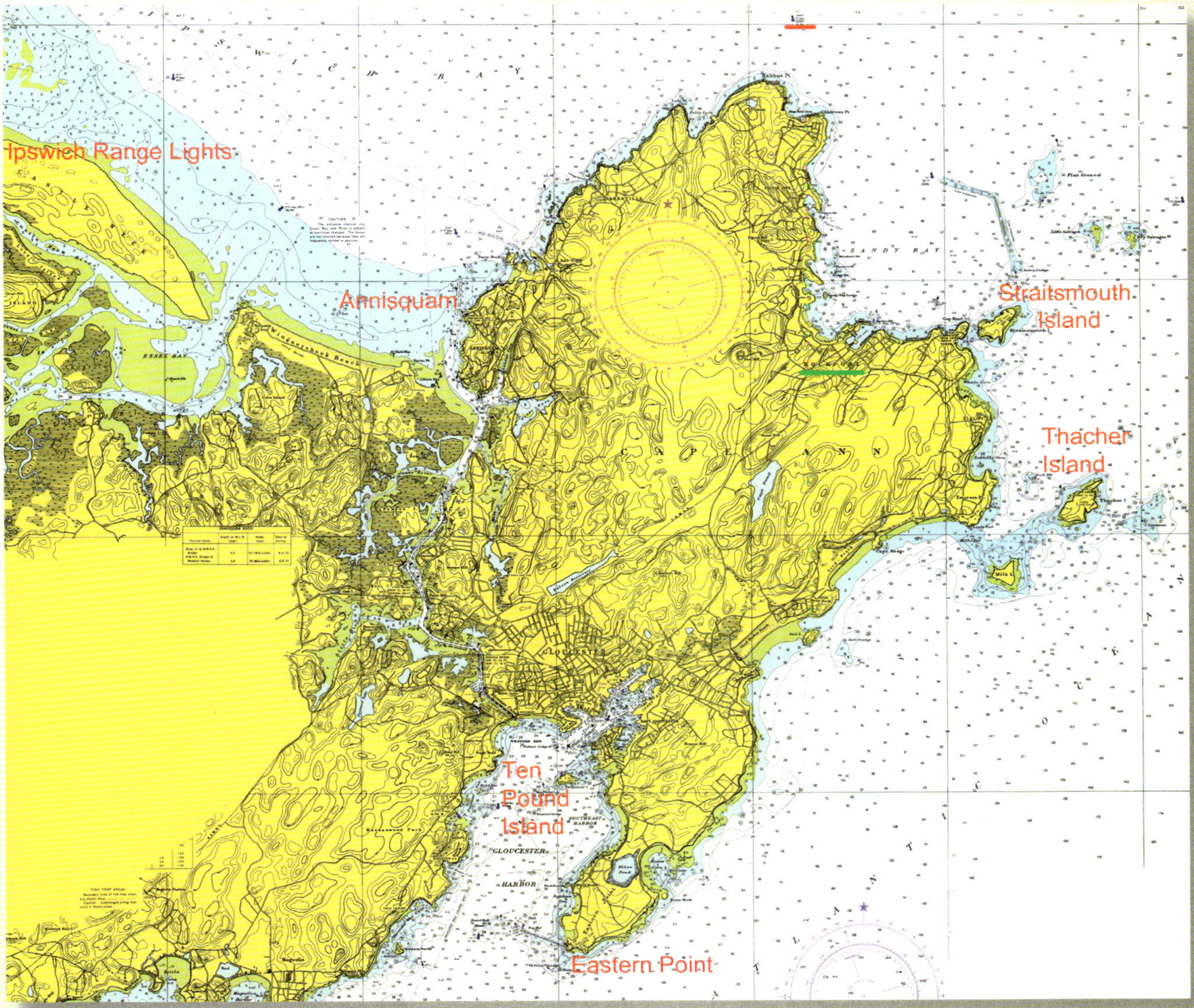

This chart of Cape Ann shows the aids to navigation on this peninsula. Eastern Point marks the entrance to outer Gloucester Harbor; Ten Pound Island marks the inner harbor. Two island lighthouses, Thacher and Straitsmouth, identify the eastern boundary of the Cape. Underlined in red at the top of the chart is a large navigational buoy. Annisquam Light marks the entrance to the river on the north side of the Cape. Identified but no longer in existence is the location of the former Ipswich Range Lights. Underlined in bright green is Rockport and its fishing harbor. Also, Pigeon Cove is just to the north along the coast. *(Courtesy of NOAA)*

Compare this aerial image, looking north, with the previous chart and locate the following aids to navigation: **1)** Eastern Point, **2)** Dog Bar, **3)** Ten-Pound Island, and **4)** general area of Thacher Island. Gloucester Harbor is beyond 3.

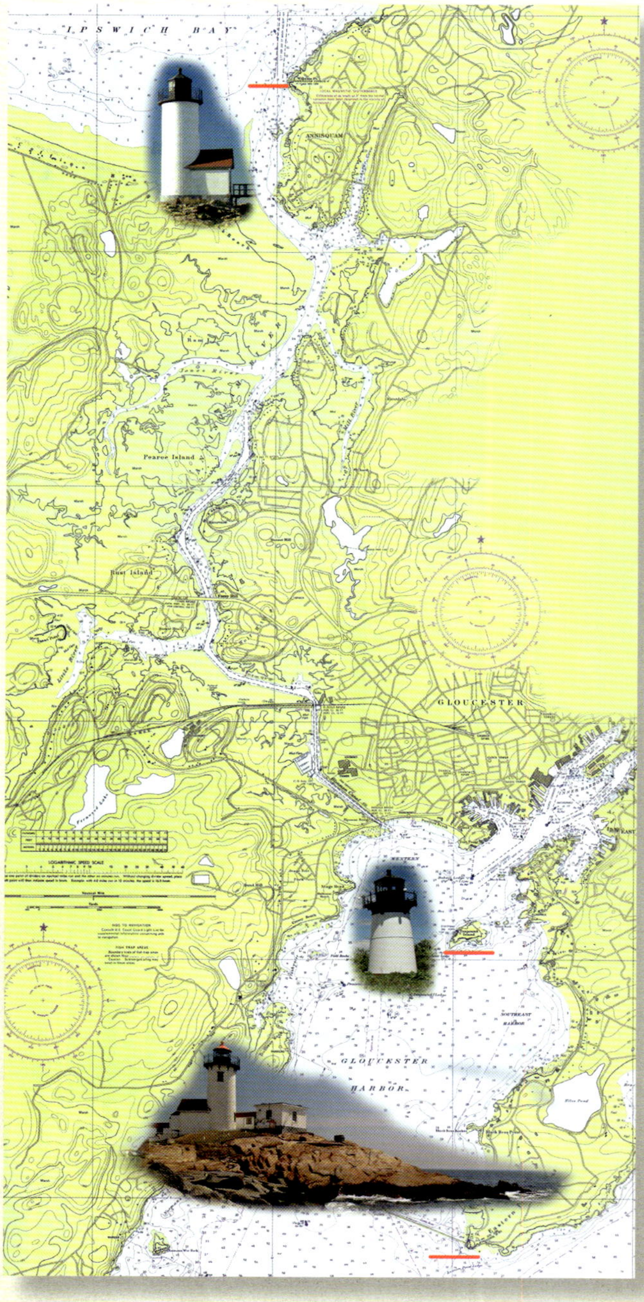

Above: This 1879 chart identifies the location of the two lighthouses (red underline) and their image that mariners would have seen at that time. *(Courtesy of NOAA)*

Left: A present-day chart showing the three current lighthouses. The Annisquam River is the connecting waterway. *(Courtesy of NOAA)*

EASTERN POINT

It soon became obvious that the light on Ten Pound Island was not adequate for vessels sailing along the coast. Unless you were directly in line with the upper end of Gloucester Harbor, the beacon on Ten Pound Island was not visible. To compensate for this lack of an aid near the outer harbor, Eastern Point Light was built in on a rocky promontory on the east side of the harbor entrance. The first lighted tower was erected in 1832 with a fixed white light. The twelve-inch parabolic mirrors were replaced by a 4th order Fresnel lens. A second tower, thirty-four feet tall, was built in 1848. The present-day brick tower was built in 1890. The Fresnel lens was removed in 1946 and replaced with a rotating aerobeacon. The light was automated in 1986.

Through the years, several structures were built at this site: a combination Gothic Revival/Queen Anne style keeper's house in 1879, a brick oil house in 1894, a radio beacon tower in 1932, a garage in 1947, and a fog-signaling building in 1951. The characteristic signals of Eastern Point light are a white flash every five seconds and a fog signal once every ten seconds. While the lighthouse, listed on the National Register of Historic Places, is not open to the public, the grounds surrounding the tower and the nearby breakwater offer excellent views.

Two images, both from the National Archives, show opposing views of the complex in the late 1800s.

A black-and-white postcard highlights the fog-signaling device located at the end of the rocky shore.

Above: As part of the HABS study in the 1930s, this image illustrates the location of Eastern Point Light and the rough rocky coast it's on. *(Courtesy of LOC)*

Left: Two colorized postcards showing different views of Eastern Point Light.

These two Coast Guard aerial images of 1945 show the lighthouse complex. In one, Gloucester Harbor can be seen in the background. *(Courtesy of USCG)*

Compare these two images of the tower taken from opposite sides more than thirty years apart. *(Black-and-white image courtesy of MHC)*

Almost a half-century ago, the Massachusetts Historical Commission did a survey of lighthouses; this image looking from the tower of Eastern Point was shot at that time. *(Courtesy of MHC)*

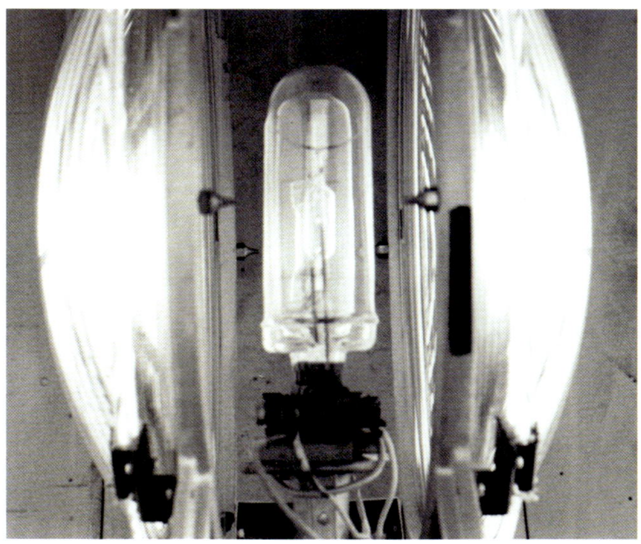

A close-up of the lamp taken in the 1980s; the optic is now a modern plastic beacon. *(Courtesy of MHC)*

From the keeper's house, a short flight of stairs and an enclosed walkway lead to the tower.

A final set of metal stairs leads to the lantern room.

Above & below: The present-day beacon in the lantern room.

Looking toward the jetty with the Breakwater Light at the end.

This water view was captured in 1980. *(Courtesy of MHC)*

Still an active aid: Eastern Point Light at the end of this rocky site.

A present-day aerial image of the Eastern Point Lighthouse Station.

GLOUCESTER BREAKWATER / DOG BAR

On the harbor side of Eastern Point Light was the Dog Bar Reef, and ships continued to ground on these rocks as they sailed into the harbor. Something had to be done to prevent further wrecks. Even before the breakwater had been totally completed, more than forty ships crashed into it. Between 1894 and 1904, a breakwater, more than twenty-two hundred feet long was built along the west side of Eastern Point Light. At the end of the breakwater, an iron tower building on a metal framework was constructed to house the light. The 4th order lens was first lit in 1905 with a fixed white signal. A Daboll trumpet was the fog signal. Keepers from Eastern Point were responsible for this light and during heavy weather reaching the tower was extremely dangerous. Automated the same time as Eastern Point, 1985, the tower now shows a fixed red signal. A fog signal is activated by a sensor.

Above: This shot of the tower was taken in 1980. *(Courtesy of MHC)*

Left: Once the jetty had been completed, it became necessary to mark its outermost end, and the resulting structure can be seen in this 1914 image. Notice, as seen in many of the old images, the keeper, who is standing near the right railing with the bell on the seaward side. *(Courtesy of NA)*

Top & above: The Breakwater Light is mounted on rocks slightly higher than the jetty and marks the east side of the harbor entrance.

The red beacon is mounted at the top of the wooden tower; access is by the metal stairs on the side.

Above: Along the shore of inner Gloucester Harbor is the distinctive statue dedicated to "They that go down to the sea in ships."

Left: The Breakwater Light can be seen at the end of the long jetty.

TEN POUND ISLAND

Named for the number of enclosures that farmers kept their sheep in, Ten Pound Island on the east side of inner Gloucester Harbor has had two lighthouse towers. In 1820, funds were appropriated by the Commonwealth of Massachusetts, and the following year a forty-foot stone tower with a covered passageway to a keeper's house was erected. The site also included a stone and slate oil house and storage shed. The second and present-day thirty-foot brick-lined, cast-iron tower replaced the original tower in 1881. The original optic was a 5th order Fresnel lens that was replaced with a 4th order lens in 1925. In turn, it was replaced shortly after, when a stronger light signal was required. The light tower was deactivated in 1956 and the optic moved to a nearby bell tower. In the late 1980s, the tower was restored and relit in August 1989. A modern plastic optic is now present in the tower. In the 1990s funds were raised to restore the oil house, one of America's oldest. The light signal is isophase (equal periods of light and dark), three seconds red and three seconds dark. Almost sixty feet above the waterline, the light is visible for five nautical miles. All that remains on the island, covered with vegetation, is the tower; only birds are the residents.

Two old photographs show the tower and keeper's house from different views. It was common during the early 1900s to paint towers other than white. The dark colored towers though had problems: they were too hot; condensation increased inside causing rusting; and sometimes they were not as visible as the white tower. Eventually, all the towers were painted white. *(Both images courtesy of NA)*

An image captured in the late 1800s of the original Ten Pound Island Lighthouse with the bird-cage lantern room. *(Courtesy of NA)*

The renowned artist Winslow Homer painted many of his works in the Gloucester area. *(Courtesy of LOC)*

Popular with postcard photographers, this vista is just one of the many available of this lighthouse.

About sixty years ago, the Coast Guard photographed many of the local aids to navigation. These are two of the images of Ten Pound Island. Compare these photos with present-day images seen elsewhere on these pages. *(Courtesy of USCG)*

Compare these present-day aerials to the above Coast Guard photographs and notice the differences.

Compare these two images taken more than a century apart; only the tower remains, with the island now covered with vegetation.

Top two images: Two views from opposite sides of the tower; the first from behind looking out of the harbor, and the second looking into the harbor. Note the solar panels that provide the power for the light.

Above left: The original oil house is now nearly covered with vegetation.

Left: On the back side of the island, this corner of a building foundation is all that remains.

THACHER'S ISLAND

The twin lighthouses on Thacher's Island, when built, had several distinguishing characteristics: they were the last lighthouses built (1771) under Colonial rule; they were the first lighthouse to have two towers (to make them more distinctive); and instead of marking a port, they warned of a nearby hazardous ledge. These were the eleventh lighthouse(s) built under British rule, the third by the Massachusetts Bay Colony after the first, Boston Light (1716) and then later Plymouth Light (1716). The original towers were forty-five feet tall and about three hundred yards apart on the northern end of the island. The first keeper, since this was before the start of the American Revolution, was a Tory, who was quickly forced out by local residents when the Revolution began. The lights were dark for the duration of the war.

The island was named for Anthony Thacher, who in 1635 while commanding the vessel *Watch and Wait,* was wrecked during a storm. He and his wife were the only survivors. This rocky fifty-acre land mass with little or no vegetation or soil is located less than a mile off the east coast of Cape Ann and about halfway between Eastern Point Light and Straitsmouth Island Light.

In the early 1860s, the original towers were replaced and rebuilt with granite and stone to a height of 124 feet. These towers had 1st order Fresnel lenses and the twin lights were sometimes referred to as "Ann's Eyes." When a submarine cable connected the island in 1932, the north light was deactivated. In 1989, the north light was re-lit as a private aid to navigation, with a fixed yellow light. The south light was automated in 1980 with a flashing red light every five seconds. Both lights are now modern plastic optics. They are the last set of twin lighthouses in existence in the United States. The Thacher Island Association provides tours during the summer season.

Some of the oldest images of the twin lights on Thacher Island were on stereo cards and dated October 4, 1869. These two images show the north (left) and south (right) towers. Compare these images with the present-day photographs of the keepers' houses. *(Courtesy of LOC)*

Another set of pictures of the twin lights, undated, probably shot at the end of the late 1800s. Compare these images with the present-day photographs and notice the changes. *(Courtesy of NA)*

Compare these two pictures, one a colorized postcard, showing the Thacher Island Lighthouses from a water view. Notice the location of the houses in relation to the towers. *(Sepia courtesy of NA)*

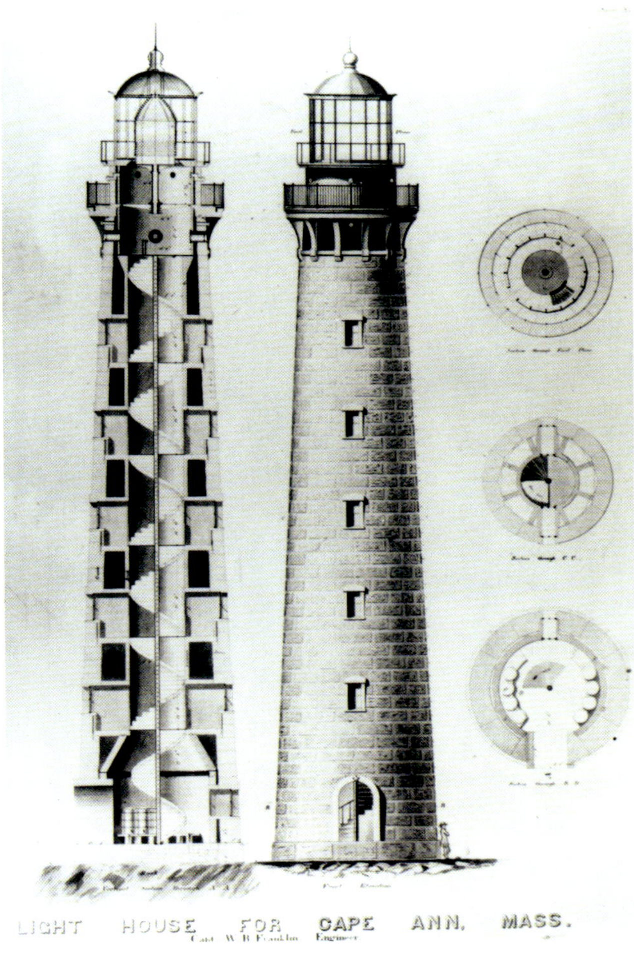

A plan for one of the towers. *(Courtesy of LOC)*

A present-day view of the north tower.

Three aerial photographs taken in the mid-1900s of different views of the island. Note the rails set up to move supplies on the island to different locations. *(Courtesy of USCG)*

Below: A view of the north tower captured in the 1960s when a survey was done of Massachusetts lighthouses. Information and images are available for study at the Massachusetts Historical Commission at the State Archives in Boston. *(Courtesy of MHC)*

Stairs inside the tower lead to the top; note the black band in the background. These rows of bricks decrease the diameter of the inside space within the tower; the thickness of the tower wall has increased to withstand high winds.

A view of the roof of the lantern room with the relatively small plastic beacon.

A short flight of stairs leads to the lantern room and the outside walkway.

Looking north from the lantern room, Straitsmouth Island and the lighthouse (underlined in red) can be seen to the left.

A view outside one of the windows on the south side of the tower; note the remnants of the foundation marking what was once the keeper's house.

From the walkway of the south tower, the north tower sits at the end of the island; in the distance Straitsmouth Island Light is barely visible. In the foreground left is the oil house; in the foreground right, on the edge of the cliff is the whistle house.

Volunteers, one day a week during the season, work on several projects; rebuilding and maintaining the rail system is one.

From the walkway of the north tower, the oil house, whistle house, and south tower with the keepers' houses are in the distance.

A walkway with local residents on the railing leads to the whistle house.

A view of the south tower and the only two houses that remain on the island.

A short walkway inside the south tower leads to the stairs to the top. Notice the same design in this tower where the inside diameter has been reduced.

With the brick wall in the background, a short flight of stairs leads to the lantern room.

Black curtains hang in the lantern room to block out or allow specific sectors of red light.

Looking underneath the base of the lantern room, the cast-iron plates have been bolted together and supported by a center post.

The north tower is visible in this view from the lantern room.

A vista from the south tower of the island and the Rockport shore in the distance.

The two keepers' houses; volunteers live here during the season.

In the white house, in the previous image, is a museum that documents the history of the island and the lighthouses.

From the walkway, the two houses, a helicopter landing pad, and near the flag in the distance, the ramp and boat house where the launch lands on the island.

A parlor in the white house decorated as it would have been in the past.

From the kitchens of the two houses, it is possible to see the towers.

Top & center: Knowing the houses are near the south tower, when looking at these aerial images we can determine our direction of view.

Left: Rockport, the closest harbor to the island, is filled with both recreational and commercial craft; the red building on the dock, motif #1, is one of the area's most photographed landmarks.

STRAITSMOUTH ISLAND

On the northeast coast of Cape Ann, two quintessential harbors, Rockport and Pigeon Cove, have had fishing fleets for centuries. Just offshore and to the east of these two harbors is Straitsmouth Island with its lighthouse, first built in 1835. The twenty-nine-foot-tall lighthouse located at the tip of the island also included a Gothic Revival keeper's house and a slate covered oil house. In 1851, a twenty-four-foot tower replaced the original lighthouse; the keeper's house was replaced in 1878. The present brick tower, thirty-seven feet tall, was built in 1896. A Fresnel lens (6th order) was installed in the 1850s. The light was automated in the 1930s, with a modern plastic lens installed in 1967, and was converted to solar power in 1985. Not accessible by the public, the island is owned by the Massachusetts Audubon Society. The tower is listed in the National Register of Historic Places. The present light is a green flash every six seconds. The foghorn blasts a signal once every fifteen seconds.

This classic image from probably the 1880s shows the lighthouse with its birdcage style lantern. Four individuals (one in the tower) are included in the image. *(Courtesy of NA)*

This archival image of the tower was taken in 1914. *(Courtesy of NA)*

Once a popular resort destination, Straitsmouth Island had numerous buildings; the lighthouse can be seen in the distance to the left. *(Courtesy of Paul St. Germain)*

Two parlor cards from about 1900 show the station from the water and a close-up of the keeper's house. *(Courtesy of NA)*

The tower and walkway were captured in 1925. *(Courtesy of USCG)*

A colorized postcard from 1910 showing the light, the keeper's house and other buildings on the island.

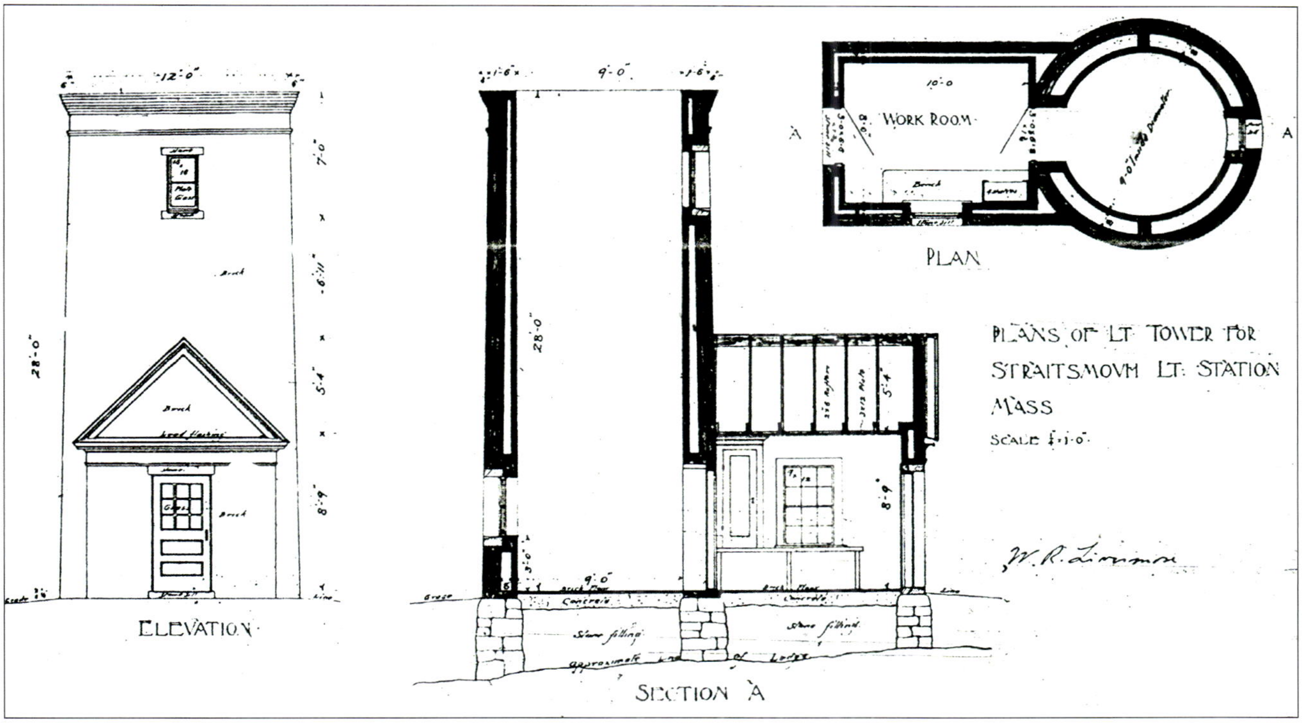

Plans for the tower. *(Courtesy of NA)*

This aerial was taken by the Coast Guard in the early 1950s. *(Courtesy of USCG)*

The Massachusetts Historical Commission surveyed lighthouses in the early 1960s. The keeper's house, the oil house, and a view of the tower are just some of the sights captured on Straitsmouth Island. *(Courtesy of MHC)*

Two views, one from the water and one from the air, of the island looking north.

This is a relatively close-up aerial of the eastern end of the island.

Looking south with the twin lights of Thacher Island in the distance. *(Courtesy of Paul St. Germain)*

Distinctive Straitsmouth Island Light is built right next to the rocky shore. *(Courtesy of Paul St. Germain)*

A present-day view of the station with the keeper's house in the background. *(Courtesy of Paul St. Germain)*

The keeper's house and (right) a view out one of the windows. *(Courtesy of Paul St. Germain)*

Circular stairs lead to the watch room where a short flight of stairs leads to the lantern room. *(Courtesy of Paul St. Germain)*

A modern green beacon flashing every six seconds is found in the lantern room. *(Courtesy of Paul St. Germain)*

A view from the lantern room, looking west. Rockport and Pigeon Cove are behind the rocky points. *(Courtesy of Paul St. Germain)*

With the rocks of Straitsmouth Island in the foreground, a view of the the one-time life-saving station on the Rockport shore. *(Courtesy of Paul St. Germain)*

ANNISQUAM

On the northern shore of Cape Ann where Ipswich Bay and the Annisquam River meet, Congress in 1800 appropriated funds to build a lighthouse on the eastern side of the river at what was known as Wigwam Point because it was a summer gathering place for Native Americans. The original wooden tower was thirty-two feet tall and displayed a fixed white light. Nearby a two-room keeper's house was built. By the late 1840s, the tower was so in need of repair that it was decided to replace the structure. By 1851, there was a new forty-foot white octagonal tower and the keeper's house had been repaired. In 1857, a 5th order Fresnel lens was installed in the tower. The present brick tower was built in 1897 on the site of the previous beacon. A foghorn was established in 1931, but only operated from October 15 to May 15 so as not to disturb the summer residents. By 1949, the foghorn was year-round but only during the daytime during the summer. Automated in 1974, the keeper's house is used by Coast Guard personnel, and the foghorn is controlled by a switch at a local police station. Still an active aid to navigation, the light flashes white every 7.5 seconds (with a red sector), the fog signal is two blasts every sixty seconds. Access to the tower is limited; it is best viewed from across the river.

Several lighthouses have red sectors that indicate hazardous courses. The chart shows the red sector of Annisquam Light. Underlined in red, at the bottom of the chart, is Ten Pound Island Light in Gloucester Harbor. Red plastic in the lantern room marks that sector. *(Courtesy of NOAA)*

A view of the protected Annisquam River and the some of the vessels that are moored there.

This second Annisquam tower was built in 1851; notice the lantern room. *(Courtesy of NA)*

Another archival image of the 1851 tower. Note the covered walkway that has been added and the change in the lantern room. *(Courtesy of NA)*

Above: Taken after 1897. The photographer captured the present-day brick tower that replaced the previous wood structure. The original keeper's house still stands; the covered walkway no longer exists. *(Courtesy of NA)*

Left: A Coast Guard aerial image taken in the 1950s. *(Courtesy of USCG)*

Compare this century-old postcard to the archival images.

A present-day aerial image of Annisquam Light.

In the early 1960s, these two images were shot as part of a study by the Massachusetts Historical Commission. *(Courtesy of MHC)*

Two views of the stairs leading to the lantern room.

The present modern-day optic is a VRB-25.

A winter scene of the Annisquam Lighthouse Station.

Two views of the tower on the rocky shore.

IPSWICH RANGE

With a fishing fleet, local shipbuilding, and coastal maritime trade, an aid to navigation was deemed necessary on what is now Crane Beach, Ipswich. Located on an east-west line, the first set of range lights was built in 1838; the two twenty-nine-foot brick towers were about 550 feet apart. A one-and-a-half story brick keeper's house was also built. With numerous lamps, the first lights were fixed white. Like other aids constructed in exposed sandy areas, it wasn't long before shifting sands required moving the towers. In 1867, the front tower was replaced by a relatively small wood structure so that it could be moved as the channel shifted. By 1881, the rear brick tower was badly cracked; it was replaced by a cast-iron tower. The front light was decommissioned in 1932; the rear tower was replaced in 1938 with a steel skeleton tower. The cast-iron tower was loaded on a barge, shipped to Edgartown on Martha's Vineyard, and replaced the lighthouse that was destroyed by the hurricane of 1938.

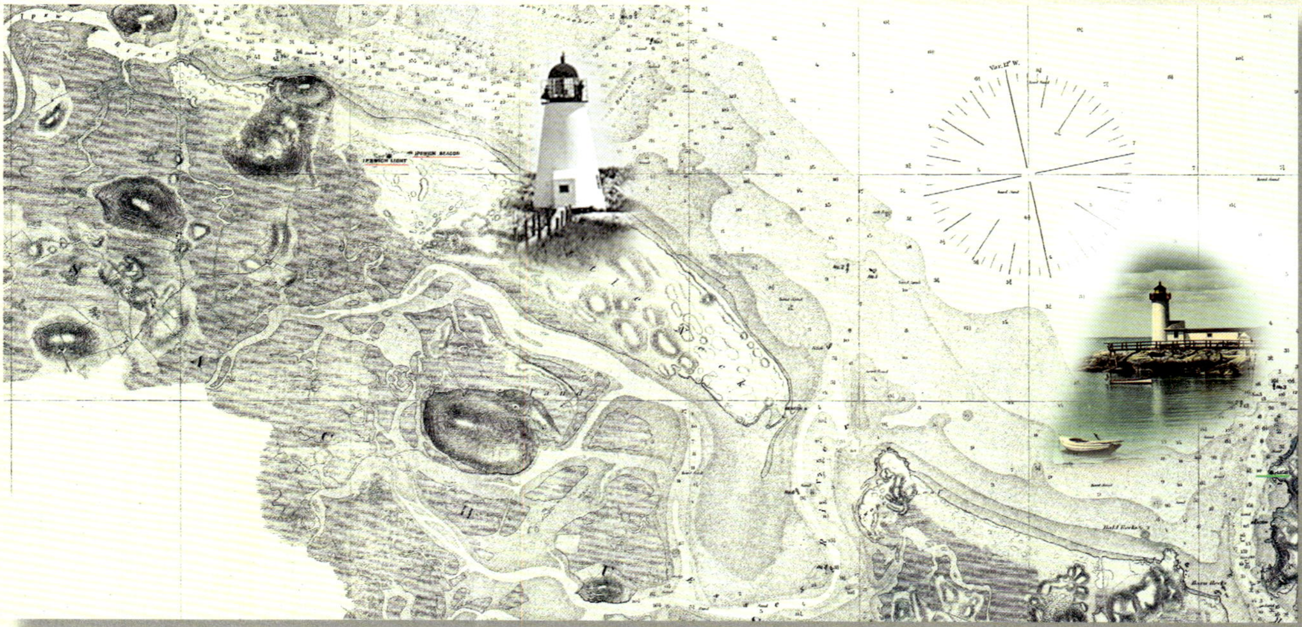

This is an 1857 chart of the Ipswich River and the two closest aids to navigation. On the right is the Annisquam Light and its location identified in green; on the left is one of the Ipswich Range Lights and its location identified in red. *(Courtesy of NOAA)*

A view of the front wood range light taken in 1914. Research indicates that George A. Howard or A. A. Howard were keepers in the 1910s; perhaps that is one of the men standing on the deck. *(Courtesy of NA)*

The 1881 tower probably taken sometime in the late 1800s. *(Courtesy of NA)*

Dated 1914, this wide-angle view shows the two range lights; the front light in the foreground was sometimes referred to as a bug light. *(Courtesy of NA)*

A view showing both range lights and part of a walkway that connected them. Continually shifting dunes were a problem. *(Courtesy of NA)*

Dated 1925, this is the keeper's house and the rear range cast-iron tower. *(Courtesy of NA)*

A present-day aerial image of Castle Neck, Crane Beach.

The present-day aid to navigation on Crane Beach. Note the castle in the background.

A modern plastic beacon flashes red every six seconds; Edgartown Harbor is in the distance.

This 1939 image shows the cast-iron tower after it was rebuilt in Edgartown on Martha's Vineyard.

An aerial view of Edgartown Light; the inner harbor is to the left.

Compare this image to the black-and-white 1925 photograph on page 207.

Decorated for the holidays, the Edgartown Lighthouse at sunset.

NEWBURYPORT REGION

PLUM ISLAND

For the vessel sailing north and passing Annisquam Light which led to Gloucester and the Ipswich Range Lights near the mouth of the Ipswich River, a nearly nine-mile-long barrier island had to be passed before encountering the Merrimack River. Originally called Plumb Island, Plum Island today is now parts of the towns of Newbury, Ipswich, Rowley, and Newburyport. In the mid-1700s, fires would be set on the beach at the northern end of the island to guide mariners into the Merrimack River. Local merchants after 1783 erected two day beacons, and lanterns were hung at night. With these measures not adequate, Massachusetts in 1787 approved the building of two lighthouses provided it didn't cost more than 300 English pounds. Each tower was to have a fixed white light thirty-seven feet above the water. When finished and lit in 1788, these were the thirteenth lighthouses built in America and probably the first set of range lights. The towers were turned over to the Federal Government in 1790. Rebuilt in 1809—when they blew over after a severe storm, probably a tornado—they were also the first beacons to be equipped with Argand lamps.

After the towers were rebuilt, during the next ninety years several changes occurred: one tower burned down in 1856, a rail system was proposed to deal with shifting channel changes, the towers were relocated in 1874, a more powerful light was recommended, a tower built in 1887 failed to meet requirements of being an aid, and in 1898 the present-day tower was refurbished. Jetties, built in the late nineteenth century on both sides of the river, helped to stabilize the shifting shoals so the lighthouses wouldn't have to be constantly moved. In 1927, electricity replaced the kerosene that had been used since 1877. Across the river were the Salisbury Beach Range Lights, and the keeper at Plum Island had the additional duty of maintaining those signals. The light was automated in 1951.

Now owned by the City of Newburyport, the tower is leased to The Friends of Plum Island Light, who open the lighthouse for scheduled tours in the summer. Still an active aid to navigation, the tower has the 1856 4th order Fresnel lens (a beautiful piece of glass) with an occulting green light with two eclipses every fifteen seconds. The nearby 1898 keeper's house is now used by the Parker River Wildlife Refuge. The grounds around the tower are open year-round, with excellent views.

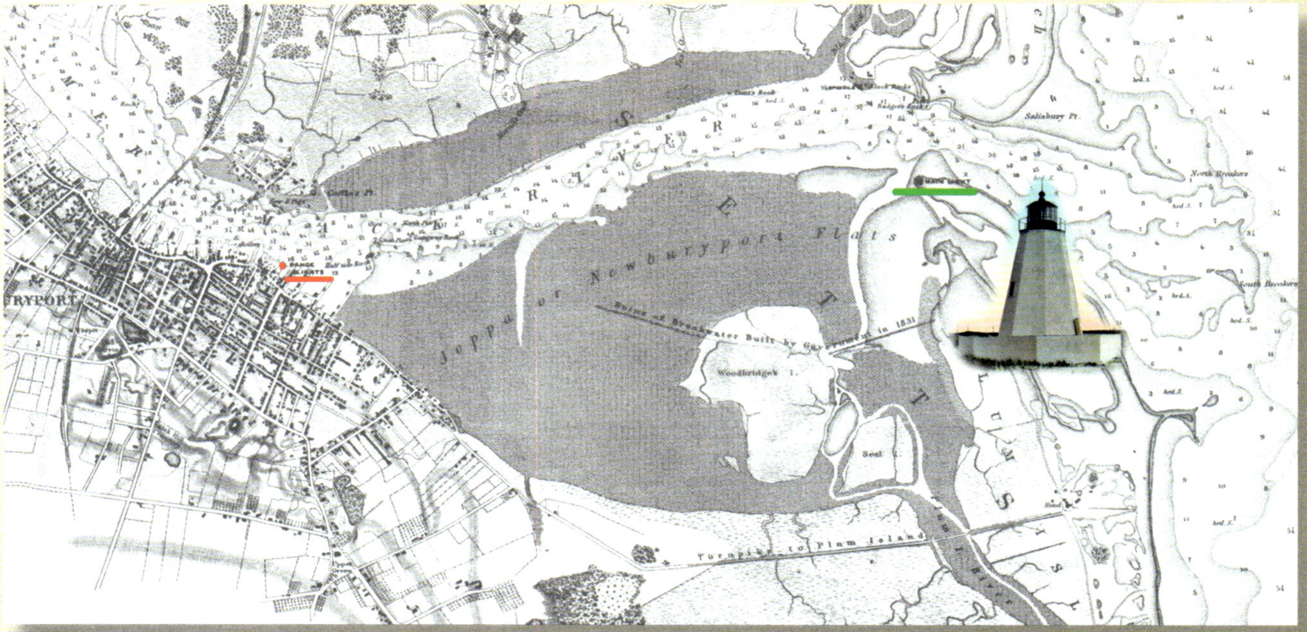

This 1855 chart of the Merrimack River shows Plum (Plumb) Island Light as it would have looked at that time and its location underlined in green. This is before the jetties were built at the mouth of the river to prevent the shifting sands from changing the inlet. Underlined in red is the location of the inner harbor range lights. Once the mariner had passed the lighthouse it was nearly a straight course to the docks. On the north side of the channel in Salisbury, a set of range lights was established in 1891. They were discontinued in 1950. *(Courtesy of NOAA)*

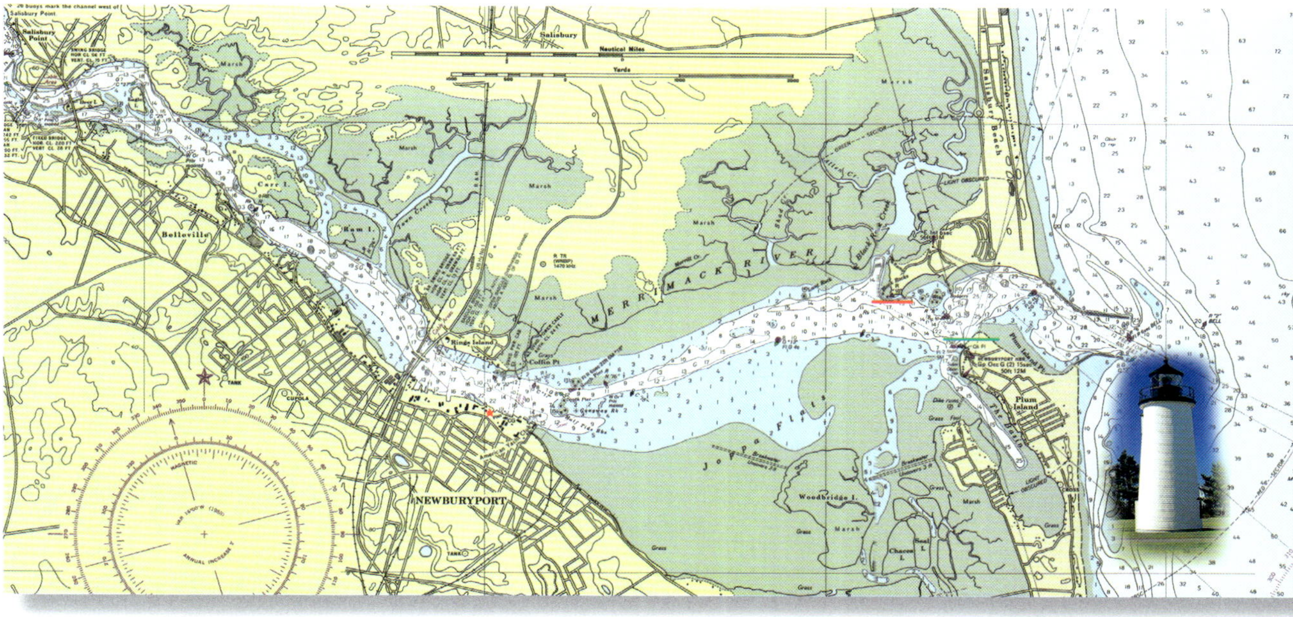

A present-day chart with the refurbished 1898 lighthouse and its location underlined in green The red dot indicates the general location of the range lights since the front light has been moved from its original position. Notice the jetties that extend out and control the shifting sands in the inlet. A sandbar (light blue) is indicated just north of the mouth of the river; this is an indication of the shifting sand along the coast. *(Courtesy of NOAA)*

An iconic photograph of Plum Island probably captured in the late 1800s. *(Courtesy of NA)*

An old postcard of one of the original octagonal towers.

Compare this old postcard at right, showing the present-day tower with the keeper's house, with the two black-and-white images above. Close examination of the left photo's background shows the Merrimack River. Also notice there is nothing but sand in the images; the keeper was paid extra because he couldn't grow any crops in a garden. *(Black-and-white images courtesy of USCG)*

Two aerial views from the 1950s. *(Courtesy of USCG)*

Left: This image was captured on the north side of the Merrimack River in Salisbury, looking west towards Newburyport Harbor. The inner harbor range lights would have been in the distance. The white church steeples, visible on the horizon, would have been an aid during daylight hours. This day beacon indicates to navigators "red right returning." The Salisbury Range Lights (page 221), simply lanterns on a pole, would have been found in this vicinity. In 1922, there were two pyramidal towers present, with the front tower at twenty-two feet and the rear tower at thirty-two feet. By the 1940s the heights were increased to aid mariners.

Two present-day aerial images of the Merrimack River. Looking east, the jetties extend out from the beaches and protect the inlet. Plum Island Light on the south is underlined in green; the day marker in Salisbury on the north shore is underlined in yellow. The second view is looking north across the river. Barely visible, the Plum Island Light is surrounded by homes.

Looking across the Merrimack River, the Plum Island Light with its distinctive green signal marks the left side of the channel.

Top row: These two pictures show the tower that is maintained by The Friends of Plum Island Light.

Center & bottom: Excellent images and views of the tower can be captured year round.

A close-up of the door; bricks in the walkway can be purchased to help maintain the tower.

Two views of the impressive stairs that lead to the lantern room. Inside walls have been removed to show the wood construction techniques; photos have been hung within the tower to show its history.

Two views from the lantern room. The red-roofed Coast Guard boathouse can be seen in the river view; the blacked-out section is in the image looking west.

Above: A short flight of stairs leads to the lantern room; more photos offer the visitor historical perspectives of the light.

Top right: The distinctive architecture of the first floor window.

Right: The 1856 4th order Fresnel lens is surrounded by green Plexiglas.

NEWBURYPORT REAR RANGE

From the time when it was first settled in 1635, Newburyport was an active harbor involved in maritime trade, shipbuilding, and a large fishing fleet. Little remains of the docks where clipper ships were built. With vessels navigating the Merrimack River, it was of importance to have aids to guide the mariners. At the mouth of the river were the Plum Island Light and the Salisbury Range Lights. In the inner harbor, range lights privately maintained by the merchants as early as the 1790s consisted of relatively simple lamps. Examine the early chart and note that once a vessel was through the treacherous inlet of the river, it was a relatively straight course to the docks in the inner harbor. During the day, church steeples could be used to navigate; at other times range lights would aid the navigator.

In 1873, the Lighthouse Board approved the construction of two towers with lights on Bayley's Wharf that could be lined up when sailing upriver. There were three sets of range lights built in Massachusetts, and this is only remaining pair in existence. The Front Range light, now moved from its original location, consisted of two sections: the fifteen-foot cast-iron bottom section that was lined with brick, and a twenty-foot hexagonal upper section made of wood and covered with shingles. At some point in time, the tower was changed from a range light to a harbor light and an octagonal wooden lantern was added. The tower is presently located on the grounds of the Coast Guard Station, built in 1972, and access is restricted.

The Rear Range Light, located a few hundred feet south on Water Street, is a fifty-three-foot tower that is made of brick, cast iron, and wood. Originally painted white on the top third on the north side facing the river, there was also an additional vertical white stripe. The octagonal lantern room is made of cast iron; the four rear- facing panels are blacked out while the four facing the river are clear. Both lights were discontinued in 1961 and are now listed on the National Register of Historic Places. The front tower has been moved onto Coast Guard property and both towers have been restored.

Nearby is the Custom House Maritime Museum which includes not only three hundred years of Newburyport history, but beginnings of the U.S. Coast Guard that date back to 1789. Also of interest and on display is the 4th order Fresnel lens that was originally at Pomham Rocks Lighthouse in Providence, Rhode Island.

This 1914 image captures the range lights in Newburyport; notice the tower in the background.

An active Coast Guard Station, Merrimack River provides assistance and maintains navigational aids on this potentially hazardous waterway.

Two images of the former front range light, no longer an active aid to navigation. This tower is not in its original position; it was moved to the Coast Guard Station in 1964. There's only a door for access to the cast-iron tower.

The two short flights of stairs lead to the lantern room; the signaling lens was removed when the tower was decommissioned.

The view from the lantern room of the front range light, looking out onto the Merrimack River. Note the buoys visible in the center panel that mark the channel and the blacked out panels on the shore side direction of the tower.

Stand in front of the tower and the distinctive rear range tower can be seen in the background.

Now privately owned, the rear range tower is available for dining. Reservations required.

Taken about sixty years apart, these two images show the side of the tower facing the river. Painted white, it was more visible to mariners as a day marker. *(Black-and-white image courtesy of USCG)*

Two vistas from the dining room; find the stairs and the Front Range tower in these pictures.

The side of the tower that faces the street with the door for access; the Merrimack River can be seen in the background.

A view of the stairs that lead to the dining/lantern room. Hung with archival photos, the brick tower has limited space.

Right: An aerial image of the two towers, highlighted in red, along the river in Newburyport Harbor.

SALISBURY RANGE

Located on the north side of the entrance to the Merrimack River, this set of range lights was established in 1891, rebuilt in 1906, and deactivated in 1950. Initially, the front light was a lantern with a red light on a twelve-foot pole. By 1922, the range lights had been removed and there was a red pyramidal skeleton tower eighteen feet tall; by 1941, a there was a skeleton tower with a white daymark. No evidence remains of this aid.

The Salisbury Range Lights, located on the north side of the Merrimack River, were basically lights hung on a pole. *(Courtesy of NA)*

MASSACHUSETTS LIGHTSHIPS

INTRODUCTION

Although many lighthouses on the Massachusetts coast have been built, maintained, moved, and in many cases restored, numerous lights still exist and provide enthusiasts with an opportunity to visit and examine these noteworthy pieces of local maritime history. That is not true for the lightships that guided mariners through the treacherous waters. The last lightship in Massachusetts waters left its station in 1983. There are no lightships in Massachusetts that are open to the public. Several lightship museums are open for tours of these floating aids to navigation, but none are located in New England. These historic maritime vessels are slowly disappearing.

(Author's note: The book *Cape Cod Lighthouses and Lightships* [Schiffer Publishing, 2010] describes in detail the lightships found south of Cape Cod, in Vineyard Sound and Nantucket Sound, while this book details the lightships in Buzzards Bay and Massachusetts Bay. Some of the lightships found in the first book are also mentioned here to provide a historical perspective.)

An increase in sailing vessels and maritime traffic in the eighteenth century resulted in a significant number of ships being lost to offshore navigational hazards. Something had to be done, something that went beyond the local lighthouses and their relatively short range signals, to protect and guide mariners to their destination.

The first light boats, light vessels, or as they are referred to today, lightships, can trace their history back more than twenty-three centuries when Roman galleys patrolled coastal waters They were visible during the day to aid commerce and protect merchant ships from pirates, and at night a lighted fire-basket hanging from the mast identified the vessel. Fast forward to the 1730s when the first modern light vessel was developed and patented by a wealthy merchant, Robert Hamblin, and was placed near the Nore sandbank at the mouth of the Thames River in the South of England. Under a lease from Trinity House, Hamblin, in 1732, placed a lightship near that sandbank and would collect a tariff from each passing ship. Small and primitive, the early lightships would hang two ship's lanterns from the yardarm to guide mariners into port. Countries could now provide lightships to aid navigators as an additional assistance to completing their journey safely in hazardous conditions.

In the early years, lightships were faced with several noteworthy difficulties. One of the original problems was the design, or more correctly, the lack of it. A sailing vessel of the time, converted to a lightship, was not suitable to stay moored in one location and provide comfort and safety for the crew. Vessels needed to be designed and constructed that could carry out their duties in heavy weather and hold the necessary equipment to accomplish that mission. At a significant distance off the coast, lightships had to be larger with a longer chain and a heavier anchor to maintain their position. In addition, the crews that manned the early lightships were recruited from nearby communities and many were not skilled or qualified to complete the required duties. They were not trained seamen and not competent in living aboard a lightship and maintaining the signaling apparatus.

In America, there were also difficulties with the governmental organization and administration, impacting not only the lighthouses (as previously discussed), but also the lightships. When the Lighthouse Board was formed in 1852, conditions improved, but it wasn't until 1910 that the U.S. Lighthouse Service came into existence and then the situation really improved. Technology also had to be developed that would improve the signaling devices. Distinctive daymarks easily identified the vessel and the station during the daylight hours, but at night, in fog, or in heavy weather, the lightship needed distinctive illuminating lamps, some type of sounding device both above and below the water, and a distinctive code that would identify the lightship to submarines.

Lightships were constructed of wood because it was considered more seaworthy than metal hulls, and it was believed that they could respond better to heavy weather. Wood vessels were cheaper to build and supposedly afforded better living conditions inside the ship. The first lightship to be built using a composite of metal and wood was the *LV 43*. The *LV 51*, built in 1892, was the first steel hull lightship with a steam engine for propulsion. Also of importance is that she was the first vessel using electric incandescent lamps. She had sister vessels *52*, *53*, and *54*.

England, France, and Ireland led in the development of the lightship and by 1870, Britain and Ireland had 59 lightships along their coasts providing aids to navigation. England still maintains several lightships, unmanned but visited regularly for maintenance.

The American administration of the lightships, also known as light vessels, was controlled by the same governmental organizations that adminstered the lighthouses. In succession, these were the Fifth Auditor, Stephan Pleasanton, from the early 1800s until 1852; the nine-member Lighthouse Board until 1910; then the Bureau of Lighthouses, which was created by Congress, until 1939, when lightships came under the governance of the Coast Guard.

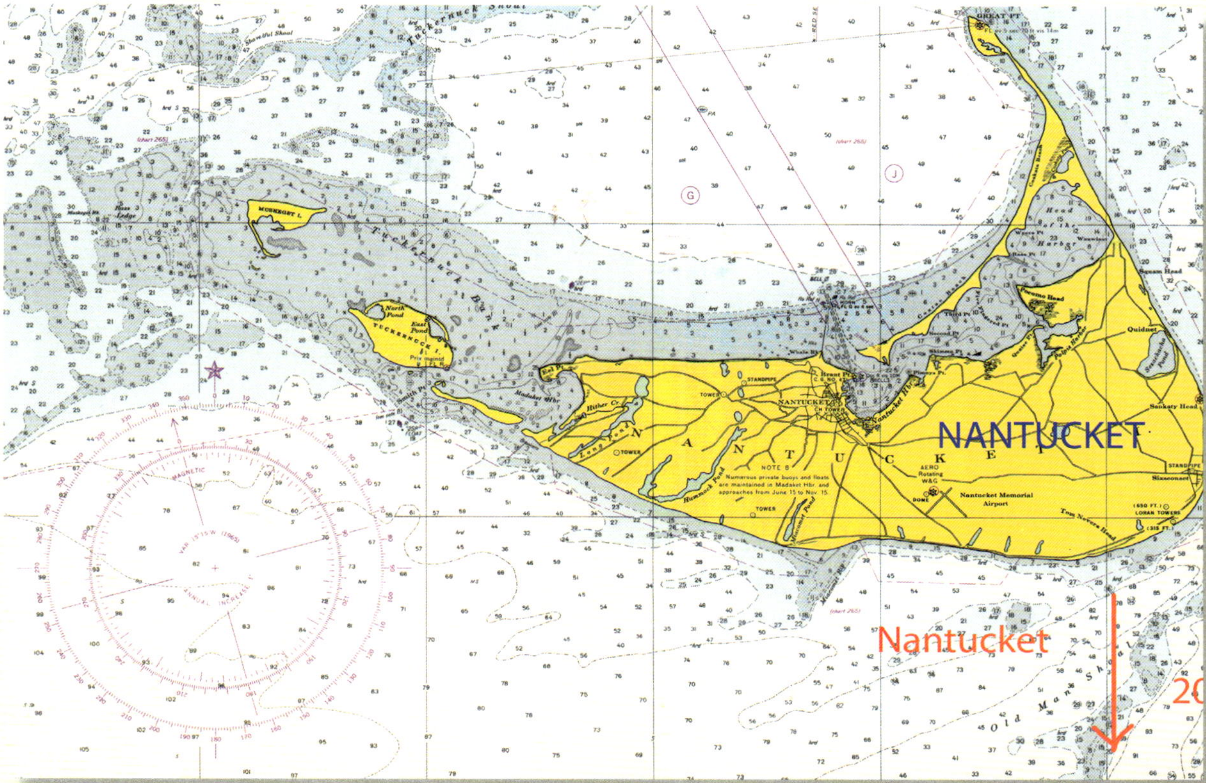

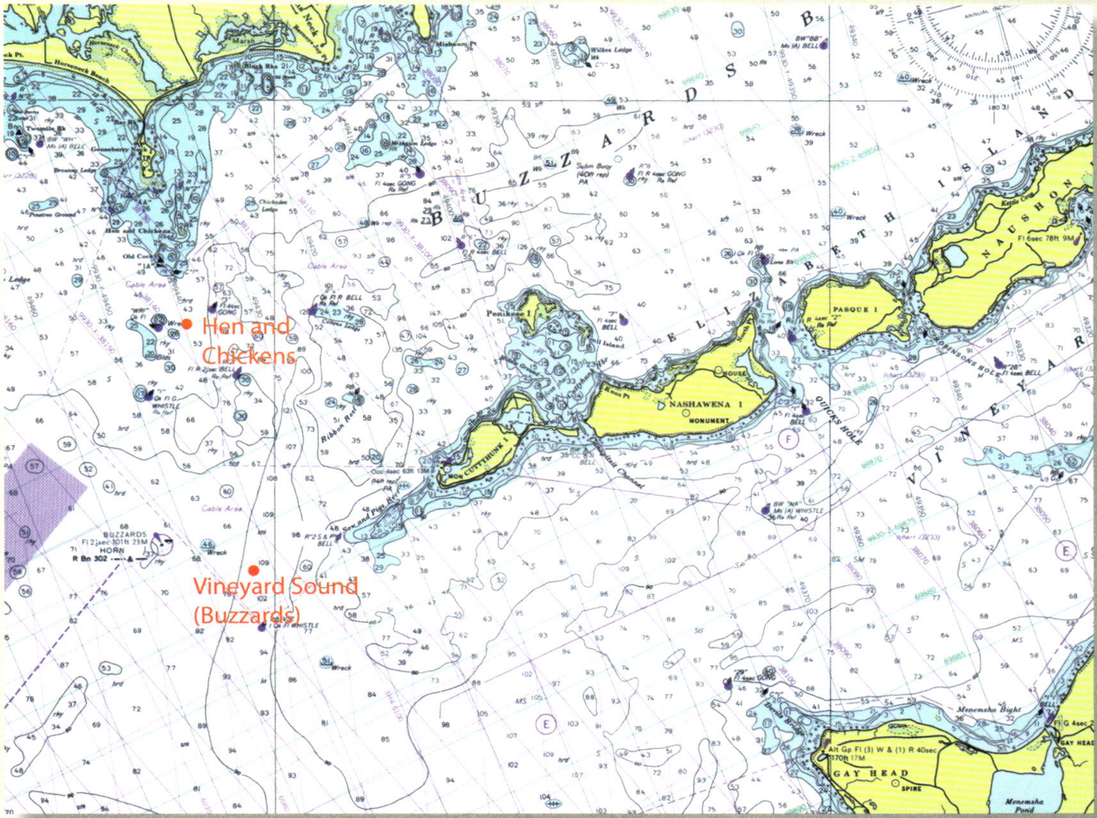

The following charts, including Cape Cod, offer insight into assignments and characteristics of where the lightships were stationed. The waters south of Cape Cod had the greatest concentration of lightships in the United States. These two present-day charts show the approximate sites of the lightship stations that were found in the waters on the south coast of Cape Cod. There were no lightships on the north side of Cape Cod in Cape Cod Bay. In Massachusetts waters, only two lightships were found north of Cape Cod, the first marking Minot's ledge, and the second marking the entrance to Boston harbor. *(Courtesy of NOAA)*

This Coast Guard archival image shows *LV 1* during its service time as a light vessel. Built in 1855 in Kittery, Maine, *LV 1* had a schooner rig with a fore and main mast and two lamps with eight oil lamps and reflectors. From 1856 until 1892, she was stationed and identified as Nantucket New South Shoal and then was used as a light vessel in North Carolina, South Carolina, and Georgia. The second image shows her on Frying Pan Shoal in North Carolina. She was retired from duty in 1930 after seventy-five years of duty, and was donated to the Sea Scouts in Haverhill, Massachusetts. *(Courtesy of USCG)*

This waterlogged hulk of a vessel which is only visible at low tide in the Merrimack River may be all that is left of the *LV 1. (Courtesy of CGHM)*

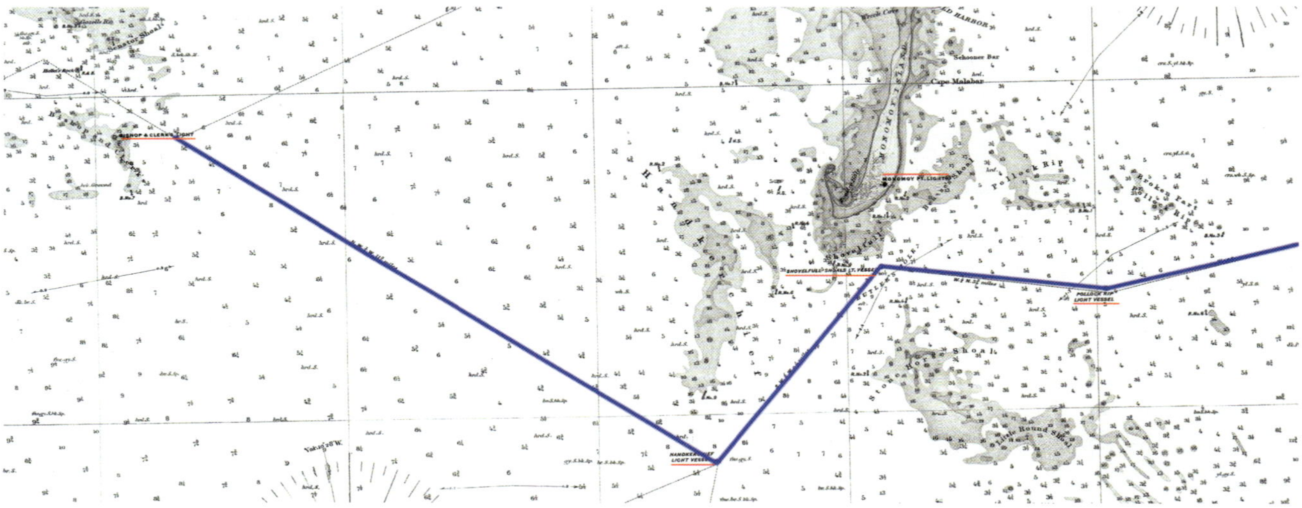

This chart could have been used to sail these coastal waters. The aids to navigation are underlined in red and from left to right are Bishop and Clerks Light, Handkerchief Light Vessel, Shovelful Shoals Light Vessel, Monomoy Light on the island, and the Pollock Rip Light Vessel. The blue highlighted line indicates the course the vessel would take through the sound. A ship leaving Hyannis would take this course to reach the open Atlantic. Captains and navigators also had available the latest publications identifying the local aids to navigation. This excerpt from *The New American Coast Pilot, 1883* can be coordinated with the chart. *(Courtesy of NOAA)*

"After passing East of Cross Rip Light-ship about 2 miles, you will be to the Red Buoy on the SE. part of Horseshoe Shoal; it should be 3/8 of a mile North of you. You will go clear of it if you open Cape Poge Light 100 yards South of the Lightship. You can then steer E. ¾ N for the Handkerchief Light Ship, distance from this buoy 8 ¾ miles. Keep her on your Port Bow and pass her on that hand, when your course to Butler's Hole or Shovel Light Ship is NE. by E., distance 4 miles. Pass her on your Port hand and on your Starboard hand you will see a Black Buoy on the North part of Stonehorse Shoal. From the Shovelful, steer E. by S. for Pollock Rip Lightship, and, to go out in the main channel, keep her on your Port and pass her on that hand, and continue the course until past a Red Buoy, distance from the Light-Ship 1½ miles, when you can haul up to N. by E. all clear of the Broken parts of Pollock Rip. When Chatham Two Lights bear N. by W., you are clear of the Broken parts."

Like lighthouses, lightships encountered difficulties with equipment, maintenance, and personnel training. In America, the first lightship station was in Chesapeake Bay in 1820. The following year four more lightships were stationed in the same area. In 1823, the first outside vessel was moored seven miles off Sandy Hook and aided vessels entering and leaving New York Harbor. By 1839, there were thirty lightship stations, with only one in Cape waters, the Cross Rip, previously called Tuckernuck Shoal, just north of Martha's Vineyard. Originally named *Tuckernuck Shoal,* from 1828 to 1852 the lightship provided a navigational aid for ships transiting to and from Nantucket. In 1858 there were forty-eight lightship stations, but by 1885 that number had decreased to twenty-two. All along the coast, navigators had publications and charts available that allowed them to plot a course using the local lightships as guides.

Many of the early "inside" lightship stations in the Mid-Atlantic region, especially in Chesapeake Bay, were eventually replaced by screw-pile lighthouses which could be built in shallow water and would safely mark navigational channels. The only lighthouse built to replace a lightship on Cape Cod was the Bishop and Clerk's station on the rocky reef just south of Hyannis Harbor. Minot's Ledge Light, off the Cohasset coast, was originally a lighthouse that was destroyed by a storm, and was replaced by a lightship until a permanent lighthouse could be built. No screw-pile lighthouses were built in Cape Cod waters, although one had been proposed to replace the first Billingsgate Lighthouse in Wellfleet. In 1904, *Nantucket* had the first lightship to be equipped with radio communication. This proved fortuitous in 1905, when the *LV 58 Relief* marking the station developed leaks during severe weather. While being towed to port by a tender, the vessel foundered and sank.

By 1909, there were fifty-six lightship stations, the most ever stationed off the United States coast. In 1932, there were forty-four active lightship stations, and by 1939 that number was down to thirty. From that date on, the number of lightship stations declined as locations were disestablished or discontinued and, in some instances, replaced by "Texas Towers" or buoys. By 1983, the Nantucket South Shoals was the last active station and it was replaced by a large navigational buoy (LNB) on December 20 that year, at 8 a.m.

WLV 613, seen here in Wareham, Massachusetts, was the last lightship on station Nantucket and alternated with *WLV 612* until December 1983, when it was replaced by a lighted buoy. With *WLV 612,* this vessel was the last United States lightship on active duty as an aid to navigation. The *WLV 613* is privately maintained and not open to the public.

The last two lightships built by the Coast Guard were the *WLV 612* and the *WLV 613.* The *WLV 612* after it had been totally refitted and outfitted as a luxury yacht is seen here at a berth in Boston.

These six images are of the *LV 101 / WAL 524* and trace her history from her being built through her three station assignments, and then to her final destination as a museum. Built in 1916 in Wilmington, Delaware, the vessel was unique in that her length was 101 feet (hence she was named the *LV 101*), with a beam of 25 feet and a draft of 11 feet. The hull was made of steel with the distinctive whaleback design to shed water. Her sister vessel, the *102*, had assignments at Brenton Reef and Cross Rip before she was decommissioned. **A and B)** These two images show the *LV 101* as she was being constructed. **C)** A photograph of the *101* on her sea trials before she was placed on station at Cape Charles, Virginia, 1916–1924. During that time, her illuminant was changed from kerosene to acetylene (1917) and she was equipped with a radio (1919). From 1925 to 1926 she was occasionally used as relief vessel in Virginia. **D)** From 1926 to 1951, the vessel as seen in this image (mid-1940s) was assigned to Overfalls station in Delaware. During that time, she was equipped with a radiobeacon (1931), her lamps were upgraded to increase candlepower (1931), and she was repowered with a maximum speed of 8.2 knots (1944). **E)** Seen in this image, the last active station assignment for the *LV 101* (1951–1963) was Stonehorse Shoal located just south of Monomoy Island in Nantucket Sound. After Overfalls in 1951, the *LV 101* was overhauled in Boston before she took up station. She remained at Stonehorse until 1963 when the station was discontinued. The vessel was decommissioned in March and donated in September of 1964 to the Portsmouth Lightship Museum. **F)** Presently, the *LV 101* is now open to the public in Portsmouth, Virginia, at the Naval Shipyard Museum. There was no documented lightship or lightship station named Portsmouth. *(Black-and-white images courtesy of USCG)*

A BRIEF SURVEY OF EARLY LIGHTSHIPS

The following section of this book considers a distinct selection of lightships, their original plans and design, improvements that made vessels safer, and technological advances (most times not visible) that increased their ability to perform as an aid to navigation. Several archival images are presented of the depots that supported and maintained these offshore aids to navigation. With more than two hundred lightships assigned to our waters and many that were sunk, destroyed, or decommissioned before the advent of photography (1840s–1850s), it is not possible to illustrate each vessel.

The earliest light vessels were identified with either names, or, for historical records, letters, with limited reference data available. Designation of these ships are as follows: *LV* was used by the U.S. Lighthouse Service (for "Light Vessel") until 1939 when the Coast Guard took control and used *WAL (*the *W* indicated a Coast Guard vessel, the *A* was for "anchored," and the L was for "Light"). Finally, *WLV* was used for Coast Guard light vessels that were built after 1939. These designations have been maintained by historians to ensure correct information, and have been used in this book's text to designate those lightships.

The earliest images, starting in the late 1800s, of these ships are now archived and available to researchers at several historic locations, including the National Archives, the USCG Historian's Office, the Coast Guard Heritage Museum (Barnstable, Massachusetts), and the Library of Congress, College Park, Maryland. The images in this book are from those sources.

The earliest lightships were conscripted into duty with no forethought toward the condition of requiring a vessel to remain at one location for an extended period of time. In addition, because the first light vessels were schooner-rigged ships similar to commercial craft, identification was difficult; as an aid to navigation they were inefficient and undependable.

There was no distinction as to hull color in the first light vessels, and it wasn't until the 1850s that a systematic approach was taken to color-code aids to navigation. Popular colors for lightships first included gray, yellow, and then—to mark the sides of a channel—red and black. In 1940, the Coast Guard adopted a standard color scheme for a lightship: a red hull with white lettering, a white superstructure, and for the remaining ship parts, a buff color.

Most of the lightships in these images have been stationed at one time or another in Massachusetts waters; others are vessels that have been involved in the development of significant improvements or have been involved in a noteworthy event. Compare these ships and notice how they evolved so that they could successfully complete their mission. Even today in Europe lightships remain on station (although unmanned) as aids to navigation.

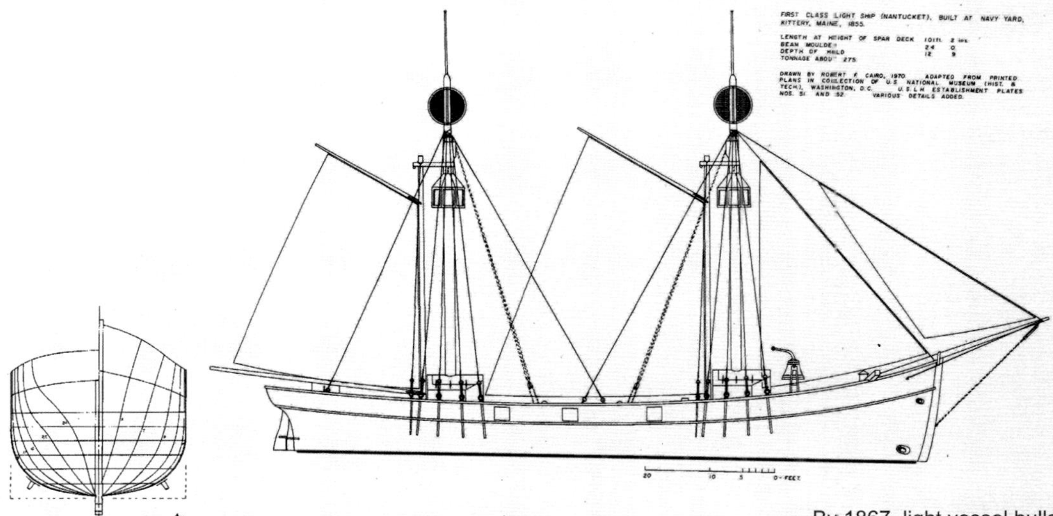

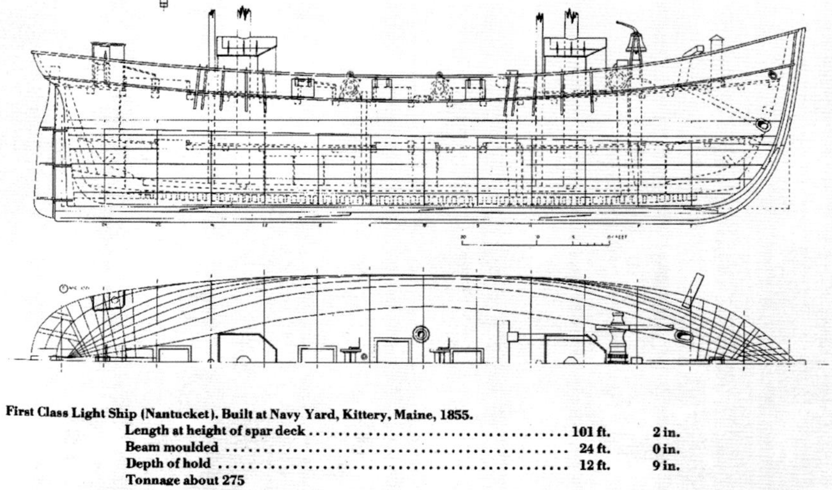

By 1867, light vessel hulls were assigned and painted not only with the name of their station but also with a designated number. This number could be used to maintain records of the vessels, the stations they served at, and any construction notes with modifications and improvements made to that hull. Many of these early light vessels were one of a kind and lacked any uniformity of design. This line drawing shows the plans of the *LV 1*; compare these to *LV 83*, built in 1904, which also had several sister ships. This light vessel was built in Kittery, Maine, in 1855, and was identified as Nantucket prior to 1867. Designed for offshore stations, *LV 1* was 103 feet long with 275 gross tons which aided her seaworthiness in heavy weather. *(Courtesy of USCG)*

LV 2, slightly smaller than *LV 1*, was built in 1849 with no record of who built her or where she was built. When built and launched, the vessel was identified as the *General Taylor.* Prior to 1867, she was identified as Pollock Rip and was stationed there from 1849 till 1875. This archival image shows *LV 2* about 1900 when she was stationed at Hens and Chickens at the entrance to Buzzards Bay. She was also stationed in Virginia and as a relief vessel until 1922, when she was decommissioned and then sold for $76. *LV 2* had a storied career with several significant events: broke adrift in 1863 and 1873, was pulled from station by ice in 1871 and 1874, was rammed in 1867 and 1873, and was rammed by a tug in 1915. None of these incidents resulted in any loss of life. *(Courtesy of USCG)*

The *LV 39,* built of oak and locust in 1875, was about 120 feet long and schooner-rigged with two masts plus two auxiliary steam boilers. Her five assignments included Vineyard Sound (1875–1876), Five Fathom Bank (New Jersey) (1876–1877), Relief (both Massachusetts and New York), and as seen in this image, her last assignment at Brenton Reef, Rhode Island, from 1897 to 1935. She was the first lightship to be equipped with a 12-inch fog whistle that was steam driven. The image above right shows a hatch on the sunken *LV 39.* *(Courtesy of CGHM)*

Seen here in this image from about 1900 is the *LV 44,* built in 1882 in Wilmington, Delaware, for less than $50,000. It was the first lightship built with an unsheathed metal hull. Sail rigged, she was 116 feet long, with a draft of 25 feet and weighing about 200 gross tons. She also had several problems; one was the paint on the hull that failed to prevent corrosion of the metal, requiring her to be painted yearly. Also, her steam boilers were replaced three times within the first 18 years. Her second station was Cornfield Point, Connecticut, from 1926 to 1938 when the vessel was severely damaged by the hurricane that devastated the coast in 1938. When decommissioned, she was the last manned lightship without machinery available to propel the vessel. *(Courtesy of USCG)*

This image was taken of the *LV 71* while she was on Diamond Shoal, North Carolina, station sometime between 1898 and 1918. Built in Bath, Maine, in 1897, the vessel was originally designated for the Overfalls station in Delaware Bay. While on Diamond station, she was dragged off several times and was involved in a number of rescues. In 1917, in coordination with the USN and Weather Bureau, she transmitted meteorological reports twice a day by radio. On August 6, 1918, while on duty, *LV 71* reported that a German submarine which had sunk a freighter was in the vicinity. This may have saved some of the more than twenty ships that were in the area at the time. When the message was intercepted by the U-104, the commander fired on the lightship and gave the crew the opportunity to abandon ship. The *LV 71* was sunk by the submarine with several well-placed surface shots. There was no loss of life. *(Courtesy of USCG)*

Unique in the evolution of lightship design, the *LV 58* was built in 1894 in Toledo, Ohio, of an iron plated, steel-framed hull that was 121 feet long, with a draft of 28 feet and almost 450 gross tons. She was the first ship to have a deck above the main deck. This not only added higher freeboard for a drier and safer ship, but also permitted the crew's quarters to be placed in a more hospitable environment. In addition, the lanterns located on spring-loaded platforms could be raised and lowered through hatches in the weather deck. The *LV 58* for all its improvements had a relatively short life span. She was assigned to two stations, Nantucket South Shoals (1894–1896), Fire Island, New York (1896–1897), and then as a Relief (1897–1905) in Massachusetts. While on Relief duty at Nantucket South Shoals on December 10, 1905, the *LV 58* developed a serious leak, and when the suction pumps clogged, the boilers were extinguished. For twenty-four hours the crew bailed the vessel by hand until a tender could respond. Of note, this was the first U.S. ship to use a radio to transmit a distress call. Help arrived early morning on December 11, and proceeded to tow the lightship to port. While underway, the lightship took on more water, and after the crew of thirteen was rescued, she sank in 150 feet of water south of Nantucket with no loss of life. She was only eleven years old. *(Courtesy of USCG)*

Seen here are two of a total of four sister lightships built in the early 1890s in West Bay, Michigan, for less than $55,000 each. The vessels were 119 feet long, with a draft of 10 feet, a beam of 26 feet, and a displacement of 375 tons. These ships were significant for several reasons: they were the first vessels built with an all steel hull and fastenings; the first lightships built with electric illuminating apparatus permanently attached to each masthead (four gimbaled lanterns with combined 4,000 candlepower); and the first to have a hawespipe aligned with the centerline of vessel to increase stability when retrieving mooring chain. Burning coal as a fuel, these ships burned as much as thirty tons a month. The *LV 51* seen here on her second station assignment at Sandy Hook (1894–1908), was subsequently a Relief ship in the 3rd District. Notice the sailing vessel through the rigging in the background. On April 24, 1919, while on Relief duty at Cornfield Point, Connecticut, the lightship was rammed and sunk by a Standard Oil barge. The ship sunk in less than ten minutes, with the crew being rescued by the tug; they managed to save only two log books. Compensation from Standard Oil paid for the construction of the *LV 111,* which is discussed later. That vessel was also involved in a collision. The second image shows the *LV 54 / WAL 502* on her Boston Station (1894–1940, 1943–1946), which was also her last station. Her first station assignment was Nantucket New South Shoal from 1892–1894, replacing the *LV 9.* She was in turn relieved by both the *LV 58* and the *LV 39* for her respective repairs and maintenance. In terms of technological advances, *LV 54* (as well as her sister ships) in 1910 had a submarine bell installed; in 1915 a fog signal was changed to air siren; in 1919 she was equipped with a radio; in 1921 the oil illuminant was changed to acetylene; in 1923 a transmitting radio beacon was installed; in 1929, acetylene was converted to electricity; and in 1945, radar was installed. *(Courtesy of LOC)*

These two photographs from the late 1800s show the Woods Hole depot where two lightships were tied up at the dock to be repaired and refitted. One of the vessels may have been the *LV 9*. *(Courtesy of NA and CGHM)*

Shown here while assigned to the San Francisco station (1930–1942 and 1945–1951), the *LV 83 / WAL 508* is one of the oldest extant lightships. Built in 1904 in Camden, New Jersey, she still has her original steam engines. Now named the *Swiftsure (Relief)*, the vessel is open to the public at the Northwest Seaport Maritime Heritage Center in Seattle, Washington. *(Courtesy of LOC)*

A view taken in the early 1900s of the depot at Tompkinsville on Staten Island, New York, with three lightships tied up at the docks. *87 / WAL 512* on the right was assigned to four different stations as well as being a relief vessel and an examination ship during World War II from 1942 to 1944. *93* in the background was built in Quincy, Massachusetts, at the Fore River Shipbuilding Co. in 1908 for $107,000. She had sister vessels *90, 91,* and *92,* and was constructed to the same general plans as *LV 84–88*. This image must have been taken sometime in 1908 before the *LV 93* (and the *LV 88 and LV 92,* along with three tenders) was assigned to the west coast with stations in Washington. (Courtesy of LOC)

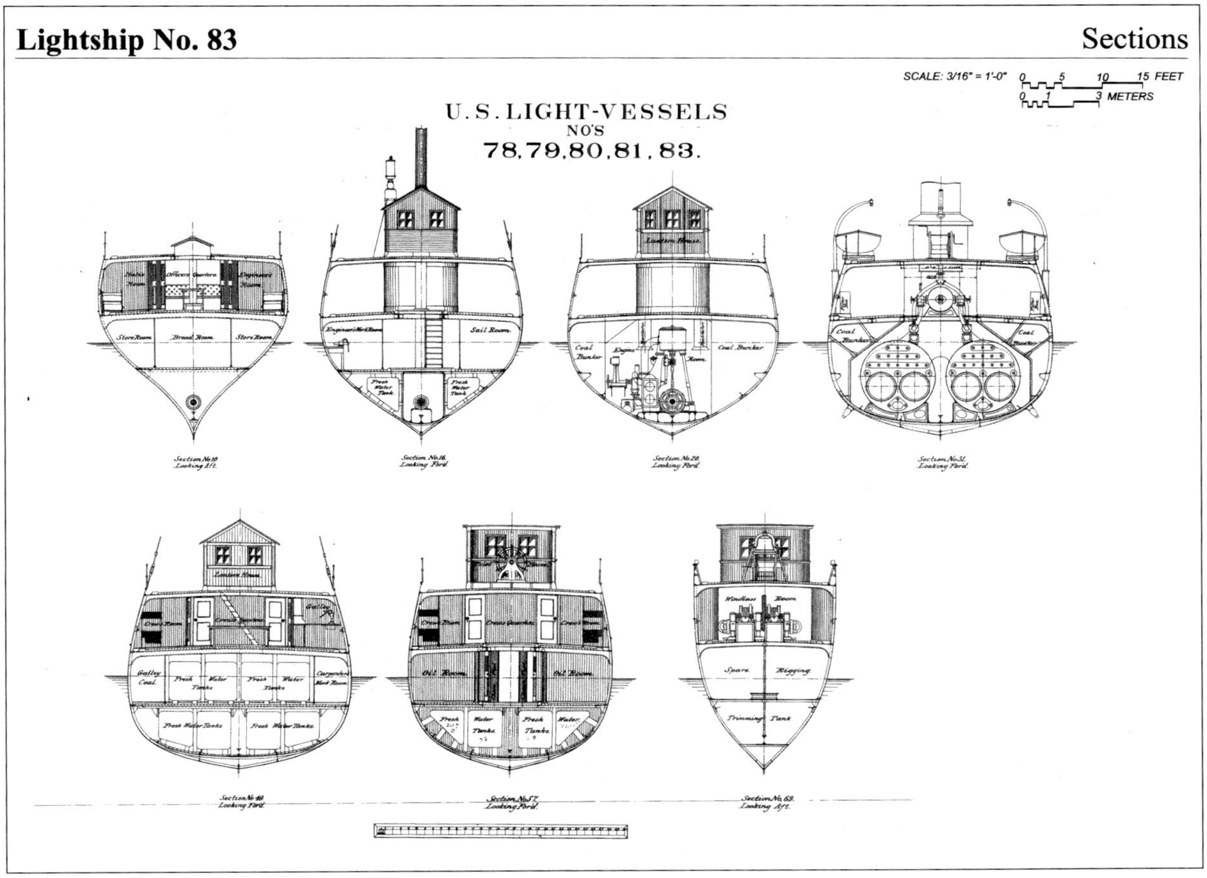

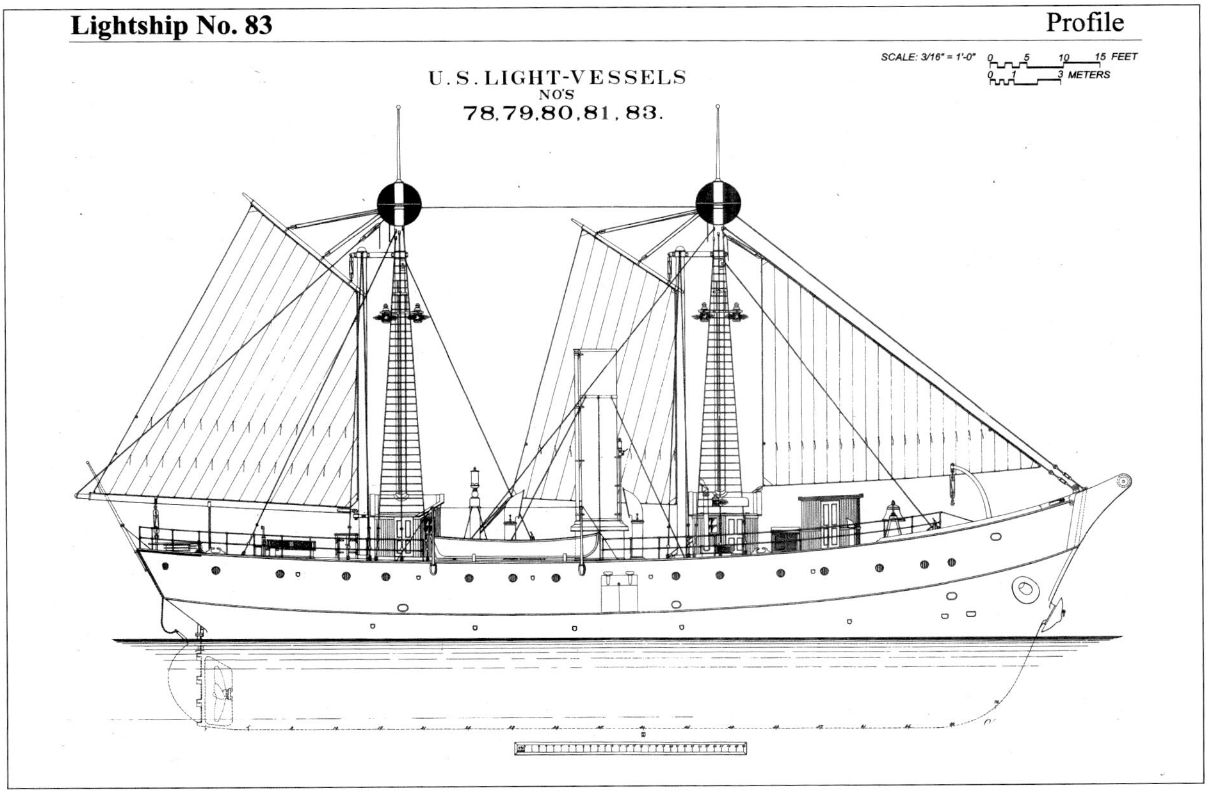

As more lightships were being built, it made good sense to have several vessels built from the same design. These plans are a copy of the original design of 1903 for lightships *79* through *83*. Vessels now were being deliberately planned with specific characteristics to ensure their seaworthiness and their ability to be a proficient aid to navigation. Notice how these plans compared to the *LV 1* and how the ships have been designed and developed to perform their mission. *(Courtesy of LOC)*

Sometimes lightships were converted to perform other duties. **A)** As seen here, *LV 87*'s first duty station was Ambrose Channel from 1908 to 1932. In 1944, she replaced the *LV 73* which was sunk in September by a hurricane while assigned to the Vineyard Sound station. **B)** During WWI and WWII, many offshore lightships were removed from station to prevent attacks from submarines. The *LV 87* during WW II (1942–1944) was assigned as an examination vessel to Fort Hancock at Sandy Hook, New Jersey. The *LV 88*, seen in this image, a sister vessel of the *87*, was an examination ship assigned to Seattle, Washington. Her armament included a forward mounted 3-inch gun, three antiaircraft cannons hidden under the tarps, and a depth charge projector on her stern. *(Courtesy of USCG)*

This image from the mid-1900s shows two lightships berthed at the United States Coast Guard facility in Boston Harbor (probably the Chelsea Depot). The vessel closest to the dock is likely the *LV 102 / WAL 525,* Brenton, which was assigned to the station at the entrance to Narragansett Bay, Rhode Island, from 1935 to 1962 when it was discontinued. The Relief vessel also tied up at the dock is the *LV 112 / WAL 534.* More information on this vessel can be found in the discussion of the station Nantucket South Shoals. *(Courtesy of J. Owen)*

Two views of the *WLV 613,* the last lightship ever built (1952) by the Coast Guard. Her first duty station was Ambrose Channel, New York (left), from 1952 to 1967, when the station was discontinued and replaced with a buoy. After a tour as a Relief (1967–1979), she was designated Nantucket II and alternated every twenty-one days with the *WLV 612* (Nantucket 1). She was the last lightship on duty when she replaced the *612* on December 20, 1983, and in turn was replaced by an LNB (large navigational buoy). The righthand image is of the *613* at a dock in Wareham, Massachusetts. *(Courtesy of USCG)*

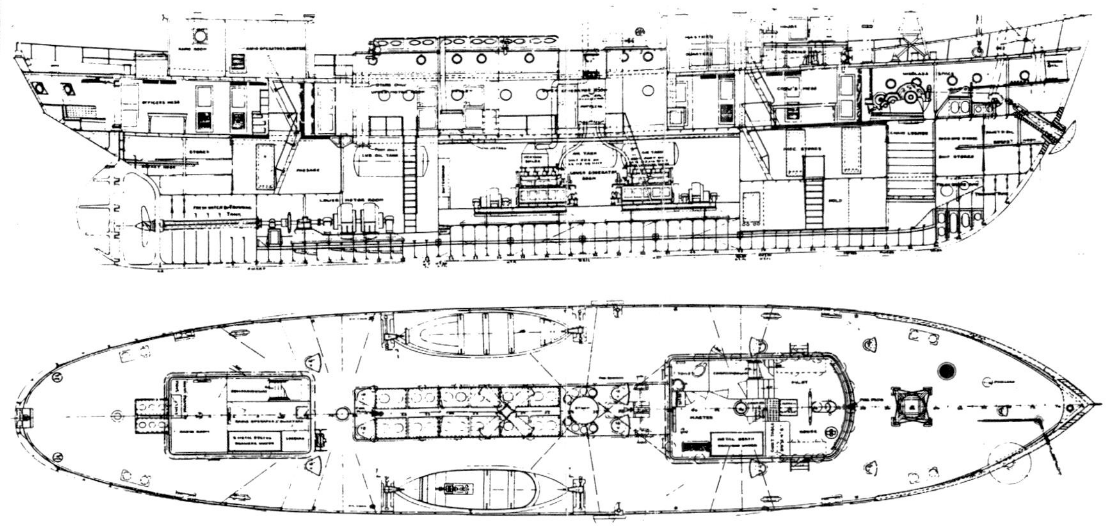

These plans are for the 133-foot lightships that were built in the United States. Compare these to the other plans shown on the previous pages. *(Courtesy of USCG)*

Seen when she was launched on October 16, 1946 (left), and when she was on station in 1965 (right), the *WLV 189* was unique in her construction in that she was 1) the first of six designed and built for the Coast Guard; 2) the first of only six all-welded lightships ever built; and 3) the first of only six lightships built with a system of alternating electrical current. Built specifically for Diamond Shoal, North Carolina (1947–1966), her last station was Boston (1972–1975), when the vessel was decommissioned and the station was discontinued. *(Courtesy of USCG)*

Not only collisions but weather conditions had an effect on numerous lightships. Some were sunk and, in this case, the *LV 69* was blown on shore. During the late 1800s, the *LV 69* was blown off station at least twice while at Diamond Shoals, North Carolina. *(Courtesy of USCG)*

Duty on a lightship was not without numerous hazards. The *LV 111 / WAL 533* is seen here at the dock after she collided on September 17, 1935, with the SS *Santa Barbara* while on the Ambrose Channel Station, New York. The captain of the lightship, when the liner made its course intentions known, changed the direction of the lightship to strike the liner bow to bow. If no change had been made, the *LV 111* would have been struck amidships and probably sunk. This lightship, built in Bath, Maine, in 1926, was constructed in reparation for Standard Oil sinking the *LV 51*. This was the first lightship built with full diesel propulsion. Her final duty station was Portland, Maine, from 1952 to 1969, when she was decommissioned. An image of her possible fate is seen on page 247. *(Courtesy of CGHM)*

MASSACHUSETTS LIGHTSHIP STATIONS

Nationwide, there were 116 lightship stations between 1820 and 1983, with 179 lightships assigned to those stations. Sandy Hook, which was later renamed Ambrose Channel and which leads to New York Harbor, was the longest active lightship station, with 144 years of service. During that time, eight vessels were assigned to the station, until the Ambrose Light Tower was built in 1967.

The last active lightship station was Nantucket South Shoals, which was replaced by a lighted buoy in December 1983. Lightship stations and the vessels were assigned numbers by the Lighthouse Board, starting from north to south. The northernmost lightship station, identified as number 1, was Portland, Maine (Cape Elizabeth), number 2 was Boston, and number 3 was Minot's Ledge in Cohasset (maintained only nine years until the present-day lighthouse was built)

This book includes the lightship stations located in Buzzards Bay—Vineyard Sound, Hens and Chickens, and Buzzards Bay—as well as the two in Massachusetts Bay, Minot's Ledge and Boston.

Depending on the actual station assignment, vessels would be moored in mid-channel, and with the fully extended anchor chain, collisions were a frequent occurrence when sailing ships passed by. There have been over 150 documented serious collisions, with the loss of five lightships.

Although vessels were painted with the station name on the sides, and later (1867) were assigned hull numbers, lightships in their lifetime may have been at multiple stations. Because there were more lightships assigned to Massachusetts waters than anywhere else along the Atlantic coast, vessels assigned to those stations were distinctively painted in different colors to distinguish their location and to aid mariners as they navigated through these waters.

In the early 1900s, twelve lightships found in these waters were painted as follows:

Pollock Rip, red
Great Round Shoal, lead colored with black markings
Shovelful, green, then black, and finally red
Handkerchief, straw-colored with black markings
Cross Rip, black with a white streak and white markings
Succonnessett, red with white squares with red markings;
Bishop and Clerks, straw with black marks
Vineyard Sound, red with a yellow streak and white markings
Hens and Chickens, lead colored, then black with white markings

The images that follow are the vessels that were assigned to those stations at some point during their career. In some cases, the same image is used twice, as that vessel may have been assigned to both stations and had historical significance at each of those locations. Images of sister ships which might have served at that station are also included, when available. Some lightships were also converted to Relief ships that replaced active lightships when they needed maintenance and the updating of equipment. The Relief had to have the same signaling apparatus as the ship that it was replacing at that station.

Refer to the charts earlier in the text to see the general location of the lightships and their relation to other vessels. More detailed information regarding specific stations can be found by referring to the bibliography.

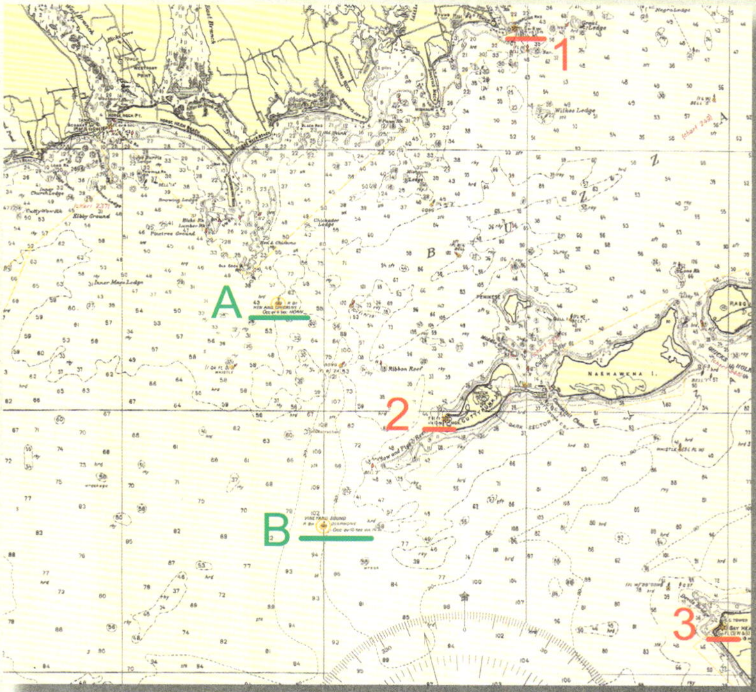

This 1942 chart identifies five aids to navigation that mariners could have used to chart a course at the western end of Buzzards Bay. Only one, Gay Head **(3)**, is still active. **A)** Hens and Chickens and **B)** Vineyard Sound were the two lightships that guided vessels into upper Buzzards Bay. Closer examination of the chart near Vineyard Sound would reveal R Bn (radio beacon), diaphone, and an occulting light every ten seconds that was visible for fourteen miles. Hens and Chickens, to distinguish it, had an occulting light every four seconds. Additional buoys are also on the chart to mark the channel. Two lighthouses, **1,** Dumpling Rocks, and **2,** Cuttyhunk, no longer exist. *(Courtesy of NOAA)*

When the station was first established in 1847, vessels were assigned letters and the first ship was the "Z." She was built in Washington, D.C., and was a 78-foot-long wood hull vessel with a beam of 20 feet, and displaced nearly 160 tons. She was fitted with two lamps. I have found no images of the ship. The vessel seen in this image (1895) is the *LV 7* when she was on station off the coast of New Jersey. The vessel was built for $22,000 and her first assignment was Minot's Ledge. She was at Vineyard Sound from 1861 to 1875. During those years, she was twice dragged off station in 1886 by storms, and carried off station in 1874 by ice. She became a Relief vessel in 1875. *(Courtesy of USCG).*

Two images of the *LV 41*: one taken in the late 1800s when she was on station (she replaced the *LV 39* on her first tour), and the other with the lightship leaving Boston Harbor sometime around 1920. From 1876 to 1910 and 1915 to 1924, the lightship was assigned to Vineyard Sound. During those early years, several times the *LV 41* broke her chain and drifted free in addition to the occasional collision. She also had duty stations at Hedge Fence (twice) and Handkerchief Shoal before she was retired in 1933. *(Courtesy of USCG and CGHM)*

The third vessel to serve at the Vineyard Sound Lightship Station was the *LV 39* and this was for only one year, 1875–1876. *(Courtesy of USCG)*

Tenders provided supplies to the lightships on a regular basis. This image shows a tender tied up to a lightship at Vineyard Sound; notice the flag straight out and the wave in the background.

Another lightship assigned to Vineyard Sound was the *LV 90* (1910–1915), and she served without incidents. She was built based on the *84–88* plans, and had two masts with a cluster of three lights on each. *(Courtesy of USCG)*

Built in 1901 in Baltimore, Maryland, the *LV 73* is seen here on station at Pollock Rip. Her stations included Pollock Rip from 1902 to 1913, Pollock Rip Slue (station moved after channel was dredged) from 1913 to 1923, and then back to Pollock Rip from 1923 to 1924. She was then assigned to Vineyard Sound in 1924. *(Courtesy of USCG)*

Lightships would be routinely taken off-station for maintenance, repairs, and the updating of equipment; this is the *LV 41* at a dock in Woods Hole. *(Courtesy of NA)*

BOSTON, THURSDAY MORNING, NOVEMBER 12, 1925

LIGHTSHIP AT HEDGE FENCE SUNK IN CRASH

Rammed by Steamship M. C. Holm, Crew Saved, Master of Surviving Vessel Reports by Radio

HEDGE FENCE LIGHTSHIP SUNK BY DANISH FREIGHT STEAMER M. C. HOLM

On March 6, 1925, the *LV 90* struck a rock in Quick's Hole and sank. She was later raised, repaired, and returned to duty. According to this newspaper article, the *LV 90* was rammed and sunk while on station. *(Courtesy of USCG)*

This image shows the *LV 73* when she was assigned to the Vineyard Sound station beginning in 1924. *(Courtesy of USCG)*

The *LV 87 / WAL 512* on station at Vineyard Sound. *(Courtesy of USCG)*

The *LV 87 / WAL 512* was at the Vineyard Sound Station for only three years, 1944–1947, and historical notes indicate no difficulties. She was built in 1907 in Camden, New Jersey, for less than $100,000. Images and discussion of her sister vessels (*84, 85, 86,* and *88*) can be found elsewhere in the text. Most of her sea time was spent in the New York–New Jersey area where she was stationed at Ambrose Channel, New York, and Scotland, New Jersey. During the early years of WW II, 1942–1944, she was an examination vessel. These images were taken when she was assigned to Ambrose Channel, sometime before 1932, which marked the passageway into New York. The liner, *Olympic*, moves past the lightship. *(Courtesy of USCG)*

About twenty years after the *LV 73* sank, a group of divers from Fairhaven with the help of side-scanning sonar discovered the wreck in eighty feet of water near her station three miles from Cuttyhunk. The ship's binnacle, compass, lamp, and bell have been recovered. The *LV 73* is United States government property and salvage prohibited. The mast light is on display at the Coast Guard Heritage Museum in Barnstable, Massachusetts. The bell of the *LV 73* seen here in New Bedford Harbor is dedicated to the seamen that served on the *LV 6, LV 117,* and the *LV 73.*

BUZZARDS BAY

VINEYARD SOUND

These three stations were found at the westerly entrance to Buzzards Bay, and guided mariners towards the busy harbor of New Bedford and then later (after 1914) to the Cape Cod Canal. When the Canal was built, ships no longer had to transit the dangerous shoals north and south of Nantucket.

The first two stations, Vineyard Sound and Hens and Chickens, were subsequently replaced by the station Buzzards Bay, which in turn was deactivated in 1961. Vineyard Sound was established in 1847 about two miles southwest of Cuttyhunk Light, and marked a group of rocks called Sow and Pigs. It was involved in four collisions and dragged off station at least a dozen times. The station's most tragic incident was on the night of September 14, 1944, when a hurricane was responsible for the sinking of the *LV 73*, and a crew of twelve was lost. Nearly two weeks later, the lightship was discovered, still attached to her mooring chains, on the bottom of the Sound in seventy feet of water. Nearly twenty years later, the vessel was relocated using side scanning sonar. The secondary anchor, never released before the onset of the storm, had swung into the hull and caused a large gash, which perhaps had contributed to the sinking. It was replaced on station by the *LV 87 / WAL 512* from 1944 to 1947, and then the *LV 110 / WAL 532*, until the station was discontinued in 1954 and replaced by the Buzzards Bay lightship at a slightly different location.

VINEYARD SOUND LIGHTSHIPS ASSIGNED & YEARS AT STATION

Station established 1847

1847–1860........................"Z"
1861–1875........................LV 7
1875–1876........................LV 39
1876–1910........................LV 41
1910–1915........................LV 90 / WAL 514
1915–1924........................LV 41
1924–1944........................LV 73 / WAL 503
1944–1947........................LV 87 / WAL 512
1947–1954........................LV 110 / WAL 532
Discontinued 1954

The first lightship assigned to Hens and Chickens was the *LV 5* and then for only one year, 1866–1867. This image was taken in 1895 when she was at the Cross Rip station in Nantucket Sound. Built in 1864, she was named "Hens and Chickens" and served on that station before she was assigned the number "5" in 1867. The *LV 5* was a sail-schooner rig and was about 80 feet long with a beam of 21 feet. From 1867 till the decommissioning in 1930 she was stationed at Cross Rip, Stonehorse, and Handkerchief. The second lightship, *LV 8,* assigned to this station (again, only for a year, 1866–1867), was a former navy vessel that was converted to a lightship. Built in 1854–1855, the *Arctic* was designed to carry out polar rescue operations before her transfer to the USLHS. She was about 100 feet long and had a beam of 23 feet. In 1860 she had been captured and sunk by Confederate forces. Raised and repaired, she then served lightship stations off the Massachusetts coast. By 1878, she was old and worthless. *(Courtesy of USCG)*

Built in 1849, and previously assigned to Pollock Rip and Winter Quarter Shoal (Virginia), *LV 2* spent thirty years at Hens and Chickens, from 1877 to 1907. This 1895 image of the vessel on station is typical of late-nineteenth-century lightships. Previous to being assigned a number in 1867, she was named the *General Taylor* when launched. In 1897, two crewmen were lost at sea when returning from New Bedford on the liberty boat. Twice during the thirty years she was assigned to the Hens and Chickens. The ship was pulled off station in heavy weather. *(Courtesy of USCG)*

After the early 1900s, photographers were able to capture lightships (as well as lighthouses) during their many years of service. These two images of the *LV 42* show the visible changes that have taken place on the vessel. Built in 1877, the *LV 42* was large—121 feet long, 26-foot beam, 10 foot draft, and over 400 tons—and was originally assigned to offshore stations (Pollock Rip and Great Round Shoals). In 1877, it was reported that she was the largest and strongest lightship in the service. Her last station was Hens and Chickens before she was retired in 1931. In 1926, her two masts were removed and a steel lattice structure amidships was built to house an acetylene lantern. She was sold in 1932, and on July 4, 1940, she was burned in Boston harbor as part of the celebration. *(Courtesy of NA)*

Shown here at an offshore station, the *LV 66* spent five years (1908–1913) at Hens and Chickens as a Relief vessel. Similar in size to the *LV 42*, she was the first lightship (1904) to have radio equipment permanently installed. Previously (1901), a Marconi wireless was installed for experimental use. Built in 1896, she was retired in 1934. *(Courtesy of NA)*

Another vessel that only spent a year at the station was the *LV 74*, seen here at a dock when she had been assigned to station #1, Cape Elizabeth, Maine. Built in 1902, she served in Maine until 1931 when she became a Relief vessel, and then her last assignment was at Hens and Chickens. While no problems or incidents occurred at her last station, the *LV 74* was blown off station several times in Maine. *(Courtesy of NA)*

Another lightship that was assigned to this station for only a year (1933–1934) was the *LV 49*. Built in 1891, she had the sister vessels *47, 48* and *50*. The image shows her (1891–1916) at Cape Charles, Virginia. The most significant event in her career was in 1925; while at Hedge Fence (Massachusetts) station she was rammed and sunk by the steamer *K C Holn*. She was replaced by the *LV 5* until the *LV 49* could be raised, repaired, and returned to service at that station. *(Courtesy of NA)*

HENS AND CHICKENS

The second station in Buzzards Bay was the Hens and Chickens, which marked the north side of the channel. Nearly 4 miles from Cuttyhunk Light, the lightship was named after the nearby rock reef. Just 2 miles off Horseneck Beach, eight different lightships were maintained at this station between 1866 and 1954 when the Buzzards Bay replaced this location. Unlike other stations that were either offshore or closer to shipping channels, the vessels assigned to Hens and Chickens served mostly without any severe incidents.

HENS AND CHICKENS LIGHTSHIPS ASSIGNED & YEARS AT STATION

Station established 1866

Years	Lightship	Years	Lightship
1866–1867	*LV 5*	*1932–1933*	*LV 74*
1867–1877	*LV 8*	*1933–1934*	*LV 49*
1877–1907	*LV 2*	*1934–1954*	*LV 86 / WAL 511*
1908–1913	*LV 66 / WAL 511*	*Discontinued 1954*	
1913–1932	*LV 42*		

The *LV 86 / WAL 511,* as shown in these two images, spent two tours at the station, 1908–1913 and 1934–1954, when the station was discontinued and the vessel was renamed the Buzzards Bay. From 1883 to 1940, the hull color was black, but at that time it was changed to red. The hull with the "86" on the sides may have been black; hulls with no number may be red. Sometime in the 1940s (before 1947), the vessel was repowered with a 600hp diesel engine; at the same time the stack was shortened. *(Courtesy of NA)*

Dated 1947. Lightships were routinely returned to port for maintenance and updating of equipment. No incidents to the lightship were reported while at Hens and Chickens, but it was blown off station in November 1956 when at Buzzards Bay. *(Courtesy of USCG)*

BUZZARDS BAY

This last lightship station established by the Coast Guard in 1954 was deactivated in 1961 after only 7 years in service. Only 2 lightships were assigned to this location, the LV 86/WAL 511 from 1954 to 1959, and the LV 110/WAL 532 from 1959 to 1961. Buzzards Bay station replaced both the Vineyard Sound and the Hens and Chickens stations at a new location that better served the traffic lanes moving in and out of Buzzards Bay; it also provided a marker for Vineyard Sound traffic. In addition to an air horn fog signal, the vessel had 2 groups of flashing white lights that were 65 feet above the water and visible for 14 miles. In the early 1960s, the Coast Guard began a program to replace lightships with offshore towers. Construction of a 100-ton 85-foot-high frame began in 1961 and was placed on location four miles from Cuttyhunk Island. At completion, the deck of the tower which allowed helicopters to land, was nearly seventy feet above the water and the lamp produced a flashing white light over 100 feet above sea level. The crew's quarters were below the deck. Named the Buzzards Bay Entrance Light, this was the first offshore lighthouse built over deep waters. The light was automated in 1980 by the Coast Guard. By 1994, the helicopter deck was condemned and the tower dismantled and replaced with a buoy. When the tower was razed, it was moved to Long Island, sunk, and became part of an artificial reef. In 1996, another smaller tower was placed on station; it flashes a white light every two and half seconds and two blasts every thirty seconds as a fog signal.

BUZZARDS BAY LIGHTSHIPS ASSIGNED & YEARS AT STATION

Station established 1954
1954–1959.........................LV 86 / 511
1959–1961.........................LV 110 / WAL 532
Discontinued 1961

The *LV 110 / WAL 532* sitting at the dock at the Coast Guard base in Boston in the 1950s, and one photograph while she was on station. This was the *LV 110*'s final station. *(Courtesy of CGHM)*

A relief lightship (*WLV 613* at the Ambrose tower) passes by the "Texas Tower"–style light tower that replaced the Buzzards Bay station. The tower was constructed in 1961, automated in 1981, and deactivated and dismantled in 1996. *(Courtesy of USCG)*

Two views, probably taken by the USCG in the early 1950s, of the Buzzards Bay platform with the tower and lamp. The lamp, a DCB-224 aerobeacon, was over 100 feet above sea level and had a range of almost twenty miles. *(Courtesy of USCG)*

Two color images, also by the Coast Guard, show the tower from sea level and the landing pad. Delivering supplies and repairs to the tower after it became automated became a problem as both the deck and stairs had to be condemned. *(Courtesy of USCG)*

MASSACHUSETTS BAY

MINOT'S LEDGE

After the tragic collapse of the steel skeleton tower during the storm of April 1851 that resulted in the death of the two keepers, it was necessary to provide an aid to navigation into the busy and active Cohasset Harbor. For more than a month the Boston tugboat *R. B. Forbes* was on station, until it was replaced by the light vessel "N" in late May of that year. Built in 1823 in New York, the "N" was 72 feet long, had a beam of 20 feet, and displaced 120 gross tons. The two-masted vessel had oil lamps with cylindrical wicks that displayed two lights 42 feet and 45 feet above the water. A hand-operated 450-pound bell was used as a fog signal. She had been originally assigned to Brandywine Shoal (Delaware) from 1823 to 1850 and was known as "Old Brandywine" or "lightboat Brandywine." For three years, 1851 to 1854, she was designated as Minot's Ledge until funds ($22,000) were appropriated for the *LV 7*.

Specifically designed for this lightship station, the *LV 7* was built in Somerset, Massachusetts, and took up station at Minot's Ledge on November 3, 1854. Compare her dimensions with those of her predecessor, "Old Brandywine": *LV 7* had a length of 96 feet, a beam of almost 23 feet, and a displacement of 150 tons. The signaling apparatus on the *LV 7* was similar: two masts, both about 42 feet with red daymarks, and two lights consisting of eight oil lamps with 12-inch reflectors and a 500-pound hand-operated bell.

These early lightships were most often schooner-rigged sailing vessels. An October 1854 notice to mariners indicated that the *LV 7* was painted cream color with black lettering. An archival image of the *LV 7* at Minot's Ledge probably does not exist.

The *LV 7* was removed from station on November 15, 1860, when the present lighthouse was activated. After her six-year service off Cohasset, the *LV 7* was transferred to Vineyard Sound (1861–1875) and then became a Relief vessel in the First, Third, and Fifth districts. Her only other station assignment was the Wreck of the Scotland (New Jersey) from 1881 to 1902. She was finally retired from service in May 1909, and sold for $155.

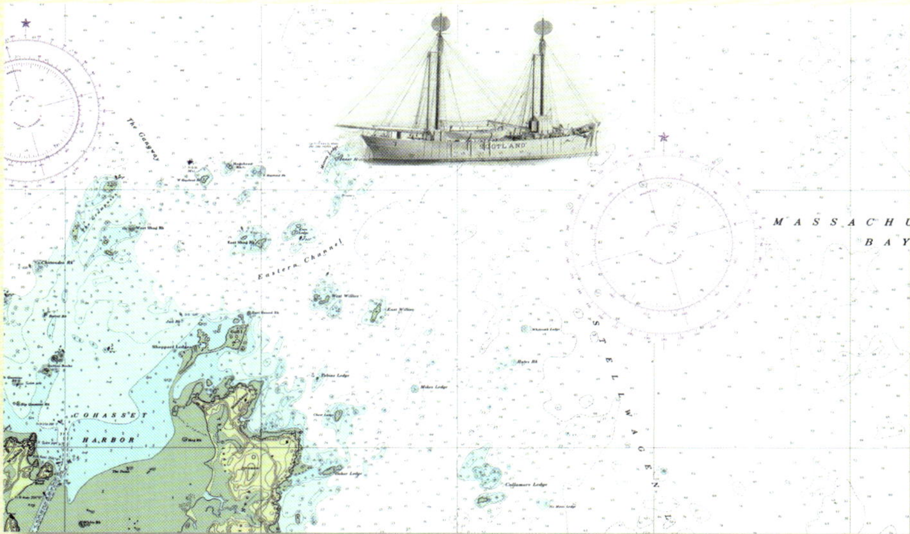

This chart shows the *LV 7* and where her location would have been in relation to the rocky shoal, Minot's Ledge, which is located just to the left of her stern. Most lightship stations through the years were moved due to changing conditions; Minot's Ledge lightship, on the other hand, was always at 42° 17' 0" north latitude and 70° 56' 6" west longitude. *(Courtesy of NOAA)*

This archival image of the *LV 7* was taken sometime between 1881 and 1902, when she was assigned to the Wreck of the Scotland (New Jersey). The Light List, available to mariners, contained photographs including this one of the different aids to navigation. *(Courtesy of USCG)*

MINOT'S LEDGE LIGHTSHIPS ASSIGNED & YEARS AT STATION

Station established 1851
1851 (3 weeks) Steam tug R. B. Forbes
1851–1854 "N"
1854–1860 LV 7
Discontinued 1860

BOSTON

Almost seventy-five years after the first lightship station in the United States was established (Willoughby Spit, Chesapeake Bay, in 1820), the first Boston lightship—*LV 54 / WAL 502*—was placed on station, on October 1, 1894. Originally located about six miles ESE from Boston Light and about three miles due north from Minot's Ledge Light, the *LV 54* was anchored in eighty-four feet of water. It may not be the exact spot, but close examination of the present-day chart indicates that same depth where the lightship would have been.

Unlike Minot's Ledge lightship that was always in the same latitude/longitude location, the Boston lightship was moved several times (see chart). The first move in 1900 was about a mile north to better mark the channel when the SS *Ultonia* stranded on the rocks off of Point Allerton, Hull. She was also moved temporarily during World War II. Her final move in 1973 was to aid ship traffic with the separation scheme for the two approaches (one from the north, one from the south) to Boston Harbor.

A more complete description of the *LV 54* can be found on page 229. Along with her sister ships, the *51, 52,* and *53,* the *54* was built in West Bay, Michigan, and they were the first lightships with a complete steel hull and fastenings. (The first lightships were made entirely of wood, primarily oak, but *LV 48* and *49* were built of a composite frame that included both steel and wood.) There were five lightships assigned to the Boston station in the eighty-one years that it was maintained.

BOSTON LIGHTSHIPS ASSIGNED & YEARS AT STATION

Station established 1894

1894–1940	*LV 54 / WAL-502*
1940–1942	*LV 81 / WAL 507*
1942–1943	*Buoy on station during WW II*
1943–1946	*LV 54 / WAL 502*
1946–1951	*LV 81 / WAL 507*
1951–1962	*LV 85 / WAL 510*
1962–1972	*LV 118 / WAL 539*
1972–1975	*WLV 189*

Discontinued 1975

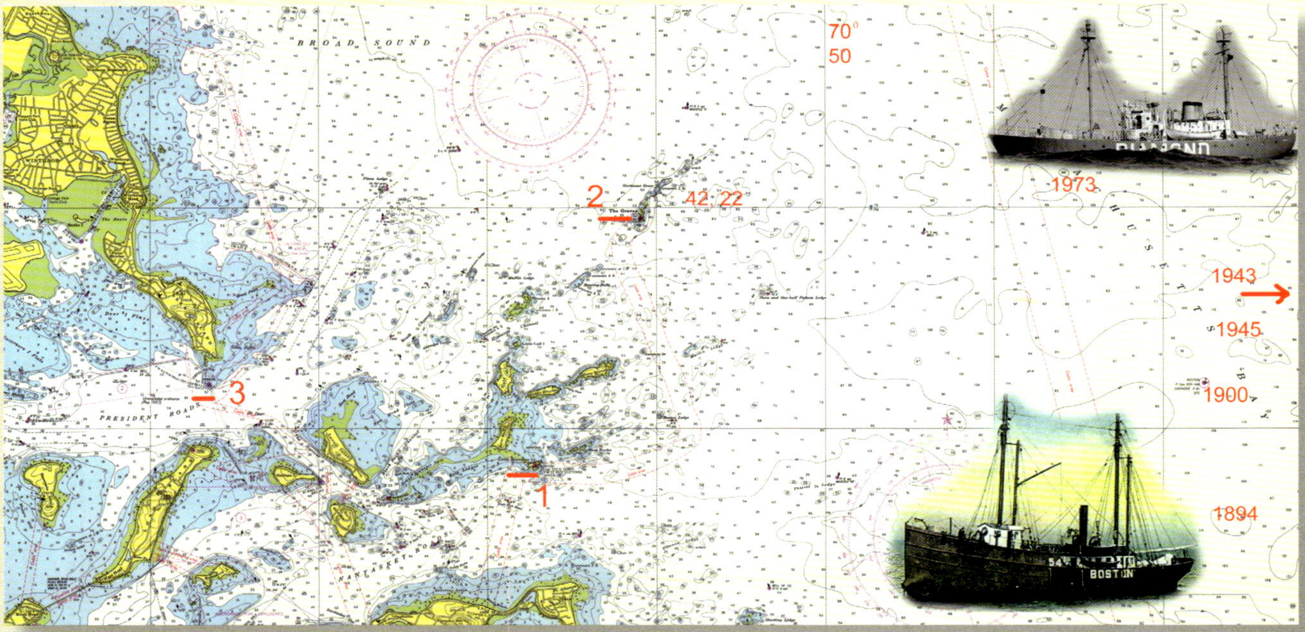

This present-day chart of outer Boston Harbor shows two of the lightships that were assigned to this station and their location. At the bottom right is the first, *LV 54*; the red year off her stern indicates her original position. Boston Light, number 1 underlined in red, was about six miles to the west, and the Minot's Ledge lighthouse was a little more than three miles to the south. At the top right is the image of the last lightship assigned to this station—*WLV 189*—and the year 1973 indicates her location. Because the complete chart has been cropped to include only necessary locations, the latitude 42° 22' and longitude 70° 50' are designated on those specific lines. The number 2 indicates the location of Graves Light which was built in 1905. Deer Island Light is number 3, with the island just to the north. *(Courtesy of NOAA)*

These three images, one a colorized postcard, the other two file photographs from the Library of Congress, show the *LV 54* on station. Interestingly, it is possible to see the hawespipe at the bow with the anchor chain that could be brought into the bilge in the center of the ship; this increased stability. Masts behind the mainmasts could be rigged to allow the vessel to sail. The circular daymarks can be seen at the top of the masts. *(Courtesy of LOC)*

Improvements and modifications were continually being made to lightships. In the case of the *LV 54,* sometime in 1914–1915 her two masts were removed and replaced with a single lantern mast that had an incandescent oil-vapor lantern; she was also repowered with a diesel engine. Through the years, her aids to navigation were changed: 1910, submarine bell added; 1915, fog signal changed to air siren; 1919, equipped with radio; 1921, equipped with radio beacon; and 1945, fitted with detection radar. Many images found in historical files are undated, but the stern shot we know was captured in December 1921. *(Courtesy of LOC)*

Before and after World War II, 1940–1942 and 1946–1951, *LV 81 / WAL 507* was assigned to the Boston station. During the war, she was an examination vessel and had a 3-inch gun. Her first assignment (1905–1936) was at Heald Bank (Texas), but she spent her last years in the Boston area. Extensive repairs and refitting were carried out at the Fore River Shipyard in Quincy. She was decommissioned in 1951 after forty-seven years of service, and sold. *(Courtesy of NA)*

This image of the *LV 85 / WAL 510* was taken while she was on the Boston station sometime between 1951 and 1962. Built in 1907, she was at Nantucket Shoals from 1907 to 1923 and then was assigned as a relief vessel until 1951. During the war, 1942–1944, she was an examination vessel in the Norfolk, Virginia, area. After the Boston station, she was decommissioned. *(Courtesy of NA)*

This image shows the *WLV 189* on Diamond Shoal Station, North Carolina. This was the last lightship assigned to the Boston station. She was unique in several ways: 1) the first of six vessels designed and built specifically for the Coast Guard; 2) the first of only six all-welded lightships ever built; and 3) the first of only six lightships built with a system of alternating electrical current. Built purposely for Diamond Shoal, North Carolina (1947–1966), her last station was Boston (1972–1975), when the vessel was decommissioned and the station was discontinued. *(Courtesy of USCG)*

From 1962 until 1972, this was the final station of the *LV 118 / WAL 539*. Details such as the lamp are visible. After she was decommissioned in 1972, she was donated to the Lewes Historical Society, Delaware, and is now a museum and open to the public. *(Courtesy of NA)*

A present-day image of the *LV 118* in Lewes, Delaware.

These two Coast Guard images were captured of the *WLV 189* when she was at Boston station (1972–1975). She was replaced by the "B" buoy sometime in the spring of 1975. *(Courtesy of USCG)*

Decommissioned in 1975, she was delivered to Atlantic City, New Jersey, as a training vessel, converted to a museum in 1980, and, as seen here, the *WLV 189* was scuttled in 1994 as part of an artificial reef.

LIGHTSHIPS TODAY

When the last lightship station was deactivated and replaced with a buoy in 1983, lightships inexorably became maritime objects of the past. Some were sold to other countries to continue to operate in the same capacity, while others were decommissioned and became fishing vessels, restaurants, and otherwise were privately maintained.

Although more than two hundred lightships assigned to United States waters beginning as early as the 1790s, only a handful remain today. Most are integral elements in maritime museums located on both coasts and on the Great Lakes. One lightship has become a luxury yacht. The photos show several lightships that are open to the public. Also, one may tour the *WLV 612* which is available for charter.

NANTUCKET *WLV 612*

The *WLV 612*, formerly identified as Nantucket 1, was built in Curtis Bay, Maryland, in 1950. Her duty assignments included San Francisco (1951–1969) and Blunts Reef, California (1969–1971), before she returned to the east coast. From 1971 to 1975 she served at Portland, Maine, and then was subsequently assigned to Nantucket Shoals.

From 1979 until 1983 when this last lightship station was deactivated, the *612* and *613* alternated on station about every three weeks. After thirty-three years of lightship duty, the *WLV 612* was retired, and sea trials were performed to determine her usefulness as a support vessel. Found not to be cost effective in other roles in the Coast Guard, the vessel was decommissioned in March of 1985. After passing from one organization to another, the lightship was posted on E-bay in the year 2000. The present owners won that auction with a bid of $126,100 and a new paradigm in preserving and maintaining classic ships was born. This ship would be given a total restoration, and rebuilt to perform a distinctively different function.

Taken to New Bedford, the lightship was stripped of its inoperable engines, all the plumbing and wiring, thousands of gallons of contaminated diesel fuel, and the asbestos that covered numerous interior surfaces. Then shipwrights and artisans began the task, with the guidance and direction of the owners, of converting the *612* into a luxury yacht. The finest woods (birch, cherry, and mahogany) were used throughout the vessel, in addition to granite countertops. With over four thousand square feet of interior space, the ship has six staterooms, each with its own private head; a salon and parlor that easily accommodates twelve guests; and a gaming room with a flat-screen TV and the original gaming table that was used when she was on station. The decks, with over two thousand square feet of space, allow guests to relax and enjoy the vistas. This is truly a luxury yacht with a memorable history, and is available for charter as The *Nantucket Lightship*.

Nearly sixty years apart, the above two images show the *WLV 612* when she was launched in 1950 at the Curtis Bay, Maryland, shipyard. Decommissioned in March 1985, she was the last lightship in the Coast Guard. The present-day image shows the lightship in Vineyard Haven, Massachusetts. *(Black-and-white image courtesy of USCG)*

A modern diesel power plant provides power, and with two additional generators available, the eight heating and air conditioning zones provide climate control to the vessel.

Two present-day images, looking sternward, of part of the over two thousand square feet of space on the decks of the lightship. Boston Harbor is in the background.

The bridge, totally refitted, includes not only the original equipment but additional modern electronics hidden from view. The eight-balls were manufactured by the Lionel Corp. in 1942.

The spacious and elegant parlor and salon is located near the bow.

There are six staterooms, each with its own bathroom, offering a variety of sleeping accommodations.

The stylish kitchen includes modern appliances with portholes looking out the starboard side.

CHESAPEAKE *LV 116 / WLV 538*

One lightship that is possible to visit is the Chesapeake (*LV 116 / WLV 538*) that is tied up to the docks in Baltimore, Maryland, in the National Heritage Area. Listed on both the U.S. National Register of Historic Places and U.S. National Historic Landmarks, she is owned by the National Park Service. Built in 1930 in South Carolina, the LV116 had four duty stations before decommissioning in 1971. An interesting sidelight: during World War II, she was assigned duties as an examination vessel in Sandwich, Massachusetts.

When lightship stations were discontinued, there was still a need for an aid to navigation. In this image, an LNB (large navigational buoy) is in the foreground, with the *WLV 604* lightship, Columbia River, Oregon. The buoy replaced the lightship.

The *WLV 612* tied up at a dock in Vineyard Haven Harbor.

Mast and lamps from the *WLV 612.*

Throughout the world, lightships have been preserved at maritime museums. This is the *Finngrundet* which was built in 1903 and replaced by a caisson lighthouse in 1969. She is now open to the public at the Vasa Museum (masts in the background are of the seventeenth-century warship) in Stockholm, Sweden.

CONCLUSION

The future of lighthouses in Massachusetts is bright. Many are still active aids to navigation maintained by the Coast Guard, and some of those are open to the public. For the enthusiast, there are over two dozen lighthouses that can be seen relatively easily. Others are maintained by preservation groups and historical societies dedicated to the proposition that these wonderful and illustrious aids to navigation will be available for future generations. Still others are privately owned and maintained as silent and unlit sentinels.

The future of lightships is not as bright. Throughout the world, the number of active lightships has declined, as improved and modern technologies have made navigation safer. Still, in some countries, unmanned lightships are, nevertheless, maintained to assist traffic in shipping lanes. Great Britain, as well as other European countries, continues to use these aids to navigation. Here in the United States, decommissioned lightships have a bleak future. Some are preserved as museums and are open to the public. A few are privately owned and used as pleasure vessels, restaurants, or some other form of maritime activity. Others have fallen into disrepair and have been either scrapped or sunk to make future artificial reefs. For over 150 years, lightships in the United States were an important and indispensible aid to navigation. Now, they are a fading part of our maritime history. I hope this book will keep their memories alive so they will not be forgotten.

AUTHOR'S NOTE

Of all the books that I have completed, this one has been the most time-consuming and has also been the most remarkable. I have met more people, visited more museums and historical sites, and accessed more information than for all my other books combined. There were several trips to the National Archives in College Park, Maryland, as well as to the United States Coast Guard Historian's Office in Washington D. C., to collect not only existing information and plans, but also historical images, some over 130 years old, that have never been published. Closer to home, visits to the Historian at the Cape Cod National Seashore, as well as to the Massachusetts State Archives, have produced additional facts, figures, and images. Previous books, including the highly regarded *Wide* series, deal basically with the here and now. The images in those books were photographed at the present time as they now exist. With the exception of a few Library of Congress panoramic photographs and a few old postcards, what you see in those books is as it is presently, early in the twenty-first century. This book is different, as many of its images are black-and-white because color photography hadn't yet been invented. As early as 1910, images in color were produced by a variety of techniques, but it wasn't until the mid-1930s that Kodak produced Kodachrome and the world of color photography began.

The focus of this book is to provide the reader with an illustrated history of Massachusetts lighthouses and lightships for the last 190 years. This book does not concentrate on the narrative history of those topics. A very basic time frame for these subjects is as follows: lighthouses, very primitive in the 1600s, became important and substantial in the late 1700s and are still functional as aids to navigation. Lightships, first developed in England in the mid-1700s, became common in the United States by the mid-1800s, the last station was discontinued in 1983, and now only a few vessels scattered across the country, remain as museums. Included in this book are plans of lighthouses that were drawn in the early 1800s before the development of photography in the 1830s, 1840s. Preserved at the Library of Congress and the United States Coast Guard's Historian's Office, many of these documents and images illustrate the aids to navigation during the glorious and golden age of sail.

In addition to photographs of Massachusetts lighthouses and lightships, I have also integrated images I have taken in my travels whenever these subjects were available. The last lightship was built more than sixty years ago and only a few remain open for visitors. I have included the *Chesapeake*, located in Baltimore Harbor,

as well as several other vessels that are open to the public.

It is my hope that this book will inspire and motivate the reader to visit and enjoy the locations found in this book and treasure their histories.

ACKNOWLEDGMENTS

Frank Sinatra came to mind after I finished my first lighthouse book, *Cape Cod Lighthouses and Lightships,* because "I did it my way." I basically went to each lighthouse that I could and took the photographs that I needed. With this book, it was more like the Beatles' "I get by with a little help from my friends." Actually, a lot of help from new acquaintances that I hopefully can call friends in the future. This book would not have been possible with the contributions of the following individuals: Jeremy D'Entremont, Joseph Langlois, Christian Gomes, Christina Stevens, Dolly Bicknell, Bob Gallagher, Dave Ball, Sally Snowman, Charles Delafero, Mike Parr, Phil Karwowski, Emily Levin, Daniel Sunday, Paul St. Germain, Barbara Kezer; and the organizations the United States Coast Guard (USCG) and The Friends of the Boston Islands. As I spent more time and effort on this project than on my prior publications, it is understandable that more individuals have contributed to the success and completion of this endeavor. The errors are mine. I have visited numerous places and where I have found inconsistencies and a lack of data in the records, I have tried to present to the reader what is the most likely the correct information. Like many other maritime enthusiasts, I have been intrigued by lighthouses for many years and have captured images of these structures not only in Massachusetts, but around the world. Most of the modern images found in this book are mine. Additional photos have been provided by those individuals previously mentioned. Thank you. Historic images were found primarily in three sources which any interested researcher can access. The National Archives (NA) in College Park, Maryland, is a national treasure, with a substantial collection of images, plans, and supporting documents regarding lighthouses. To all those individuals on the third and fifth floors who provided assistance, thank you. Another resource that proved invaluable was the United States Coast Guard Historian's Office in Washington, DC. To Scott Price and Chris Havern who provided direction and assistance that proved most helpful, thank you. A third major resource was the Coast Guard Heritage Museum in Barnstable, Massachusetts. Bill Collette, Jack McGrath, and all the other "Coasties," thank you for all your help. To all the guides, historians, and escorts at the lighthouses and museums that I have visited who answered my questions and provided guidance, thank you. To Mr. and Mrs. Golden, for your hospitality, thank you. To Carol for all her help, both in traveling to all these locations as well as reviewing, editing, and discussing the final document. To Tony Pane, as always, for trying to teach me the finer aspects of the written English language (I hope I get there), thank you. To Jim Owens, who provided additional modern images of lightships, thank you. To Salty Dog, my best friend and a companion for many of these trips to lighthouses: hopefully, more treats for the next book.

BIBLIOGRAPHY

Adams, W. H. Davenport. *Lighthouses and Lightships, A descriptive and historical account of their mode of construction and organization.* London: T. Nelson and Sons, 1878.

Bachand Robert G. *Northeast Lights Lighthouses and Lightships, Rhode Island to Cape May, New Jersey.* Norwalk, CT: Sea Sports Publications, 1989.

Clark, Admont G. *Lighthouses of Cape Cod, Martha's Vineyard, and Nantucket—Their History and Lore*. East Orleans, MA: Parnassus Imprints, 1992.

Davidson, Donald W. *Lighthouses of New England.* Secaucus, NJ: The Wellfleet Press, 1990.

D'Entremont, Jeremy. *The Lighthouse Handbook New England.* Kennebunkport, ME: Cedar Mill Press, 2008.

Holland, Francis Ross Jr. A*merica's Lighthouses: Their Illustrated History Since 1716*. Brattleboro, VT: The Stephen Greene Press, 1972.

Kochel, Kenneth G. *America's Atlantic Coast Lighthouses: A Traveler's Guide.* Clearwater, FL: Betken Publications, 1996.

Pratt, William A. *The New American Coast Pilot*. Boston, MA: F. W. Lincoln & Co, 1884.

Putnam, George R. *Lighthouses and Lightships of the United States, New and Revised Edition.* Boston, MA: Houghton Mifflin Company, 1933

Snow, Edward Rowe. *The Lighthouses of New England.* New York: Dodd, Mead, 1945, rep. 1973.

Thompson, Courtney. *Lighthouses of Southern New England, Massachusetts, Rhode Island and Connecticut: A Pictorial Guide.* St. John, New Brunswick: Cat Nap Publications, 2002.

INDEX

Annisquam Light 201–205
Baker's Island Light.......152–156
Bird Island Light...........61–62
Borden Flats Light........22–26
Boston Harbor...............96–98
Boston Light 104–113
Boston Lightship Station 244–247
Brandywine....................133
Brenton Reef
    Lightship Station 228
Broad Sound Range Lights
    244–247
Buoys, design and history 18–19
Butler Flats Light..........39–44
Buzzards Bay 27
Buzzards Bay Lightship Station
    241–242
Buzzards Bay Tower 242
Cape Ann Region..........175–176
Chesapeake Lightship ...251
Clark's Point Light 34–38
Cleveland Ledge Light..49–51
Columbia Lightship 250
Cuttyhunk Light 28–29
Deer Island Light..........114–116
Derby Wharf Light.......162–166
Dumpling Rocks Light .30–32
Duxbury Pier Light / Bug Light
    65–68
Eastern Point Light.......177–182
Egg Rock Light.............138–140
Fort Pickering / Winter Island Light
    157–161
Fort Taber......................36–37
Fresnel, Augustin...........7
Gloucester Breakwater / Dog Bar
    182–184
Gosnold, Bartholomew..28
Hens and Chickens Lightship Station
    240
Hooper Strait Light 15, 131–133
Hospital Point Light 167–174
Ipswich Range Lights....206–209
Lighthouse, introduction
    and history 7–10
    tower design 11–18
Lighthouse Board..........8
Lightship, introduction and history
    222–226
    early design 227–233
Lightship depots............230, 232, 236
Lightship plans..............227, 231, 233
Lightship tenders 235
Lightships by vessel number
    LV 1..........................224, 227
    LV 2......................... 228, 238
    LV 5......................... 238
    LV 7......................... 235, 243
    LV 9......................... 230
    LV 39....................... 228, 235
    LV 41....................... 238
    LV 42....................... 239
    LV 44....................... 228
    LV 49....................... 235, 239
    LV 51....................... 229
    LV 54....................... 229, 244, 245
    LV 58....................... 229
    LV 69....................... 233
    LV 71....................... 228
    LV 73....................... 236, 237
    LV 74....................... 239
    LV 81....................... 245
    LV 86....................... 230
    LV 87....................... 232, 237
    LV 90....................... 230, 235, 236
    LV 110......................241
    LV 111..................... 233, 240
    LV 116..................... 251
    LV 118..................... 246
    LV 101..................... 226
    WAL 508 230
    WLV 189................. 233, 246, 247
    WLV 612................. 248–250, 252
    WLV 613................. 225, 232
Lightship Stations 234–247
Long Island Head Light 119–124
Lovell's Island
    Range Lights............125–127
Marblehead Light 141–150
Massachusetts Bay North 138
Massachusetts Bay South 63–64
Minot's Ledge Light 88–95
Minot's Ledge
    Lightship Station 243
Nantucket *WLV 612*......248–250
Narrows Light /
    Bug Light.................128–130
Ned's Point Light 52–57
New Bedford 33
New Bedford Lightship.9
Newburyport Harbor Rear
    Range Lights...........217–220
Newburyport Region.....210
Nix's Mate 117–118
Overfalls Lightship........247
Palmers Island Light 45–48
Pleasanton, Stephen 7
Plum Island Light 210–216
Plymouth Light /
    The Gurnet..............69–76
Salem 151
Salisbury Range Lights..221
Sanibel Light.................16
Scituate Light................77–87
Spectacle Island
    Range Lights...........134–137
Straitsmouth Island Light 196–200
Ten Pound Light 185–187
Thacher Island
    Twin Lights.............188–195
The Graves.....................99–103
United States
    Coast Guard.............8
United States
    Lighthouse Service...7–8
Vineyard Sound
    Lightship Station 238
Wing's Neck Light........58–60